micro:bit Projects with Python and Single Board Computers

Building STEAM Projects with Code Club and Kids' Maker Groups

Martin Tan

Apress®

micro:bit Projects with Python and Single Board Computers: Building STEAM Projects with Code Club and Kids' Maker Groups

Martin Tan
Doncaster Heights, VIC, Australia

ISBN-13 (pbk): 978-1-4842-9196-2   ISBN-13 (electronic): 978-1-4842-9197-9
https://doi.org/10.1007/978-1-4842-9197-9

Managing Director, Apress Media LLC: Welmoed Spahr
Acquisitions Editor: Aaron Black
Development Editor: James Markham
Coordinating Editor: Jessica Vakili

Distributed to the book trade worldwide by Springer Science+Business Media New York, 233 Spring Street, 6th Floor, New York, NY 10013. Phone 1-800-SPRINGER, fax (201) 348-4505, e-mail orders-ny@springer-sbm.com, or visit www.springeronline.com. Apress Media, LLC is a California LLC and the sole member (owner) is Springer Science + Business Media Finance Inc (SSBM Finance Inc). SSBM Finance Inc is a **Delaware** corporation.

For information on translations, please e-mail booktranslations@springernature.com; for reprint, paperback, or audio rights, please e-mail bookpermissions@springernature.com.

Apress titles may be purchased in bulk for academic, corporate, or promotional use. eBook versions and licenses are also available for most titles. For more information, reference our Print and eBook Bulk Sales web page at http://www.apress.com/bulk-sales.

Any source code or other supplementary material referenced by the author in this book is available to readers on the Github repository: https://github.com/Apress/micro:bit-Projects-with-Python-and-Single-Board-Computers. For more detailed information, please visit http://www.apress.com/source-code.

Printed on acid-free paper

Table of Contents

About the Author

Martin Tan wrote the first Code Club Moonhack projects in Scratch and Python, used by over 10,000 kids in Australia. He has taken kids to demo robots and coding projects in parliament, delivered training to Code Club Australia, and contributes to various Maker communities online. Martin blogs on Maker topics, runs a Maker store, and works in IT security, contributing to various open source projects and community conferences. Most of his endeavors feed into his hobbies, which also include music, locksport, and various techy pursuits.

About the Technical Reviewer

Ioana Culic is currently a PhD candidate in the field of Internet of Things and the cofounder of Wyliodrin, a company that offers educational and industrial IoT solutions. She is a Teaching Assistant at the Politehnica University of Bucharest and has also been teaching IoT technologies to high school and university students at different events for the last five years. Despite the technical background, writing has always been Ioana's passion, and she managed to mix the two. She has published several articles in magazines such as *The MagPi* and *Make* and books on Internet of Things technologies. Ioana has been porting JavaScript to TockOS.

Acknowledgments

During our journey helping kids to learn programming (coding) and other maker skills, there were many people who helped as we strived to empower kids to push themselves further and leverage their newfound skills to express their imagination and ideas. Whether it be donating time, knowledge, or even just being supportive when I would excitedly rant about how proud we were of the kids, it made a lasting difference to the kids, and for that we are thankful. In this section, I also wanted to mention some specific contributions.

Firstly, thanks to David Mander at Milgate Primary School for taking the initiative and leap of faith to register a code club and for the many hours spent after school making sure that the code club would run and helping with all our extra excursions and events and dealing with the anxiety of all the administrative requirements that came with these. Thanks for your support in the face of much frustration at trying to prepare things and push our club to eventually embrace text-based coding and electronics.

From the early days: Thanks to Jay for your consistent presence in the early years of our code club and starting the trend of alumni school kid volunteers. And thanks to Ryan for lighting a fire under everyone in that first year and onward with your unique game demos, and in later years, Jamie for breaking out your super fun multilevel games.

To all the parents who volunteered their time over the years, especially Glen and Rula who stuck around for multiple years and provided great support and belief, which made such a difference, and helped us fumble through some frustrating times.

ACKNOWLEDGMENTS

Some special people from Code Club Australia were instrumental in providing such powerful encouragement, support, and feedback to myself and our club over the years. Thanks to Kelly Tagalan for all your belief and enthusiasm and trusting me with presenting our club's demos and to write all those projects, including the first Moonhack to get 10,000 kids coding. Thanks also to Nicola and Tom for your support, encouragement, and feedback. To Rik from Code Club UK, thanks for your help, feedback, and very knowledgeable tips and all the work you put into writing all those code club curriculum projects over the years.

Without the advice and inspiration from other authors, including Michael Rash, Al Sweigart, and many other technical authors, I would not even have considered contributing a book – thanks for paving the way with your inspiring writing and experience!

I would also like to thank those who made podcasts that encouraged me when driving to work, especially Michael from "Talk Python to Me," Kelly and Sean from "Teaching Python," and Chris from "The Real Python Podcast." And also, thanks to Michael from Kitronik for supporting our club with various samples and keyrings. Thanks to *micro:mag* and Code Club World for publishing my articles.

In addition to Jay, all the other alumni students who came back as volunteers over the years – thank you so much for just turning up and making such a fantastic difference to our code club kids. You are the best inspiration because you have done what they are doing and continue to do so. Some extra special thanks must go to Ethan, Emily, Thom, Noah, Yasmine, and Yamen for the extra consistency, time, and effort you invested. You helped our code club to persist over the years and made sure that so many got the help and support when they needed it!

Huge thanks to my family for putting up with all my ranting, stress, and frustration during the writing of this book, especially my kids for coming to code club week after week, year after year. This book would not be possible without all your love and support.

Introduction

Although programming (coding) was once a skill for a very specific role, nowadays, computers or microcontroller chips are ubiquitous; when coupled with today's human-friendly modern coding languages, the scope for applying this skill is now much broader. However, in the same way that reading or writing is useful for recreational and personal interests rather than relegated to purely academic applications, coding and creating with technology is now much more accessible to everyone. By embracing these skills for creative and artistic pursuits or just to help simplify the way we interact with our tools, the areas that once took us away from enjoying life can now free us from the restrictions that technology previously placed on us. For kids, this is realized through maker groups and code clubs, which meld a previously academic skillset to apply for our own recreation or to express our ideas into something tangible to others. Sadly, we often hear of a disconnect between people who want to learn and the more technical folk – the latter explaining things in their own context, without realizing their use of jargon and what seems like abstract terminology for those that bridge into other disciplines such as teaching. When listening to teachers, I've often heard things like, "IT people don't get it when they try to explain to us" or "How do I implement this for a class or group?" Similarly, our code club kids ask for project examples within their life environment, so they could see how maker skills could be immediately useful.

Over several years, a group of volunteers and I have muddled our way through adventures with our Australian code club, hosted at the local primary school. This has taken us to conferences, Parliament, and our code club kids were featured on TV and online media; had begun to incorporate their code club skills into their social lives and school projects. Along the way, we struggled with logistical and IT-related challenges and the quest to make sure kids were engaged and constantly challenged to grow, rather than just occupied. We sought to give kids ownership of these skills so that these would not just be something they "learned about at school" but rather something that empowered them to use across other aspects of their lives, rather than just an academic topic. Sometimes, we failed or ran out of time, but the net effect was that we gradually progressed over the years. As I looked back and had my memory jogged by others as we tried to remember the details, we realized that we had come a long way from that first day of code club. When David, one of the school teachers; Jay, a former student recently graduated to high school; and myself initially shuffled into a room with a small group of kids and some computers, we wondered whether we could even get a working program to run – now, almost a decade later, we're seeing kids using these skills at home and able to interact with AI interfaces, hopefully more seamlessly and with a little less trepidation.

The Purpose of This Book

Although there are many books filled with activities for a lone person, or replicated for many working individually, there were not many that showed how to take a project and scale it for pairs or groups of kids. Most books show projects created in isolation rather than tested with class groups. Rather than providing deep technical discussions or a technical reference, this book aims to give a relatable context to the technical things while pointing you in the right direction for the deep technical information. Projects are also included and have been developed in the context of a club limited to one-hour sessions at a time. From a school perspective, I'm not a teacher, so I've provided the how-tos so you can paste these into handouts, but they may require assessment tasks to be added. From a social and maker group perspective, these can be run as provided. All the materials and tools are specified at the start of each project, and many are made to be scaled to allow group collaboration. Some will run for multiple sessions but have been designed to easily be continued in one-hour chunks. Through my recollections of our mistakes and successes with real anecdotes peppered throughout, the book also aims to help the reader with the logistics of preparation, providing a structured approach to learning the basic skills and explanations of useful tools and where to find the deep details. Most projects also have a challenge with some hints, to accommodate a range of kids' skills and experience so no one is left behind, ahead, or idle for too long! You'll learn the useful concepts and skills for running a maker group or code club, in a way that gives more of a meaningful real-life creative context rather than being purely academic.

I hope that the platform and skills we provide with will go some way toward giving kids the skills, freedom, and drive to explore and do that which we do not yet think is possible. We only need to look into the Demoscene's[1] origins and history to realize how much can be achieved with just a bit of curiosity and collaboration, to do things previously deemed impossible with electronic hardware limitations of the time.

Intended Audience

The intended audience for this book is teachers, parents, and volunteers who are running or looking to run a maker group or code club for kids aged from eight years old to those beginning high school (in Australia, the latter is generally around 13 years old). If you're a school-aged kid, you can also enjoy digging through this book for the projects and find ideas for getting your own maker group happening – all it takes is a few friends to get together! A maker group or code club is in essence two or more people getting together to learn and create. The book does not assume any technical experience, as I have aimed to explain terminology in layperson's terms before applying it – so you will both learn and be able to talk about the

---

[1] https://chipflip.wordpress.com/category/demoscene/

concepts as a universal way of collaborating then use the included references to go as far as you want with learning more. Since part of the book's objective is to help you keep kids engaged at all experience and skill levels, there are also some components that will introduce more experienced kids to more advanced concepts. However, I've also aimed to provide practical stepping stones to allow you to reach useful levels of skill and fluency in coding, before progressing to applying these in more challenging and rewarding contexts; for example, in Chapter 3, pointing to Code Club Australia lessons on simple web pages and basic Python concepts before looking at writing a "web application" that uses Python logic to create an interactive web page.

Overview of Chapters

The chapters of this book are structured as follows:

Chapter 1: Initial considerations for your code club or maker group, support resources, initial curriculums to use, logistical solutions to common problems, and how we improved over time, in practice.

Chapter 2: Finding IT resources and help for your code club and how to have the required software tools and IT infrastructure set up on computers and in your space.

Chapter 3: This covers general Python programming concepts and program structure and how to get the right Python programming environments to suit your requirements and any location limitations.

Chapter 4: I talk about using more tactile approaches with e-textiles starting from a basic electronic circuit to a programmed digital e-textile project with readily available materials, for example, a baseball cap.

Chapter 5: Going "off map" and creating your own project; included is a self-watering plant project created at our code club.

Chapter 6: Introducing collaboration with others, including a group project we tested and used and systems you can use to collaborate with volunteers or other coders. Contributing to community projects is also discussed.

Chapter 7: Introduction to some basic electronic components and electronic circuit concepts and analog vs. digital approaches. This chapter includes building an electronic badge, adding various features, and how to extend it further.

Chapter 8: Finally, we put what we've learned, together, by walking through planning a year of a code club or kids' maker group starting with a Python curriculum progressing through to workshops and next steps.

A bonus appendix is also included with a couple of projects for creating micro:bit traffic lights.

Conventions Used in This Book

In the included projects, existing code is shown for context, with the code to be added shown in **bold**. Explanations of concepts are included as breakouts to separate them from the main text. Any links with further information are referenced as footnotes. Python code that wraps to the next line is denoted with a "\" (slash). Although two-character indents are used, four-character indents are fine and accepted in Python, if the indentation is consistent throughout the program. All indents are spaces, although some editors will automatically convert tabs to spaces. The phrase "code club" is used interchangeably with "maker group" and refers to an extracurricular maker club based around coding and electronics that may be set up on its own or in conjunction with a school.

Prerequisites

The only prerequisites are enthusiasm and a few kids that want to learn. If you are already teaching kids how to code and have access to computers, even better! However, this book will outline how to access what you need and where to find help. When we started our local code club, we only had a handful of kids, a teacher, an older student, and one person (me) with programming experience. We used free resources and the school's computers to get started. During the book, I will outline how we ended up building up more electronic hardware and attracted more volunteers over the years. Although one of us had programming experience, this is not necessary as many of our volunteers learned as they progressed. Most of the free projects from Code Club Australia and Code Club World were able to be completed by adults in 20 minutes before each session.

Other Resources

Throughout this book, I've included footnotes with various online resources, including groups that publish free tools and materials for the community. I also explain where to start getting involved in contributing to community projects and how kids can also start collaborating to such projects or even methods they can use to work collaboratively with one another.

As you progress through this book, you'll find that it is equally divided into three main areas of knowledge:

- Getting started, running, and growing your own code club or maker group

- Prewritten projects and resources to use with groups of kids

- Anecdotes and learnings taken from building our own code club, attending some fabulous events, and contributing to the community – drawn from my own experience doing these things

CHAPTER 1

Getting Started

Expectations is the place you must always go to before you get to where you're going.

—*The Phantom Tollbooth* by Norton Juster

This chapter covers the initial considerations for getting started with your code club or maker space. I have included examples from the experiences from our earlier code club years with challenges faced and give an overview of our strategies to address these. Chapter 8 will dive into exploring these strategies in detail, using specific how-to examples and useful templates. As you've probably guessed, there's no technical content in this chapter, but rather it is a way of outlining some of the more essential lessons we learned after several years of running a code club.

Note Throughout this book, I refer to code club or maker group participants as "kids," whereas older school student alumni will be referred to as "volunteers," as are adult volunteers.

So, let's get started! One of the things to consider when starting a code club or maker space is roughly what your short-term and long-term goals are. I say "roughly" as any progress is a reasonable achievement, providing that the kids stay eager and keep coming back for more. Goals will change and develop as you progress. For example, an achievable goal can be as simple as making sure every kid who attends for a year learns to write a working program. Another goal may be to equip kids with a new skill – allowing them to implement or prototype their ideas to a level previously inaccessible to them. At our local club, the point at which kids became so engrossed in what they were doing, and keen to complete something, felt like a definite indicator that something good had "clicked." We almost had to drag them away from the activity so that their waiting parents could take them home.

Once your initial, and long-term, goals are established, you'll start to develop a clearer picture of the requirements for those goals. The simpler your initial goals are, the easier the requirements will be to procure – you can easily, and probably will, refine and add to your goals as you progress!

Unsurprisingly, one of the main requirements when starting off is volunteers to help run your code club or maker group sessions. Since our code club is a school-based extracurricular activity, our three initial volunteers were drawn from these three groups:

- Teachers

- Parents

- Ex-students from the school

When talking to other code club volunteers, they all mentioned challenges in finding enough volunteers to get started.

Some reasons for this are as follows:

1. People are working during the time when your code club or maker group is scheduled (typically after school or weekends).

2. Concern that they do not possess the skills required.

3. Not interested or only see a limited scope.

4. Not enough time due to existing responsibilities outside of work.

Issue 1 is becoming less of an issue as more people work flexible hours and work from home. As our local code club muddled its way through half-finished coding projects, some of the kids stood up in school assembly to show what they had made and learned. After that, some awareness and understanding started to grow that we were doing something positive for the kids. One kid explained that, while he had originally expected just games, he had learned that there was much more that he could do with the skills gained, including creating things that helped people and made a difference to the world.

Although **issue 2** has not really been a problem, with some parents volunteering to learn themselves, to prevent stagnation at least one member of your team needs some vision, enthusiasm, and a thirst to learn or implement ideas. I will aim to provide some of these in this book, in the form of working projects and simple explanations of concepts, with summaries and cheat sheets that you can reference. I've included lots of snippets of anecdotes and experiences, as people often recount such stories as adding to their learning.

Issue 3 often stems from ill-informed ideas that programming or technical pursuits are only for those who want to work in "IT" or some sort of stereotype who doesn't engage in anything except for typing at a computer. An analogy I often mention is that although we don't all aspire to become professional writers or editors, learning to read and write is very useful and enriching for our lives. The idea that programming is only for those who wish to become software developers, and that all these jobs are now performed offshore, is sometimes touted as a reason for ignoring programming, electronics, or other maker skills. Many successful products have been launched through kickstarter sites, and typically work is not offshored until more cost-effective mass-production is required. In short, a very broad range of people can benefit from learning computational thinking, automating something that may prevent them from having more time in their lives, or even just for the sheer enjoyment of creating something.

Finally, **issue 4** may be a valid blocker, although we still do see some great support from families that have lots of projects and activities going on. Understanding the reasons why issue 3 is not valid, or was misunderstood, can often change priorities here.

Note   With our code club, we never charged any money and just allowed kids to apply at the start of each year. This is part of the mission of Code Club Australia to "Get kids coding." I did initially donate a couple of old Raspberry Pis (Model 1B) that I had lying around, with the school buying some accessories for these later. In a subsequent year, the school committee asked me to write up some workshops for a school open night and bought ten BBC micro:bits[1] for this. Along the way, we were lucky enough to have some hardware gifted to us; it became apparent that some hardware was useful for teachers at the school as well. Generally, most costs (outside of the computers and network) were not excessive. When we did sometimes have a play with some of the school's more expensive robots, those seemed to be nowhere near as useful or reliable as the cheaper, simpler hardware.

---

[1] https://microbit.org/

A Quick Tale: Several Years of Mistakes – Numbers, Passwords, Computers, Accountability, and More

When a high school student, a teacher, and I decided to start our code club, we began with

- A small room at the local primary school

- A class set of laptops connected to the Internet

- Some prewritten Scratch programming activities

- A group of about 20 excited 11–12-year-old kids

At least we had the foresight to read through and try the first programming exercise prior to our first session, but soon ran into some unforeseen challenges. All the kids were facing either against the wall or toward a desk partition in the center of the room.

That day, our short-term goal was simply to make our way through our first code club session. Only three kids out of the group of 20 ended up completing their projects – each had learned programming before and had also used Scratch. A benefit of this was the other kids seeing a glimpse of the possibilities. Meanwhile, much of our time was spent frantically racing to each kid with their hand raised and asking for help, before they got distracted or frustrated. The kids' idle time was quite high at this stage, as we had to work through each previous problem before we got to them.

At this early stage, all the kids used a shared login since they had only used tablets during school, and classes weren't utilizing their computer lab time – this meant they didn't yet have logins and us having to help each kid log in. Projects were often not saved consistently or in a safe place. In subsequent weeks, this work had to be repeated, making the experience less rewarding. One week, my son brought in a game he had written and showed the group – for a couple of weeks, there was a renewed energy and enthusiasm in our club. Another of our code club kids, Tim, wrote a game where the player had to set everything on fire. Our other experienced kid, Darren, wrote a game where the player controlled a fish that ate smaller fish – at my suggestion, he later ended up adding a scoring system.

So, after our initial excitement and a slight spike a bit later, kids were still turning up, but we still had wasted sessions, which increased in frequency as we tried to add new activities. Although everyone had started with a variety of different skill levels, we still weren't seeing much measurable progression at any level, and those initial speed bumps from lack of good processes and fuzzy expectations began to wear thin.

In hindsight, the causes of increased delays in those early sessions can be summarized as follows:

A failure to anticipate logistical problems: We had limited contingency plans in place for computer or Internet problems. Credentials to gain access to computers and online services were often forgotten or shared, or kids/guardians lacked accountability for managing their credentials from week to week.

Underestimating the impact of most problems: Failing to manage login credentials to retrieve the previous week's work, working inefficiently by repeating ourselves, and a general lack of continuity or expectations of acceptable behavior in code club were to take up many weeks of our time and worked against us to stifle enthusiasm and slow down progress for kids. A side effect of this was that the more advanced kids ended up being less engaged and progressing slower.

Using processes that were not scalable or just not using processes: With only a few volunteers, it was easy to communicate, but onboarding more volunteers made it hard to be consistent. Sometimes, new volunteers would repeat our old mistakes or raise issues that we had already resolved. Not resolving a login problem or saving projects in a different place would often just repeat themselves during the next week.

A lack of experience of what did and did not work in the club environment: The idea of a club or space implies that everyone will be at different stages of learning, albeit within a chosen path. This extends to kids working on different projects to their peers at different time. Accommodating these different learning stages within a club took us a while to figure out. Using older styles of having all the kids continually being called back to the floor or trying to keep everyone on the same project just resulted in frustration.

Failing to discuss or improve our approach: Making time to regularly reflect on our sessions in a focused way resulted in ongoing improvement in our approach. To prevent us from reinventing the wheel, these included only our teacher representatives, with a small subset of longer-term volunteers. By regularly reviewing, we were able to reduce the amount of wasted session time while presenting a more unified interface for the kids. We also gained the agility to be able to accommodate unforeseen interruptions from other school events and changes in schedule, developing contingencies for these, such as bringing in a three-week activity or adjusting our calendar to suit.

A lack of accountability for guardians and kids: There was no accountability from kids or their families, and they would essentially turn up each week and wait for us to notice them not doing anything. In later years, we solved these issues by clearly stating expectations and requirements in acceptance forms.

What Is Your Baseline – Where Are You Starting From?

In the beginning weeks of our code club, we never considered whether we would have kids who had never written code before or whether anyone would find it harder because they didn't have access to a computer. We tried to talk about "drop-down menus" and "left-clicking" and were met with blank stares from kids brought up on mobile devices. It became obvious that we had underestimated some of these challenges.

Ideally, everyone participating should get something out of your code club or maker group, both in the long and short terms. It is reasonable to expect different skill and experience levels and think about how to keep kids who are between both extremes progressing at a measurable rate, achieving milestones, and of course staying engaged.

Remember   Being occupied is not the same as being engaged. Staying occupied may look like someone is busy, but they're not necessarily staying hungry to learn, satisfying their curiosity, or becoming empowered to create.

Although it can be easy to have kids turn up each week and have them copy some code into a computer or chase expensive remote-controlled robots around, ask yourself, "How much will their capabilities have progressed after six months?"

Tasks for Establishing a Baseline

Here are the first tasks to help you establish a baseline for your group.

Identify Some Prewritten Content to Start With

This could be a free series of online coding lessons or activities. I would suggest something like Code Club, Grok Learning, or Code.org as they are free and well structured. These are usually written so they can be completed in a set timeframe, which can be particularly useful for setting expectations, for example, "Look – this is just three steps, with four tasks in each." It is also one less thing to worry about when beginning. In later chapters, we'll talk about how to get a bit more creative, but for now prewritten content provides a solid structure for everyone involved.

Sit Down with Other Teachers and Volunteers to Discuss What You All Want to Achieve

This includes writing down some short- and long-term goals. A good short-term goal might be to have each kid complete one lesson or activity + challenge per weekly session. A good long-term goal might be to cover enough concepts to enable everyone to participate in a larger project by six months.

Work Out How Many Kids Your Team of Volunteers Can Comfortably Handle

If you have too many kids in your sessions, you won't get to all of them in time, leaving everyone frustrated and no one progressing to a measurable level. And then there's the other challenges to consider. A measurable level of progression lets you show kids that they are learning and what this means in terms of the greater opportunities available to them such as more complex projects. If progress is too slow, kids may lose interest, become distracted, and disrupt others from learning. Over the years, we found a sweet spot of two volunteers and a teacher for 20 kids that worked well for us, with maybe an extra volunteer handy for the more involved workshops.

Resist the Temptation to Accept Too Many Kids at First

You will always have someone who has another activity that clashes with the time, moves too far away, or even regrettably loses interest. A waiting list can be a good idea, as it also puts some value on the opportunity, and word will soon get around about how valuable a spot in your club is. Having a manageable number of kids improves the experience for the kids involved, and you will have less kids getting distracted because you can get to everyone in time. As we continue, I'll talk a bit more about how to optimize helping kids and keeping them engaged.

Discuss How to Manage the Expectations of the Kids and Their Guardians

This is not to say you're limiting what can be achieved, but rather explaining what kids can expect to achieve in your club or group. It is prudent to also talk about what constitutes unacceptable behavior, to ensure everyone gets the most out of your code club. This could include no playing of games on mobile devices and other personal conduct expectations. In our club, we found it necessary to remind kids that there was a waiting list and that adhering to the rules was necessary to keep your place in the club. We also introduced some required actions such as creating accounts and managing passwords, which we'll cover later in this chapter. Stating these ground rules up front means that everyone's expectations are set, thereby reducing later problems.

Guardians also need to understand the expectations for them and their kids. This includes having guardians understand that setting up and securely managing account passwords is a requirement of participation. It also gives them an idea of what content you will be covering and that effort is required from their kids in order to get the most out of the club or group. It also goes a long way toward reducing the misuse of the club as free after-school care or if their kid fails to put in the effort required.

Finally, make some simple notes, and check back on the preceding points, and consider the resources you will need. These will include

- Computers, Internet, support.

- A good place away from distractions.

- Checks that volunteers will require in your area to work with children – this is not negotiable and should be stated as such.

- Any facilities required for any kids with disabilities or special needs.

Health and Discipline Issues

If possible, the easiest option is to have a teacher to deal with this and make it clear where the boundaries of volunteers' (nonteachers) responsibilities are. These include understanding first aid, allergies, and processes for toilet breaks and generally keeping kids safe when arriving or leaving the session. Alternatively, if one of your volunteers has previously handled these things for a scout group or club, they will be able to guide your code club in this area.

Work Out What You Want the Code Club or Maker Group to Be

For our local code club, we wanted kids to feel empowered to realize their ideas in working projects and for them to own the skills for themselves; this means that they would recognize that skills they learn will belong to them rather than being relegated to something they did at school or had thrust upon them. My own experience is that as soon as a personal hobby or interest becomes solely work, you don't benefit from it, and it ceases to be *yours*. This is what makes a club or group different from school and lessons – kids need to want to participate and get something out of it.

Work Out Your Initial Scope: What Are Your First Milestones?

Once you have written down what you want to achieve, it's easy enough to work back from those goals to find out what needs to be done. This is where some logistics will come into play as you take your ideas and implement them in a practical sense!

Up until now, we have primarily been talking about coding, as that is a common place to begin at. For our school's code club, this was where we started. For you, it may vary, depending on the skills in your own team of volunteers and teachers. For the sake of showing a club's progression and processes for that, I will be using our school's code club for most of the examples in this book. Sometimes, it may not be immediately evident what your longer-term goals are, until you go further with your club – this was exactly the case for our school's code club. Whatever the case, be ready to acknowledge these and embrace them when you see them!

A good example of a short-term milestone is to have everyone complete their first project. Working back from this, ask yourself, "what do we need to do to make this happen?" Remember when I mentioned that everyone might be at a different skill level or progress differently? This is what keeps everything fun and challenging when you try to have everyone engaged all the time! Be prepared to have multiple activity threads and even split into subgroups in order to manage everyone's diverging milestones.

A long-term goal might be to be able to run a workshop that applies coding with a new skill, such as 3D design or electronics. As you may have guessed, there can be multiple workshops based on different interests and skills running in your club. Once you have an idea of this long-term goal, look at what skills would be required and how you will equip the kids with these.

This is where your prewritten content becomes invaluable – often, such content will also include a list of concepts or a skills matrix that explains what kids will learn from each project or lesson. If you have this, you can simply look at these and determine a list of projects required for kids to obtain the skills for your first long-term goal.

Explain to everyone roughly how long the first project will take to complete. This sets expectations and sets kids' expectations for a reasonably quick and easy first task. Before your first session, go through the project and write down any tricky parts or problems with the project code – then you can address these with the entire group at various points during the first session. This helps everyone in parallel, leaving you to help those that may have typed something incorrectly or need help debugging their programming.

One milestone that I personally love, and is super handy to achieve, is to teach everyone learn how to debug their own errors. You'll know this has been achieved when they ask you a question and, after a few minutes, say something like, "oh, it's OK – I worked it out myself." At this point, just make a mental note of the milestone, smile to yourself, and go help the next person!

A nice milestone that builds skills in other areas can involve having kids show some leadership by sharing a tip or solution they have worked out either to the group or a friend. This might involve having certain kids stand up in front of the group to explain one of the trickier parts of the project and how they solved it.

Your very first milestone should be to get everyone to log on to their computer and into the chosen programming environment, for example, Scratch or Trinket.io. The next could be to have everyone save their work so they aren't redoing the same things each week without learning.

Easy, you might be thinking, "I can just run through these lessons and then do my workshop at the end of that." Remember how I mentioned that we had a variety of skill levels and experience? If we are ever short of volunteers each year, Code Club Australia sends us volunteers to help with our registered club.[2] One time, a volunteer turned up after going through a training program. After a few sessions at our code club, she commented that it was nothing like what they had trained for, because we had such a diverse range of skill levels after a few years of code club that everyone was already working on different projects! So, the key idea here is that even though everyone doesn't progress at the same rate, that is alright. Often, I would have someone become worried if they missed a session or were

---

[2] https://account.codeclubau.org/register-a-club/

not progressing as fast as others. I would often sit down with them, letting them know that maybe next week someone else would be sick or not able to attend and that it didn't really matter as long as they were learning and enjoying themselves. Later in this chapter, I will cover some tips and strategies we learned to address some of the issues we ran into.

Equipment and Initial Setup

Now that you know what activities your club will initially involve, you will likely be starting to consider what equipment and other resources you may need.

Using a fairly common scenario and set of requirements, these could be: Room that is reasonably private and comfortable, where you can regularly run your code club and physically help everyone easily. Running your code club after school at the same school is a great way to do this, since school computers can be freed up after classes, and most rooms will be empty for splitting into smaller groups. Staff are often around just before the club starts, making it easier for kids to have a snack and get to the room and settle. Ensure that heating and cooling are acceptable, since these will affect the ability of people to concentrate and could even introduce health issues if not managed adequately. Expect some tiredness or lower concentration at the start or end of the term. Other location options include libraries, or if you can borrow a free space somewhere, this may work. Just be aware of any health and safety requirements, or other groups that may be nearby or sharing the space, and could conflict with you having a safe and quiet environment for kids to learn and create in.

Computers/Laptops

Will these be owned by the participants or at a school or other locations, such as a library? The answer to this question will determine the best way to ensure that everyone has the correct computer environment set up to participate. You may need support staff. Be aware that, although many kids have access to mobile devices, the ability to learn to look under the covers of things and pull them apart is an integral part of the coding and maker mindset. With a mobile device, most things are abstracted away from the user, which tends to be counterintuitive as your group's quest for knowledge and understanding progresses.

Optimizing Your Environment

Whiteboards, projectors, TV screens, monitors, and other accessories that let you show things to the entire group are very useful and often available at schools and libraries. However, with regard to the core activities, you'll want to try and get the kids learning the basics as soon as possible, since building a reasonable skills base will prevent stagnation or reaching a plateau later. With our local code club, failing to get kids learning the basics limited our choices in earlier years, since we didn't have enough kids with the required skills for the fun and more advanced activities. Kids ended up stagnating and doing the same old scratch games all year. They would just turn up but not really progress or say they were bored because we couldn't move them onto the more interesting projects. This is one of the main reasons for optimizing the running of your code club so that kids can focus on learning rather than getting bogged down with administrative issues.

Onboarding at the Start of Each Year

When sending out an email acceptance to guardians, outline the requirements clearly, including how to create accounts for the required services online and how to store credentials. Have a checklist that guardians must tick for the tasks, with a signature to indicate understanding. This is a good time to stipulate conditions for participation, which would include the usual school or venue requirements, in addition to any other distractions, such as playing games or not participating.

15

Computers and IT Support

If you have browser-based programming projects, these are the easiest to get started with. We used `trinket.io` to do most of the Python[3] Code Club Australia projects. Once we started on hardware-based workshops that included robots and required specific software to be installed, we had to leverage IT support people to ensure things were prepared. This is not straightforward at all; even if you are technically skilled, the time constraints and a locked-down environment can be challenging to deal with for the small window of time you may have access to the computers.

As our local Code Club began to evolve and requirements grew, I managed to get the IT folk to install Python on the school computers. This involved running through the install myself and then sending the links to download the required installation to the school IT person. Initially, we were using Apple Macs, and somehow we managed to also get a working Python setup when the school decided to move to Windows laptops. Something worth considering is that for some projects, you will likely want to start installing additional Python libraries on laptops to give you more functionality – this will require setting up Python to work with the school's proxy and firewall, through which they must access the Internet. Some of the challenges and details of how we overcame them in this area can be found in Chapter 8. The important takeaway at this point is to make sure you arrange a time to come in earlier with the school IT person present, so you can test things. Make sure this is a long time before you plan to use any installed software, since it is likely to not work. Speaking directly to the IT person allows you to determine how much information they will require to set things up. At this point, I digress, since this won't be required until

---

[3] `www.python.org/about/`

you have done a bit more learning and want to do extra workshops. There are often a few smart kids that will get extremely excited and work through all the learning content at home. This is part of the "at some point you will find that everyone is at a different stage of their learning journey," so be prepared to be surprised with additional activities being required a little earlier than expected.

Also, consider that if your content is online, kids know how to Google for things and may just copy and paste, the net effect being that they feel like they achieved more, but it effectively prevents them from learning anything. Our local code club ran into the problem of kids working ahead, which is great, and other kids copying finished projects so they could move on to other activities – the side effect of the latter was that the kids who copied projects did not have the skills for the other activities and sometimes prevented others from participating, due to number limitations. As a solution, we have used a few different systems to track progress. At a midway point during the school year, we allocated a few weeks dedicated to helping kids complete projects they might have got stuck with or forgotten to complete. We also set up a requirement for kids to have their projects checked by a volunteer, where we would ask questions about how the code worked and ask the kids to verbally describe some of the challenges they had run into and how these were solved. In addition to sorting out the cheaters from the hard workers, this also provides some recognition to those who have worked hard.

Login and Password Basics

A significant obstacle to kids getting started, saving their work each week, and generally staying engaged ended up being login problems on laptops and online services such as Scratch or Trinket.io. As a quick starter tip, I have included the flowchart (Figure 1-1) that was the result of multiple attempts to solve this problem. Feel free to adapt this to your own situation!

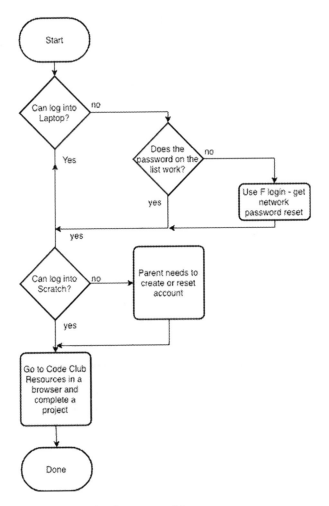

Figure 1-1. *Flowchart for login problems*

Another Alternative – Make Your Space Portable

If you have access to a small fleet of computers or are in an area where kids can bring one along, you can run your code club offline. This requires providing instructions to parents and guardians beforehand, so they can install any required software. You can provide learning materials in a file format such as PDF, which can be accessed on a mobile device.

A more modern method of running your code club or maker group can be online – since COVID-19, this is a real requirement that needs to be fulfilled. This involves using an online collaborative conferencing service, such as Zoom, Microsoft Teams, or Google Hangouts, where you can ideally share your screen. The same requirements apply for accountability and setup as I've previously described. Also, be aware of requirements for security and privacy when hosting sessions online. In short, you'll need to make sure that the conference isn't public and that personal details are not shared. Some volunteers with online-only clubs mentioned a challenge in knowing who is genuinely working – however, the method of checking completed projects could work online just as easily.

The Tech Stuff: Learn by Applying

Let's talk about the actual content we will be taking the kids through – this can often be slightly scary for some volunteers, but an important point is to be careful not to pass some of this apprehension on to the kids. I have seen volunteers openly complaining that it is impossible to work without a mouse when kids were happily using trackpads or imply that text-based programming is harder than it really is. Setting a "can-do" attitude helps kids feel empowered to complete the content and overcome any obstacles within reason. Weaning kids off block-based programming to accept the more powerful Python projects took a while for our code club. Much of this was due to some initial apprehension from volunteers, but as soon as we approached text-based Python programming in a matter-of-fact way, the kids just accepted it as being easy.

Whether you have a highly technical background or minimal technical experience, spending 15–20 minutes working through a project prior to a session increases the speed at which you can help kids solve problems. Since the projects are designed for kids, highly technical skills are not required at this time. But spending this small amount of time beforehand means you can attend to kids quicker, reducing idle or waiting time for kids and keeping them more engaged while learning and progressing and less likely to be distracted.

Examples of issues that come up during a project can include

- Ambiguities in the project text that may be challenging to interpret

- Bugs or quirks in software tools

- Skipping or mistyping lines of code

- Problems peculiar to the computer or network environment

We can introduce programming terminology and concepts while we learn – later, this will be useful for kids that may be interested in collaborating or talking to other programmers or makers.

Two Examples of Problems and Solutions

During your maker or code club sessions, some kids will put their hands up for help, some will prefer to try on their own before asking, and others may try for a short time before giving up and becoming distracted. The approaches we take to helping our kids depend on whether the issue is a common issue, such as a known bug or problem with the project, or an issue specific to the individual's own project, like a typo or leaving out a section of code. A good way of reducing the first category is to write it up for everyone to see and talk about it to draw attention to it. For the latter category, a more individual troubleshooting approach can be applied.

Troubleshooting and Debugging

As mentioned earlier, a good milestone to achieve is when our kids start to solve their own programming problems. By solving their own problems, kids stay engaged and can progress faster in their learning journey.

Here are some tips for troubleshooting with kids.

Start by asking some questions:

- "What is your program supposed to do?"

- "What is going wrong?"

- If there are error messages, "What do the error messages say?"

- "Which line of the code controls the part that isn't working?"

The last question will give you a place to start looking. To keep our kid programmer engaged, verbalize your thought processes.

Some useful phrases for this might be

- "OK, let's start by checking for typos or missing brackets."

- "Hmm, what should this variable be at this point?"

- "Where does this get set?"

- "OK, so it looks like we're using a loop to get each line of the information we read in earlier."

Once our young programmer works out the solution to the problem, check their understanding by asking some questions or by having them explain it back, for example, "So…what were we missing there?"

The Posse effect   Year after year, we often see a more experienced, louder kid develop a small group who sit near them every week. This group of kids will often progress slowly, if at all, and when pulled aside to chat, they will sheepishly admit they haven't done anything or got "stuck" and never progressed past a single roadblock and didn't ask for help. Separating the posse or sitting down with them individually for ten minutes can sometimes identify where they got stuck or get them back on track. Other times, we have found that rewarding these kids when they contribute to troubleshooting can empower them to get more involved. Again, if you have enough people running your code club or maker group, you'll be able to spot and address such issues earlier.

Strategies for Volunteer Collaboration

Online collaboration can sometimes be useful for discussing systemic logistical issues or sharing fixes that may not have been discussed during a live session. Establishing this central place to collaborate early on can help newer or less technical volunteers feel less isolated. There is less of a requirement for instant responses, but over the duration of a week, it allows volunteers to communicate without being too intrusive.

There are many ways to collaborate online. In the early days of our local code club, email worked well, but soon became difficult at times when we had a larger group of volunteers and were running more than one group of kids per week. Once we introduced additional workshops and ran these in parallel, we really need a chat system that offered individual channels to keep track of everything we talked about and also as a central source of information. For us, we tried Slack initially, but due to it being designed more for commercial developers, we soon started to hit limitations and moved onto Discord. Discord offers a good solution since it is free to run a server and can be accessed on both mobile devices and computers. If you need to have meetings online, Discord also offers quite clear group video and audio conferencing. Keep in mind that some volunteers may not be used to all collaborative platforms and will tend to forget to log in or just not participate. In those cases, a summary email can be useful to communicate key information.

A shared file folder such as a Google Drive can also be useful for sharing information to kids and distributing documentation between volunteers. Just remember to set permissions so that each is separate.

Graphical vs. Text-Based Programming

I've talked about how our local code club began with Scratch programming. We did it because that's what the Code Club Australia projects started with. It turned out that a lot of Code Clubs in Australia were also predominantly using Scratch. The limitations of a graphical language will only let you go so far, though.

Scratch is a great place for kids to start coding and leads nicely into Microsoft MakeCode and MakeCode Arcade, the former used on the micro:bit and the latter on some specifically designed consoles.[4] One of our earlier Code Club kids would write multilevel games and in later years became a volunteer. Others ended up writing some simple programs that they used for school projects. However, once we started to look at more advanced programming and tried to model various solutions to problems, Scratch became limited and required overly complex and less readable code and in other cases just could not easily interface with things we wanted to control. At our local Code Clubs and at other code clubs, it became challenging to wean kids off block-based languages and to learn more advanced concepts, such as object-oriented programming. These days, some great bridging platforms exist for this, including BlockPy[5] and EduBlocks.[6] You might be interested to know that EduBlocks was written by a 15-year-old student, Joshua Lowe,[7] and runs on computers and

---

[4] https://arcade.makecode.com/hardware
[5] https://think.cs.vt.edu/blockpy/
[6] https://app.edublocks.org
[7] www.tech4goodawards.com/finalist/joshua-lowe/

microcontroller boards like the BBC micro:bit. Here's a screenshot of some Python code written using EduBlocks in a web browser (Figure 1-2). The resulting code will be run on `https://trinket.io`.

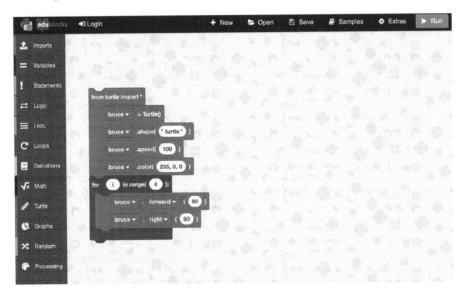

Figure 1-2. *EduBlocks Python program*

A quick explanation of object-oriented programming In a nutshell, object-oriented programming allows defining objects that can represent real-world concepts or things. This makes modeling the solution to a problem in code easier to write and read. Objects can have specific attributes and actions (methods) that can be performed. An example of an object could be an animal, with attributes such as fur `color`, `age`, or `weight`. Examples of methods that could be written include `sit()`, `stand()`, `walk()`, and `bark()`.

Python is much faster than Scratch and is both simple and powerful, but it also has over 137,000 libraries that contain Python functions to extend its capabilities while keeping the code easy to read. For example, some uses for Python are

- Controlling machines

- Interacting with things on the Internet to store or retrieve information

- Speech recognition, tracking or adding objects in video and photos, and automating many more tasks that save us time

This makes Python an easy way to show kids the scope of programming while also giving them some insight into how to integrate across hardware. Python is now one of the most popular languages and is taught at a university level. For these reasons, I really wanted to show kids how easy it was to program in Python and show them how it opened a gateway to so many possibilities! Our first efforts failed miserably, due to issues with having it installed on the school computers or the misconception that typing was hard and Python was hard. We never gave up, and I ended up running a trial group with some of the kids who we had identified as having finished the most projects. As previously mentioned, it is much easier to start with a manageable group before scaling things up. As we progressed, the kids in this group worked through the Code Club Australia Python projects, with speed of progress varying at different times. This didn't seem to matter too much as eventually everyone had a reasonable coverage of the main concepts taught in those projects.

The breakthrough moment was when I drew a diagram of a water sensor and a micro:bit on the whiteboard. Immediately, the kids' minds started to tick – someone even suggested using a pump! I explained how the sensor worked and told them to use Google to search for the code to read a value from the sensor wire connected to the micro:bit. Within ten minutes, we had some working code, and our group was deciding what value indicated that there was enough moisture in the soil. I showed our teacher volunteer, David, and we knew we had finally reached a significant milestone.

We knew that if we could get a small group of 11–12-year-olds to this level, we could potentially open the gateway to potentially thousands of projects. For that reason, this book will use Python or the embedded (used on hardware) versions of MicroPython and CircuitPython for examples.

Summary

1. Determine your initial long- and short-term goals and start with a small group before scaling to larger or multiple groups.

2. Initial number of volunteers may be low, but will grow as you progress, and people start to understand and recognize what you are doing.

3. You don't need money to get started with content from one of many groups that support teaching kids about STEAM-related areas, some even provide volunteers.

4. Don't be discouraged – my own local Code Club started with a teacher, an ex-student of the school, myself, and some super-keen kids.

5. The initial first few Code Club sessions are not too hard, but later it is important to deal with stumbling blocks before they become ongoing problems. Ongoing problems can sap kids' enthusiasm and can result in them becoming disengaged due to lack of progress and them having to repeat things that do not contribute to learning.

6. Know your baseline in terms of volunteer and kids' skills and experience and work from that.

7. Keep the volunteer/teacher to kid participant ratio at a workable level, especially when starting out. The kids will get more out of the experience, and it gives you a chance to find your way without being overwhelmed.

8. Keep communications open between you and participant guardians and between volunteers/teachers – the latter can be free online collaboration systems.

9. Set some milestones – work back from these and set yourself up for easy wins at first.

10. Anticipate that eventually everyone will be at a different level – this is fine, when everyone gets something out of it. Make sure kids work through and complete each project before moving on to the next – establish this as a standard so no one feels like they are falling behind, just because they spend more time on something.

11. Spend a few minutes to go through the content before each session – you'll be happy you did, and things will run smoother if you know where the tricky parts are likely to be, identifying any bugs that cause a project to fail. This will help you get to more kids during a session.

12. Set expectations with regard to acceptable behavior and accountability for both the participating kids and guardians. Volunteers can also benefit from understanding how things are run when they join.

13. Have processes for likely issues that will come up, such as password/account issues. This helps you deal with things quicker so that everything keeps on moving.

14. Learn the technical things by applying them. Do the exercises and help kids to debug by verbalizing your thought process as you work through problems. Keep the kids involved throughout debugging and problem solving.

15. Beware of the "Posse effect" around some more advanced kids.

16. Python can describe the real world. Scratch only has one data structure – lists – but Python has many data structures to describe real things:

     • *Dictionaries*: Lists that have an index and can be ordered.

     • *Arrays*: These are like a grid of variables.

     • *Customizable*: We can also make our own data structures to describe things and their attributes.

          • *Things*: People, animals, data to be sent over a network, audio, video, pictures, and files.

          • *Attributes*: Hair color, number of legs, type of hair, size, weight, and so on.

Chapter 1: Cheat Sheet

Sources for Free Content and Support

Code Club: https://codeclub.org

Code.org: https://code.org

CoderDojo: https://coderdojo.com/

Short-Term Goal/Milestone Examples

- Kids log in consistently to laptop and online platforms, for example, Scratch, Trinket.io.

- Kids complete the first project.

- Kids debug with help.

- Kids debug unassisted.

- Stage an event, which can be an incursion or excursion of some sort to break things up and generate enthusiasm.

Long-Term Goal Examples

- Complete a module or group of projects and have a volunteer/teacher ask questions to confirm legitimate understanding and completion of each project.

- Improve efficiency so that sessions run smoother, and kids are so engrossed in what they are doing that you have to almost tear them away at the end of each session.

- Grow awareness and understanding outside of your Code Club by having kids talk about experiences and showcase their projects to wider school or community or offer short introductory workshops during open nights.

- Move on to applying skills in more advanced workshops and collaborative projects.

- Get more volunteers and teachers involved to cover more age groups or create a second Code Club that runs parallel or during another time of the year.

- Get some additional hardware donated or bought, for example, microcontroller boards such as BBC micro:bits or CircuitPython boards, single-board computers (SBC) such as the Raspberry Pi, and electronic kits and accessories.

- Run multiple workshops in parallel.

- Add additional elements such as fabric (e-textiles) or cardboard circuits or 3D design.

Questions to Ask When Helping Kids Troubleshoot Their Code

- What should the program do?

- What is going wrong?

- What do the error messages mean?

- Which part of the code controls the problematic behavior?

Other Useful Tips for Troubleshooting

- Verbalize your troubleshooting with kids.

- Keep them involved while solving the problem.

- Ask them to explain what the problem was.

Checklist for Volunteer Onboarding

- Relevant requirements for working with children (mandatory).

- Give a brief so they know the history and how you are doing things.

- Onboard them to whatever agreed communication channel you are using.

- Find out any strengths or skills they may have and see how these can be incorporated into what you are doing.

- Explain the expectations for participating kids.

- Give them access to projects before sessions.

- Explain the process to confirm completion of projects.

Checklist for Participants and Guardians

- Signed up to required online services.

- Passwords managed appropriately so kids learn how to manage these and always can participate.

- Distribute expectations and have these signed and returned either physically or digitally.

- Ensure health and safety requirements and other housekeeping information such as disabilities, health conditions, and any other special requirements are communicated in writing and handled by the qualified volunteer or teacher.

CHAPTER 2

Getting Our Hands Dirty with MicroPython

Some of my best projects began life with me staring at some materials and tools until an idea finally took shape in my mind. Only then could I take the first step to start building. Although the time spent staring at things seemed pointless, the project would not have been completed without it. Likewise, even though establishing goals and finding content may seem tedious, eventually it will be time for you and your band of volunteers to host your first Code Club or maker group session. A little bit of thought and preparation can make all the difference, especially in saving time once you are up and running!

Your initial content will give you a chance to establish a good routine. Be aware though that even though it feels nice when everyone progresses at the same rate and is working on the same projects, the nature of a club or maker group is that, sooner or later, things start to diverge. This is where being able to write workshops and develop other activities from week to week becomes very handy. One of the aims of this book is to help you along with some examples of projects and workshops that we developed for our clubs. You should work through these projects to get an idea of how they run and what information to include – they may also have the side effect of being...*fun*!

© Martin Tan 2023
M. Tan, *micro:bit Projects with Python and Single Board Computers*,
https://doi.org/10.1007/978-1-4842-9197-9_2

An important consideration is how projects can be scaled, so that they can be run as collaborative group workshops rather than staying with individual projects. This can contribute to keeping kids staying engaged more consistently; sometimes, breaking into subgroups can offer certain advantages. In our code club, we were able to run multiple workshops in parallel, depending on how many volunteers we had that year. More engaged kids mean less distracted kids. Finally, one of the most important things to remember is to always enjoy the journey, by striving to learn and having fun. Half the battle is showing kids how enthusiastic and excited you are; keep them keen to attend and hesitant to leave!

A Quick Tale: Jumping In with Our Code Club

As mentioned earlier, some kids will race ahead or have prior experience and will finish our initial base training content earlier than others. Of course, we could ask them to help others for weeks until they catch up, but ultimately this would prevent them from progressing or learning as quickly as they probably could. Remember that a club or maker space should not be something that kids feel is *mandatory* but that they want to be involved with because it is interesting and exciting for them personally. Having worked with some reasonably smart hackers and coders in the past, my inner nerd felt that we should encourage kids to push ahead as much as they wanted, assuming they were prepared to put in the effort – this got me thinking about how I could facilitate this more efficiently and before kids lost interest!

Our first idea was to find some new content, take a smaller group of kids who had progressed faster, and look at how we could extend our Code Club scope to accommodate them. How far you manage to get with most of the kids using the initial content you started with will determine how far you can go in the next part of your creative journey. Some years we didn't get as far as we'd like, and this meant not being able to do as many workshops or extended activities. Other times, we would have a small group of budding makers and coders who were content to work away on harder projects, while the rest of the club did 3D design in TinkerCAD.[1] That particular project was planned after one meeting after which we delivered a very short five-slide presentation to the kids about building a "smart" city.

The idea of "jumping in" relates to testing small components of our projects or ideas as we go – it's easy to conceive a very elaborate idea only to find that it doesn't work. So testing often and tracing through a small, isolated component can be quicker and easier than searching through large amounts of code or circuitry to find out which part(s) caused the problem. Because Python also has an interactive "shell" that allows us to try out Python code snippets live, kids can test how commands work before incorporating them into a larger program. Then, by testing often after each section of code is added, it becomes much easier to isolate any problem code or unanticipated behavior at runtime. In short, starting with something simple that works reduces the chances of problems becoming overwhelming or code becoming overly complex.

Taking this approach of testing often before a project becomes overwhelming means that kids feel more empowered by learning to break solutions down into bite-size chunks. They also gain better visualization into how the overall system works and will later be more able to implement additional enhancements. As we progress with more projects, we can also introduce concepts such as "don't repeat yourself" (DRY) and learn how to communicate clearly with some technical terminology.

---

[1] www.tinkercad.com/

INTRODUCING SOME TERMINOLOGY

While you work your way through your initial content, it can be useful to introduce programming terminology. This helps establish a consistent way of communicating when collaborating or while debugging something that isn't working as expected. These skills will come in handy for more challenging projects. Some examples of this could be as follows:

- "So, this project is using a list structure to store the team members' names?"

- "Here's our *main loop*, and it repeats these commands – we call that *iteration*."

- "How does our script make a decision?" (assuming someone recalls a correct example; otherwise give more clues or explain the answer), "…yes, and 'if..then..else' is a *conditional* statement because it *branches* to a different place based on this condition."

- "Is this…a *variable* or a *list*?"

- "Remember that setting up all these *variables* at the start of your program is called *initialization*."

- "This variable never changes – so it's called a *constant*." There are limits though, because calling something *immutable* (not changeable) or *mutable* (can be changed) can be confusing for kids, so it's worth waiting for the object-oriented discussion to bring these in.

Tracking Progress

Knowing what level of skills each participant has reached is helpful when selecting which kids are suited to which workshops. This is especially beneficial when running these the first time and really helps stack the odds in your favor. It can be frustrating for both you and kids if they go into a workshop without enough skills to participate or contribute.

Often, when it comes to code clubs and maker groups, we learned that the loudest kids aren't necessarily the most prolific. Our experience has been that it is important to know who has completed which projects as the year progresses. Another frustrating problem came up with kids who would look up solutions online and copy and paste them, but would struggle or be negatively disruptive in the more advanced workshops where they couldn't get by just by copying the finished project.

This brings us to a question that I'm often asked, "How do you keep track of everyone's progress?" For our school-based code club, we tried to leverage resources that the school already had – one platform allowed kids to keep a diary of what they had done and take videos of completed projects. However, this still lacked confirmation that kids were understanding the code or had legitimately put in the effort rather than copying and pasting the project code.

The solution we ended up having most success with keeps things simple and efficient while ensuring that kids are understanding the code and have indeed completed the project themselves.

After a few tries, here's the process we found worked well for tracking progress:

- Use a shared Google sheet to record progress of set projects.

- Have kids demonstrate that their code works, "Can you show me the working code?"

- Require volunteers to approve completion of projects by asking the following questions:

  - "How does the code work for (specific features)?"

  - "What did you find challenging, or what parts did you get stuck on, and how did you resolve the problem or error?"

  - Ask about concepts that were used, for example, "So you used a dictionary data structure here, can you explain how a dictionary is different to a list?"

Two positive side effects of having a volunteer verify completion of projects are that we get to know individuals better and they receive acknowledgment for their efforts from volunteers. Over the years, we had seen kids who appeared to be quite distracted but knew the content and really started to focus more once we gave them some recognition. It's also a chance for the kids to get to know your volunteers, and sometimes even a quick conversation can show kids what we know, which instills more enthusiasm after seeing that we get excited and know our stuff too. One conversation I do often have relates to some of the challenges I personally had when learning. I found that sometimes it was difficult to understand something when it was explained the first time. Usually, I had to have it explained another way or experiment with things myself. It may also be that kids are wary of asking questions – sometimes in a school environment, they may feel that this shows that they weren't listening. I try to let them know that we are committed to helping them succeed and encourage them to feel comfortable with letting us know if they don't understand something, so that we can explain it in a different way that may make more sense to them.

The included projects in this book can be used without many or any changes – however, I do encourage you to improvise and improve these or customize them to your needs. I've also included various notes to explain some concepts for you – you may want to remove these before using the project in your own code club or maker group.

What Can We Do in One Hour?

During our early attempts at weaning kids off Scratch, I tried to take a group through some online Python resources. Although some of these exercises had really appealed to me, for the kids rewards seemed low in value compared to the effort required to complete them. Not everything worked on the computers or network we had. We weren't always using our time efficiently, and the path to completion was fuzzy at best. One time, one of the kids declared, "I don't like Python because Python means I have to type, and I don't want to type."

Later, we started kids off using Code Club Australia's Python curriculum – we worked hard to progress kids through the curriculum and to complete each lesson before moving on. Following along with written steps made it easier for kids to stay engaged without relying on someone to tell them what to do. This freed us up to help when needed, while everyone else continued working.

Although running through Python lessons is useful, understanding is another thing altogether. The important elements that translate from those coding lessons to more blended hardware projects are as follows:

- Create easy wins for each session

- Show the final goal and make it cool

- Keep instructions simple

- Only provide essential information

Creating easy wins means setting your kids up for success. This includes removing distractions, making tasks achievable, and making sure things work. Showing the goal, whether it is a thing that kids will make or an online interactive program, helps kids know that the effort will be worthwhile. For this reason, the goal needs to be cool, and it doesn't hurt to get excited about it yourself, either. Simple instructions keep kids progressing, and progressing is rewarding. The last element comes back to my love of cheat sheets – this is empowering for kids, because it screams "these are all the things you need to succeed!"

One of the best ways to emphasize value is to get things working quickly. Given that so many things last for roughly an hour, for example, TV shows and lunch breaks, writing projects that hit valuable milestones or complete within an hour really demonstrates value. In other words, it says, "In an hour, we will have done all this and learned tons!" The time investment then appears very much more worthwhile, especially to kids. This also builds enthusiasm when they go home and exclaim to their families, "Look what we did today!"

While we initially used some of the fancier educational tech toys that the school had access to, it turned out that some of the simpler tools gave us easier rewards while providing the learning that promoted kids to increasingly interesting projects. From some of the work I'd done in preparing the Moonhack project for Code Club Australia in 2016, I had heard about a fabulous device known as the BBC micro:bit from Rik of the UK branch of Code Club. These helped kids learn to code while allowing them to delve into electronics as well and were given out to school kids across the UK. Unfortunately, these weren't available for under $50 in Australia at the time, so I started importing these to sell at a more reasonable price. I started an online store to help kids get access to these. Eventually, everyone caught on and micro:bits are now readily available in Australia.

Introducing the BBC micro:bit

The BBC micro:bit is a pocket-sized computer that introduces you to how software and hardware work together. It has an LED light display, buttons, sensors and many input/output features that, when programmed, let it interact with you and your world.

Micro:bit Educational Foundation, 2021[2]

---

[2] https://microbit.org/get-started/first-steps/introduction/

The BBC micro:bit is a microcontroller board that doesn't run a heavy operating system like Windows, Linux, or MacOS. At the time of writing, there have been two main versions of the micro:bit released – version 1 (V1) and version 2 (V2). If you're unsure, you can find the version in the lower-right corner on the back of your micro:bit.[3]

It does run a small blob of software called firmware which, among other things, allows it to appear as a USB device when plugged into your computer. When we write programs for the micro:bit, your code is converted to a .hex file and transferred to the micro:bit's memory where it runs. For the micro:bit version of MicroPython, the .hex file also includes the version of MicroPython that is used to run your program.

Tip   Be careful about laying the micro:bit down on a conductive surface when it's powered up, especially if you have aluminum MacBooks, since it is really easy for kids to place the micro:bit on the MacBook, which will short out the micro:bit and kill it.

Setting Up an Editor

When programming Python on the micro:bit, we can edit our code using the online editor or in an editor that is installed on a computer. Each editor will also need to convert the MicroPython code into a .hex file that will be copied onto the micro:bit's storage, then run. The .hex file includes the version of MicroPython supported by the editor.

Programming in an online editor is useful when a suitable editor cannot be installed on the computers you are using. Installing a Python editor is preferable to using an online editor, as it allows programming more than just one device – once installed and set up, you can use it to program other

---

[3] https://support.microbit.org/support/solutions/articles/19000119162-how-to-identify-the-version-number-of-your-micro-bit

devices such as the range of Adafruit CircuitPython microcontroller boards. Although there are many other editors you can use, I have limited our scope to the editors that work "out of the box," that is, they don't require extra plugins or multiple changes to do what we want.

The online MicroPython editor for the micro:bit can be found at `https://python.microbit.org/v/2` as shown in Figure 2-1.

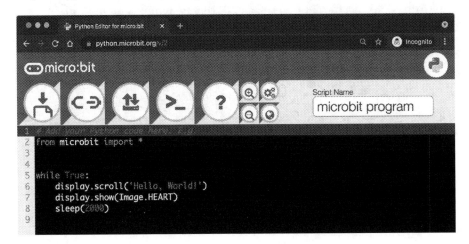

Figure 2-1. *micro:bit Python web browser editor*

The Mu and Thonny editors are quite easy to install, downloadable from `https://codewith.mu/en/download` and `https://thonny.org`, respectively. Both editors are available for Windows, MacOS, and Linux; Thonny comes already installed on the Raspberry Pi operating system.

Both Mu and Thonny editors are integrated developer environments (IDEs) that are designed to be easy for kids and beginners to use. This means that they have basic features, but don't complicate the interface with any advanced features. Features such as syntax highlighting, which colors the text to make it easier to see mistakes, command completion, and automatic indenting are included. All three editors make it easy to send the completed code and other files directly to the micro:bit or save them for editing later; they also allow easy troubleshooting, by displaying code errors that occur when running with the micro:bit plugged into the computer. Another useful debugging tool is a Python shell console or the read-eval-print loop (REPL). The former lets you try Python commands live before adding them to your code, and the latter allows you to see error messages. The Mu editor REPL is shown at the bottom of Figure 2-2. In contrast, the Mu editor is more visual, with large icons, whereas the Thonny editor is menu based, with drop-down options.

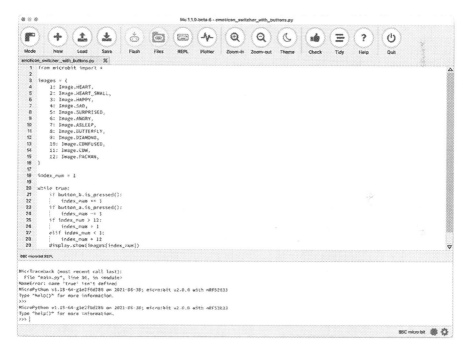

Figure 2-2.   *The Mu editor with the interactive shell and REPL interfaces*

Both editors support a range of devices and Python libraries. If you want to work with microcontroller boards other than the micro:bit or Adafruit CircuitPython boards, at the time of writing Thonny offers support for a few more devices than the Mu editor. From the View menu, select

Files to show a tree view that will let you navigate the folders[4] on your computer for upload to your device. This is shown in Figure 2-3.

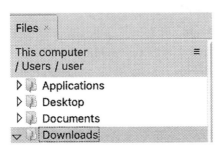

Figure 2-3. *Thonny Files view*

The Mu editor typically only allows uploading from the working directory that is set in its configuration file – if using the Mu editor, remember to ask your IT person to set the working directory to a place where you will save your files, for example, the Documents directory or a home directory on your network. The latter is especially important when your computers are shared, that is, people get a different computer for each Code Club or maker group session.

---

[4] Although this can be controversial, file folders are sometimes called "directories" and vice versa

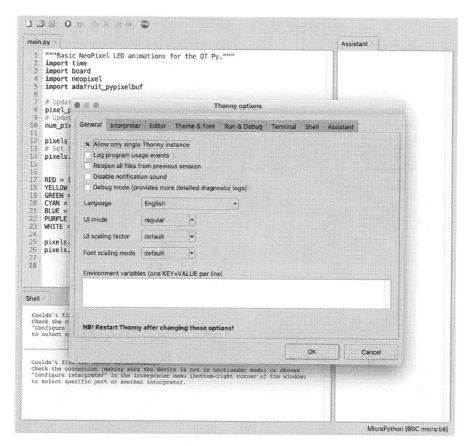

Figure 2-4. *The Thonny editor with the options window open*

Tip   If the computers you are using have restricted access to the
Internet, your editor may need to be set up to access a proxy server
that allows access to download required programming libraries. For
Mu, you can point your IT person to this information page that explains
where to find the `settings.json` file that needs the proxy server
added. Your IT person will know the proxy server URL. For the Thonny
editor, this information will need to be added under `Tools` ➤ `General`
➤ `Environment` labeled as "Environment variables" in Figure 2-4.

The initial project I am going through was also published on my blog in a more simple format and later in *micro:mag* magazine. The challenge is something I've added for this book and was adapted from other micro:bit projects we used at our code club. We have used this successfully on Windows, Mac, and Linux operating systems.

A FIRST PROJECT: BBC MICRO:BIT EMOTICON SWITCHER USING BUTTONS

Here's a simple MicroPython script that lets multiple micro:bits wirelessly send emoticons to each other!

What you will learn

- How to use a dictionary structure to store multiple emoticon images on the micro:bit

- How to structure our code to make it easier to add more features

- How to retrieve indexed images from a dictionary

- How to use radio to send information to a group of micro:bits listening on a specific channel

- How to use separate channels to group micro:bits

What you will need

- At least one or more BBC micro:bit microcontroller boards

- Micro USB cables and battery cages for each micro:bit (you'll need a USB hub or adapter to connect a USB-A cable if your computer only has USB-C)

- A computer running Windows, MacOS, or Linux

- An installed editor for MicroPython (preferable) or a web browser

Let's get started!

Displaying an image on the micro:bit can really be done in two lines of Python code:

```
from microbit import *
display.show(Image.HEART)
```

That's great to test that your micro:bit is working, but let's write our code so that it is *scalable*. This means making our code easy to add more features to and build into larger projects. We will also learn more about structuring our code to keep it manageable and readable, even once we add more features to it.

Step 1: In our editor, we will begin by writing a new script and importing the required micro:bit library module. This will let us call `microbit` functions (commands) in our code. Click New (⊕ New icon) icon in the Mu editor and ■ in Thonny), and a new editor tab will appear. Clear out any code that is in there, and type in the Python code listed as follows:

`from microbit import *`

This will import all the functions from the `microbit` library for us to use.

Note   When importing library modules, the * means we don't need the `microbit.` prefix in front of each function we will call – this makes typing a bit easier. In other words, if we type `import microbit`, we would need to type the library name before any function is called, for example, `microbit.display.scroll("hello")` rather than just `display.scroll("hello")`.

Step 2: Put the emoticons into a dictionary.

The micro:bit's image class has built-in images that we can associate with numerical keys in a dictionary structure. We'll create a dictionary called images right below the previous code. You'll notice that I will include some of the other Python code so you know where the new lines go; I will be **bolding** the new code so that you know which lines to add. The gray lines are existing lines and show where to add your new lines.

```python
from microbit import *
images = {
    1: Image.HEART,
    2: Image.HEART_SMALL,
    3: Image.HAPPY,
    4: Image.SAD,
    5: Image.SURPRISED,
    6: Image.ANGRY,
    7: Image.ASLEEP,
    8: Image.BUTTERFLY,
    9: Image.DIAMOND,
    10: Image.CONFUSED,
    11: Image.COW,
    12: Image.PACMAN,
}
```

Tip Indentation, that is, moving our text in from the left four spaces, is a way to show that commands are inside of a loop or conditional statement. You can use the tab key since all the editors we are using convert tabs to four spaces. However, this is not always the case, so be careful as it can cause errors if used in other editors.

If you are using the Mu editor, you have a few extra features:

You can click the Check 👍 icon to check that your code is indented and formatted correctly. It will display errors so that you can fix them.

You can click the Tidy ☰ icon to arrange your code in a more readable way. It will show you when your code is indented correctly by displaying a vertical dotted line.

Step 3: Create an index.

We'll use a variable to keep track of which emoticon image we have "selected" and set this to 1. Add this line under the last one:

```
images = {
    1: Image.HEART,
    2: Image.HEART_SMALL,
    3: Image.HAPPY,
    4: Image.SAD,
    5: Image.SURPRISED,
    6: Image.ANGRY,
    7: Image.ASLEEP,
    8: Image.BUTTERFLY,
    9: Image.DIAMOND,
    10: Image.CONFUSED,
    11: Image.COW,
    12: Image.PACMAN,
}
```

index_num = 1

Step 4: Main loop and receive radio data.

Now we come to the main loop that keeps repeating while the script is running. We add True so that it will run forever or until there is an error:

```
index_num = 1
while True:
```

Step 5: Do things when events occur.

The rest of the script is essentially saying "if something happens, do this," followed by displaying the selected image.

We will check for single button presses and increase or decrease the index_ num value using += and -=. Since the if statements are inside the while loop, we need to make sure they are indented (moved four spaces to the right) so they line up with the incoming line above:

```
while True:
    if button_b.is_pressed():
        index_num += 1
    if button_a.is_pressed():
        index_num -= 1
```

We need to make sure that index_num stays within the key values for the images dictionary. Checking index_num will make sure that we don't get an error when we try to display our image from the dictionary. In this case, if index_num is too high, we set it back to the first image, and if it gets too low, we set it to the highest image index.

Reading the more structured Python code might make this clearer:

```
    if button_a.is_pressed():
        index_num -= 1
    if index_num > 12:
        index_num = 1
    elif index_num < 1:
        index_num = 12
```

Finally, display the currently selected image from images and wait for half a second. Remember that we indent these last two lines four spaces only, *so that they're only inside the while loop, but not inside the* if..elif *commands.*

Again, remember to only add the bolded lines of code – the other lines are there to show the position of your new code:

```
    elif index_num < 1:
        index_num = 12
    display.show(images[index_num])
    sleep(500)
```

Let's stop and look at how we tell our code which image to select, using images[index_num]. Remember that images is the dictionary we defined earlier. We also added our emoticon image names paired with a number, for example, 1: Image.HEART is a *key* of 1 and a *value* of Image. HEART. We then tell our program which image name to choose by putting the number that is paired with our chosen emoticon in square brackets. In this case, we have a number value stored in index_num, so we put it in square brackets. We use sleep(500) to make our script wait long enough that the image can be seen by a human.

Your code should now look like this:

```
from microbit import *
images = {
    1: Image.HEART,
    2: Image.HEART_SMALL,
    3: Image.HAPPY,
    4: Image.SAD,
    5: Image.SURPRISED,
    6: Image.ANGRY,
    7: Image.ASLEEP,
    8: Image.BUTTERFLY,
    9: Image.DIAMOND,
    10: Image.CONFUSED,
    11: Image.COW,
    12: Image.PACMAN,
}

index_num = 1
```

```
while True:
    if button_b.is_pressed():
        index_num += 1
    if button_a.is_pressed():
        index_num -= 1
    if index_num > 12:
        index_num = 1
    elif index_num < 1:
        index_num = 12
    display.show(images[index_num])
    sleep(500)
```

Save and flash your code to the micro:bit

On the Mu editor

1. Click Save ■ to save the Python code to your computer.

2. Click Flash ■ to create a .hex file and send it to a micro:bit connected to your computer's USB port. For a new micro:bit, you may need to click the REPL 🖥 REPL icon twice to make the Flash icon clickable.

If these buttons are not visible at the top of your Mu editor, click the Mode button and select "BBC micro:bit."

On the Thonny editor

1. At the top of the Thonny window, click the File menu and select "Save As" to save the Python code to your computer.

2. Click the Run menu and select "Run current script" to flash the .hex file to a micro:bit connected to your computer's USB port.

If it doesn't say "MicroPython (BBC micro:bit)" in the bottom-right corner, click the Run menu, and choose "Select Interpreter" to select "BBC micro:bit."

Using a web browser

If you are using a browser with WebUSB, connect your micro:bit to your computer's USB port and click the Connect ■ icon. You will be prompted to allow your micro:bit to connect (Figure 2-5).

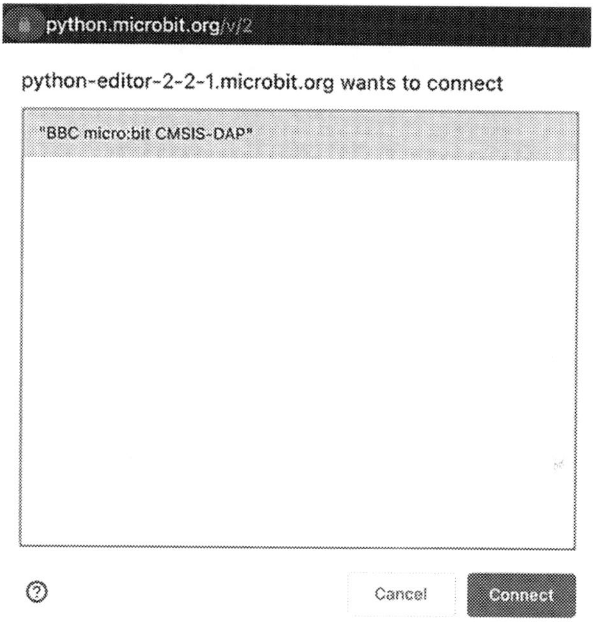

Figure 2-5. *Connecting the micro:bit to the web editor*

Once this is done, you can send your code to the connected micro:bit by clicking the Flash icon. The micro:bit light-emitting diode (LED) will flash while your code is being…uh, flashed.

If you have an older browser or one that just doesn't have WebUSB or just doesn't work, don't worry because you can just download your .hex file and copy it to your micro:bit. Your micro:bit will show up in your file manager, that is, Explorer on Windows, Finder on MacOS, and File Manager or whatever you have loaded on Linux.

Click the Save icon ■, then you can select whether to save your Python code to your computer or as a .hex file (Figure 2-6).

Figure 2-6. *Save your code as .py or.hex*

The Python (.py) file will be loadable into other editors later, but the micro:bit will need the .hex file. To copy this to your micro:bit, you should be able to plug it into your computer and see a USB storage device. Then you can copy the .hex file to the micro:bit.

Test your code!

Once you have sent your code to the micro:bit, it will restart and run your code. If you have a battery pack, you can connect it after disconnecting your USB cable. You should now be able to press the front buttons individually to change the emoticon displayed on the front LED matrix (the square grid of LEDs on the front of the micro:bit). If it works, that's great and you can continue to the section "Python Code Structure" and learn more about the code you just used.

What if my code doesn't work?

Don't worry – first, try the following steps:

1. Check your code against the code listing.

    a. Check for typing mistakes (typos) or missing symbols such as colons.

    b. Make sure that the indenting is correct, that is, the lines "inside" of your while (iterative loop) or if..then..elif (conditional) should be indented two characters to the right.

2. Make sure that there were no errors when you flashed the
    code onto your micro:bit. If you have spares, try changing to a
    different USB cable, or micro:bit, and try again.

3. You can also see error messages from your code by accessing
    the Python console (sometimes called a "shell") while your
    micro:bit is connected to your computer. Otherwise, reading the
    error messages as they scroll across the micro:bit screen can
    be more difficult!

Accessing the MicroPython REPL for Debugging

In the web browser Python editor

- You should be using a reasonably modern browser that
  supports WebUSB.[5]

- Make sure your micro:bit is connected to your computer.

- Click the Serial ▮ icon.

- Hold down the control key and press the C key (Ctrl+C).

You should see the Python read-eval-print loop (REPL) console start up
(Figure 2-7). It will show you the version of MicroPython that you are running,
including some other details about your micro:bit. If you wanted to try out
some Python code, we could type it in here to see the results. At this stage, we
are just looking at checking for any errors in our running program, so we will
restart the program.

---

[5] https://caniuse.com/webusb

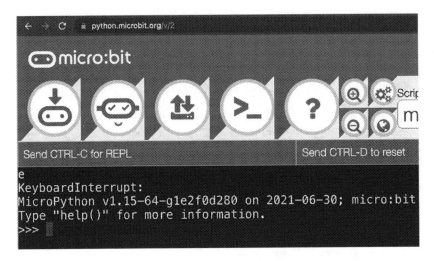

Figure 2-7. *Python REPL console on a web editor*

To restart your code on the micro:bit, hold down Ctrl+D. If there's any errors when it runs, you'll be able to see them, along with anything you decide to print() in your program. Printing variables at specific times can be handy to determine what might be going wrong. An example of an error is shown in Figure 2-8.

```
Traceback (most recent call last):
  File "main.py", line 29, in <module>
```

Figure 2-8. *Example of a program error visible in the REPL*

In the Mu editor

Click the REPL icon, and you'll see the REPL console open below. Use Ctrl+D to restart your program on the micro:bit and Ctrl+C to get back to the interactive Python prompt (also known as the *shell*). You can try out commands here, just like in the web editor REPL. Remember, you'll need to import the microbit library module to run micro:bit commands. To flash new code to your micro:bit, you will need to exit the REPL by clicking the REPL icon again.

In the Thonny editor

Go to the View menu and select Shell.

The REPL window will open below and give the same options as in the web and Mu editors; use Ctrl+D to restart and Ctrl+C for an interactive Python prompt. To exit the REPL, just untick Shell in the View menu.

Python code structure

Congratulations! You've just set up a way to continuously select emoticons using an index from a dictionary! The basic structure of our program is as follows:

1. *Initialization*: Set up variables and data structure

2. *Main loop*: Make our program continue to run until something happens

Now let's build some more features into our code!

Talking to other micro:bits over radio

Step 1: Configure and enable the radio.

First, we need to add the radio functions under our earlier import for the microbit module:

```
from microbit import *
import radio
```

To configure the radio, we need to set the radio channel to 10 and turn the radio on. We will use the .config() and .on() radio functions. Add the following commands in our initialization section, just under the line that creates our index_num variable and sets it to 1:

```
index_num = 1
radio.config(channel=10)
radio.on()
```

Note The .config() function has a *parameter* called channel passed to it, inside the brackets. The *argument* for that channel is 10.

Step 2: Receive radio messages.

Every time our while loop repeats, we want to store incoming radio messages in a variable called incoming using the .receive() function. So put this under the while True: line and indent it so that it is inside the loop:

```
while True:
    incoming = radio.receive()
    if button_b.is_pressed():
        index_num += 1
    if button_a.is_pressed():
        index_num -= 1
```

Note To keep things simple, we haven't done any validation on the incoming radio data – you should be aware that this is reading unchecked radio data into a variable, and a rogue radio transmission could potentially exploit this, make your program crash, or do something unexpected. However, for the sake of this exercise, let's assume you're well away from such transmissions and possibly in a Faraday cage or bunker of your choice.

If we receive an incoming radio broadcast, we are going to display the TARGET image, wait for half a second, then convert the incoming data back to a number using the int() function. Then we can use the display.show() and sleep() functions to display the received image long enough to be seen:

```
    incoming = radio.receive()
    if button_b.is_pressed():
        index_num += 1
```

```
if button_a.is_pressed():
    index_num -= 1
if incoming:
    display.show(Image.TARGET)
    sleep(500)
    display.show(images[int(incoming)])
    sleep(2000)
```

Step 3: Send radio messages.

Our while loop repeats over and over, letting us change the index_num to point to a different emoticon in our dictionary. To send our index_num value to another micro:bit, we'll need another button. How can we do this if we've already used both the button_a and button_b? Luckily, we can detect whether buttons A and B are pressed together by using if button_a. is_pressed() and button_b.is_pressed():.
Make sure that you type this as one line up to the colon (:).
The str() function converts the number into a character that we can send. Then we display the text "sending" so that we know that our emoticon has been sent via radio:

```
if button_b.is_pressed():
    index_num += 1
if button_a.is_pressed():
    index_num -= 1
if button_a.is_pressed() and button_b.is_pressed():
    radio.send(str(index_num))
    display.show('sending...')
if incoming:
    display.show(Image.TARGET)
    sleep(500)
```

After waiting for a couple of seconds, our code will go back to displaying the emoticon that we have selected. This is already in our code.

The entire script

To get a better idea of how this works, the whole script is listed as follows.
I have added comments – these lines begin with a hash #, and they are not
treated as commands. Comments are useful to make your code easier to read,
especially if someone else is trying to understand it.

```python
from microbit import *
import radio

# Create a dictonary of our emoticon images
images = {
    1: Image.HEART,
    2: Image.HEART_SMALL,
    3: Image.HAPPY,
    4: Image.SAD,
    5: Image.SURPRISED,
    6: Image.ANGRY,
    7: Image.ASLEEP,
    8: Image.BUTTERFLY,
    9: Image.DIAMOND,
    10: Image.CONFUSED,
    11: Image.COW,
    12: Image.PACMAN,
}
index_num = 1

# Set the radio channel to 10
radio.config(channel=10)
radio.on()

while True:
    # Capture received radio data
    incoming = radio.receive()

    if button_b.is_pressed():
        index_num += 1
```

```
if button_a.is_pressed():
    index_num -= 1
# if both buttons pressed together then send
if button_a.is_pressed() and button_b.is_pressed():
    radio.send(str(index_num))
    display.show("sending...")

# If there's incoming data, show the emoticon that's been
received
if incoming:
    display.show(Image.TARGET)
    sleep(500)
    display.show(images[int(incoming)])
    sleep(2000)

# Keep the index_num within the valid key range
if index_num > 12:
    index_num = 1
elif index_num < 1:
    index_num = 12

# Show the current image
display.show(images[index_num])
sleep(500)
```

Save and flash the code onto a few micro:bits and try sending and receiving emoticons; use the a and b buttons separately to select an emoticon, and press both together to send. The sending micro:bit will scroll "sending...," on its LED display, and the chosen emoticon will appear on any other micro:bits on radio channel 10.

The code we have produced will both *receive* and *send* radio messages to other micro:bits that are using the same radio channel – this means you can flash the same code onto multiple micro:bits to send messages between a group on the same channel! Change the channel *argument* to another number between 1 and 255, then you can have multiple groups of micro:bits receiving and sending to/ from one another, without interference with those on other channels.

Scaling Up: Adding Challenges

Something I learned from writing various projects over the years for Code Club Australia events is to always include at least one challenge at the end. This serves two purposes; it makes the basic project an achievable goal for everyone and then provides something extra for those who finish a bit earlier. A challenge must be difficult enough to push kids to think about the problem and break it down into small parts to formulate a working solution, but it should also be within their capabilities. No one likes to put effort into something that isn't possible. Some of the feedback that Rik from Code Club UK gave me was to include a hint for all challenges, to give kids a basic idea of what is required.

Here's a challenge for the preceding project. As a guide, the main ingredients for a good challenge are as follows:

- It should help with understanding of the initial project.

- It should be achievable, yet require some thought and understanding, and introduce something new.

- The hint should give enough information to set the programmer in the right direction.

- It should be fun and interesting enough to impress others.

CHALLENGE: TILT MICRO:BIT EMOTICON SWITCHER

Let's look at how we can detect when the micro:bit is tilted left and right. The micro:bit's movement sensor is called an accelerometer. We can read the movement of the micro:bit in the left/right (x axis), forward/back (y axis), and up/down (z axis). For our left/right tilting, we can use the following function call: `accelerometer.get_x()`.

Challenge

Can you upgrade your program to use left and right tilting to replace the a and b button controls?

Hints

You can check the tilt value of the micro:bit using this code:

```
x_tilt = accelerometer.get_x()
```

To check if a value is tilted to the right, you can use

```
If x_tilt > 400:
```

Challenge Discussion and Solution

This challenge example requires kids to understand how their program detects what button has been pressed and how it acts upon that event.

The following code from the previous project does this:

```
if button_b.is_pressed():
    index_num += 1
if button_a.is_pressed():
    index_num -= 1
```

We have given the hint that they need to capture the x axis value, so we can put this right at the start of the loop, just after we capture the radio message:

```
while True:
    # Capture received radio data
    incoming = radio.receive()
    x_tilt = accelerometer.get_x()
```

For the tilt controls, the values higher than 400 and lower than -400 indicate right and left tilting, respectively. So we can replace the if button_a.is_pressed(): and if button_b.is_pressed(): sections with the following code:

```
if x_tilt > 400:
    index_num += 1
if x_tilt < -400:
    index_num -= 1
```

This will let us use tilting instead of the buttons to select an emoticon. The sleep() commands slow things down enough to prevent the emoticons from changing too quickly. The latest micro:bit MicroPython has what is called a *debounce* built into the buttons, which implements a delay to allow them to be read cleanly. Otherwise, one press would potentially be easily mistaken for multiple presses. The extra sleep() commands make this more pronounced with the side effect of enabling a more usable (stable) tilt response.

Ideas for Even More Features

In addition to the two buttons on the front, our humble micro:bit also has a bunch of other sensors that we can use. If you've got the micro:bit V1, you'll have the movement, light, temperature sensors, and resistive touch.

Resistive touch works by sensing when pins 1, 2, and 3 connect to the ground (GND) pin. If you have the newer micro:bit V2, then you also have a capacitive touch sensor on the logo, which can sense when you touch the logo on the front.

Later in the book, we'll look at more of these features. This initial introduction should at least get you thinking about how to keep adding more and more features to your projects. It is much easier to write projects by first building a working program and working backward to break it down into steps. Make sure you test every time you add a new feature. We ran the project outlined in this chapter and had kids able to complete it within an hour. If you're running a workshop, try not to go over more than ten kids per volunteer/teacher. This allows you time to be able to help everyone. I have intentionally added more information than I would ordinarily add, in order to explain more concepts. Ideally, it is easier to only provide what is required to do the project and discuss more concepts in the additional challenges. Try not to give everything away until kids have made a good attempt at the challenge. I've had good results by just going to a whiteboard and drawing up ideas to expand on things – this gives kids a chance to collaborate and brainstorm. Then you can go in the direction they choose as a group.

Going Further: Adding External Components

So far, we've gone through how to scale up a project to go from a single micro:bit to using multiple micro:bits for a group and included a challenge to add features to the existing project. This should give you some ideas about how to go about putting together more activities to cater for diverging skillsets.

Our challenge utilized a feature that already existed on the micro:bit hardware – but what about interacting with the world? How can we demonstrate the incredible scope that Python opens up for us? Although, on the surface, it looks like the micro:bit only has 3 pins, a 3.3V power pin, and the GND pin, there's actually 25 pins that we can use to connect to! Although there's a lot of pins that we can use, we'll start simply. The diagrams from the Micro:bit Foundation[6] for the micro:bit V1 and V2 models show the pins more clearly in Figures 2-9 and 2-10.

---

[6] https://tech.microbit.org/hardware/edgeconnector/

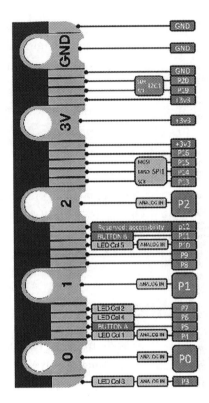

Figure 2-9. *micro:bit V2 input/output pins*

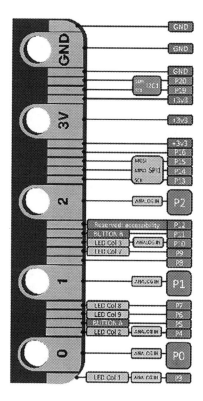

Figure 2-10. *micro:bit V1 input/output pins*

There are a few methods of connecting wires to the larger pins by using screws or crocodile clips or by using an edge connector. The edge connector is the easiest way to connect to the micro:bit pins and is also often the method used to interface accessory boards that allow connection of larger numbers of motors, sensors, power, screens, and speaker amplifiers. To make things simpler, we will start by adding a feature that connects to the larger pins with power and GND.

Adding an amplified speaker

The micro:bit V1 does not have a speaker, but on the V2 there is a small piezo speaker built in. The code to use the V2 speaker is the same as the code used to play sounds through a speaker or headphone connected to Pin 0 and GND. These solutions will not be very loud, so we'll add an amplified speaker. The Python code to make the micro:bit speak is quite similar to displaying emoticons. The following code will play a HELLO sound that comes in the microbit library module:

```
from microbit import *
audio.play(Sound.HELLO)
```

An amplified speaker board, such as the MonkMakes amplified speaker for the micro:bit or the Kitronik speaker, uses 3.3V power from the micro:bit's 3.3V pin. You can see the three crocodile clip connections in Figure 2-11.

The wire connected to input on the amplified speaker is used to send data, with the other two wires sending power and acting as a ground (GND). Even without an amplifier, you would still require input and GND to make a complete circuit for a speaker or headphones. I have intentionally chosen a very simple accessory to illustrate the way these can gradually be used to make our projects more interesting. The easiest way to write tutorials is to start simple and add one feature at a time, always testing each step.

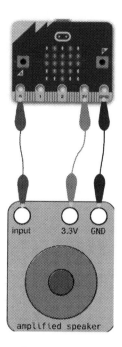

Figure 2-11. Amplified speaker

As you write up your project, it can be useful to keep programming concepts in mind – as you explain each section, feel free to describe the functions and concepts that you are using. The aim is to empower young makers to start getting creative with the skills they are learning. Later, you can simply reference previous projects that your code club kids have experienced, to give them confidence to combine what they know to make something new and interesting. Once there is a working prototype, they can start to add on extra features, one by one, just like the challenge we added.Now it's time for you to think about how you can incorporate audio into your project that already includes radio and tilt features! In the example project, we used the same code for all the micro:bits – be prepared to run out of memory to load in all the required functions into the micro:bit, at some point. When you do, you can simply spread operations across multiple micro:bits by using radio to send the required information between them!As you progress through this book, we will delve into combining more components into projects. We'll walk you through some of the workshops we have developed over our code club years.

Summary

- Aim to keep kids engaged rather than just busy – this means working on activities that are building their skills and understanding when they start at your code club.

- Understand that some kids will progress faster or have prior knowledge – although they should at least do the initial work to establish a consistent baseline of knowledge, it's OK for them to work ahead and finish faster. Just make sure everyone completes each exercise before moving to the next one and keep them accountable by asking questions. Track progress, so you know what stage everyone is at.

- You can use the web Python editor for the micro:bit, Mu editor, or Thonny editor. These all work "out of the box" and are simple by design but support the most relevant functions for kids to learn with. Your IT person may need to set the proxy as an environment variable in a configuration file for the Mu editor and in the general environment tab in Thonny. The web editor can use WebUSB to flash your micro:bit directly or save a .hex file to copy to the micro:bit in your file manager.

- Start preparing your code club volunteers for the point where some kids will finish the base-level activities. This will ensure that you're ready to get them working on more advanced tasks or even workshops if you have enough kids completing the initial tutorials after a few months.

- Let everyone know that they will all be at different stages and that it's OK. We had kids who worried that they were "falling behind" because they missed a week of code club – I mentioned that everyone would be away at least one or two weeks over the whole year, so it didn't really matter, and they got back in and later worked on some great projects!

- As you prepare a project, make that the initial basic part can be completed easily – congratulate the kids on making something that works. This will give kids confidence to keep going. Start by showing the goal to set expectations and keep kids interested.

- Write up your workshops so that kids can progress while you are helping others. This lets you leverage your time and still keep kids engaged and not 100% dependent on you.

- Add challenges that introduce a new but similar concept to what they've just learned. Give enough of a hint that they have everything they need but must think to put it together. Congratulate them on each additional feature they add.

- Once you have learned about and used all the features on the basic micro:bit, look at accessories that connect through the input/output pins. In later chapters, we will show how to expand more on this.

Chapter 2: Cheat Sheet

Introduction to the micro:bit

Table 2-1 summarises the main differences between the major micro:bit versions.

Table 2-1. *Feature comparison between micro:bit versions 1 and 2*

micro:bit Version	Audio	Sensors	General-Purpose I/O Pins	Radio
1.x	External speaker	Temperature, LED as brightness, accelerometer, magmometer, resistive touch	25 with shared pins that prevent use of certain functions concurrently	Yes
2.0	Built-in piezo speaker	As before but include microphone, capacitive touch on logo	25 without shared pins	Yes

Editors/Integrated Development Environments (IDEs)

Table 2-2 summarises the main differences between three popular editor types.

Table 2-2. *Table of Python editors*

Editor	Installed?	Works with Other Devices	Autocomplete and Suggest Commands	Supports External Library Modules
Web	Just needs a browser	micro:bit only	Yes	Yes
Thonny	Yes	Yes	Yes	Yes
Mu	Yes and has a portable version which still needs admin rights on laptop	Yes	Yes	Yes

- Talk to IT staff and test installed programs.

- Explain where to configure network proxy access.

Completing Initial Learning Projects

- Track progress.

- Ask questions to check for understanding.

- Help kids complete projects by discovering blocks.

- Give recognition.

- Set expectations of what you are trying to achieve.

Creating New Projects

- Set expectations and requirements.

- Give an overview of the structure of the program to help with understanding the design.

- Once you have a working project, break it down into instructions.

- Keep introducing terminology to encourage collaboration.

- Test and save at each milestone.

Add Features with Challenges

- Increase understanding of the initial project by adding a feature.

- Make it achievable.

- Provide a good hint.

- Make the feature worthwhile for the effort required.

Terminology

- A *dictionary* is a data structure that consists of sets of unique keys and associated values; the values can contain various other structures such as lists. The keys are used to look up the corresponding values so the dictionary does not need a specific order. Dictionaries are mutable (changeable).

- *List*: A list is a data structure that stores elements in a specific order and is also mutable.

- *Main loop*: This is the main section of the program that repeats. One repetition is called an *iteration*.

- *Conditional statements*: A decision-making statement such as if..elif..else.

- *Initialization*: Setting up data and defining variables and constants (*mutable* and *immutable* variables).

- *Saving*: Storing your Python code on your computer so you can reload it for editing later, usually as a .py file.

- *Flashing code to the device*: Converting your code into a binary file that can be loaded onto your micro:bit device through your USB port. Although editors can flash the file directly, this is often a .hex file.

CHAPTER 3

General Python Programming

Although this chapter is called "General Python," if you expected a generic and detailed rundown on "how to program in Python," then you may be sorely disappointed. Years ago, information was sparse and learning something often meant searching for multiple books or people who could explain the same thing in lots of different ways, one of which would hopefully make sense. These days, where we are practically drowning in information overload, it is very much the opposite case, that is, sometimes it can be easier to filter everything down to only the essential information we need. More specifically, in this chapter the "General" part of the title refers more to using Python on a computer that is running an operating system (OS) than on a small microcontroller board that only runs a small blob of firmware.

In our Code Club, we are teaching kids text-based programming in an after-school time slot. This means keeping kids engaged to apply concepts quickly and keep learning after a tiring day, which generally means getting straight to the guts of how things work.

This is much more a hacker-style approach, which means

- Decide which are the most relevant concepts required

- Work out the quickest path to gain skills and understand context of what we are doing

© Martin Tan 2023
M. Tan, *micro:bit Projects with Python and Single Board Computers*,
https://doi.org/10.1007/978-1-4842-9197-9_3

Rather than laboriously documenting every concept and detail, it's probably more useful to share some of the things that worked.

The strategy we ended up with is

- Give kids just enough information to be able to do cool things

- Outline what they've learned to keep it fresh in their minds

- Get them to apply these to their own projects as soon as possible

This meant getting them through the initial chosen "curriculum" at a reasonably fast rate before things became too tedious. Initially, kids would jump ahead to new lessons each week, leaving a list of incomplete lessons/projects in their wake. By abandoning projects rather than pushing through or asking for help, they were missing valuable skills gained from struggling through debugging and resolving our own code. So, although it is important to progress, it is just as important to support kids in completing projects while letting them know that it's OK to progress at their own rate because they are learning. Working through problems while verbalizing a consistent thought process is a good way to encourage self-sufficiency with debugging. We choose this as a structured way to learn basic Python skills before progressing into workshops and applying them to more advanced projects. In this case, we used the Code Club Australia Python lessons, but as mentioned earlier, there's lots of other alternatives, depending on what works best for you.

Once we have helped kids to make their way through the initial learning, we take the group through a summary of what they've learned. Even though everyone does end up at a slightly different level of skill, outlining the basic minimum concepts really empowers everyone to realize their capability at this point. Most kids don't realize how much they have learned; so, I simply map the completed lessons to concepts learned. This boosts confidence and empowers them with the understanding that they are now able to program.

I've included answers to some common questions about Python asked by kids from our code clubs, volunteers, and primary school teachers over the years. Being a star club meant that we would sometimes have visiting secondary school teachers at some sessions, including code club volunteers who would spend a few semesters helping. Some of the main benefits of using Python are also included. Next, we look at a few ways a Python program can be structured and follow up with some key concepts. These are what I've found to be most useful to get started. For those who wish to dig deeper, links to useful online resources are provided. The aim is not to rewrite all the good information available online, but rather point out the most useful things to know if you want to get started quickly and easily. My hope is that if you are considering introducing Python at your code club or maker space, you can avoid some of the mistakes we made and benefit from the lessons we learned. Perhaps this will also help to accelerate your journey and get you hitting more advanced activities earlier.

Finally, an example project is included to create a bare-bones Python web application to provide a user interface that can be accessed in a web browser. Part of my choice to include this is that it always frustrated me throughout high school when we were taught concepts without context – this project aims to put some real-world context into some of the skills kids have learned with Python, that is, you can use Python to make something that can be accessed from a web browser. Although this is not a beginner project, we have successfully given this to kids who have completed a Python curriculum that covers all the concepts I talk about in this chapter. This means that they have already worked through practical lessons where they apply all these concepts. I designed the web application project to show kids that what they have learned can be applied in a way that interacts with the real world – a web application. By completing this project, they learn that they can now apply their Python knowledge with a web interface accessible from a browser! Note that although this simple web application is initially only accessible on your computer, the concepts learned are easily transferrable for a more widely accessible version. Additionally, adding web interfaces to your projects opens many possibilities, including access from mobile devices without the need to build a dedicated mobile app. Some object-oriented concepts are introduced within the concept of the project.

A Quick Tale: Answers to Common Questions – Weaning Off Blocks and Tablets

Block-based coding is an easy way for kids to get started coding. It's big and colorful – these days, most young kids have been exposed to digital tablets, so dragging shapes around a screen leverages those existing skills. Block coding can be analogous to how we start reading; we begin with large letters and pictures, and the words we use are nice and simple with few syllables. Once we can read more confidently, we move on to more complex books with smaller letters and longer, more descriptive words and phrasing. The result is a richer and more interesting experience. When our Code Club consisted solely of Scratch block-based programming, we noticed a plateau point where our Scratch programming became quite complicated when compared to the equivalent Python. When we first started our code club, the block-based programming was nice and easy for us to teach, but in later years I assisted some younger school classes and realized that kids straight out of kindergarten were now already learning block-based coding!

Once kids can use blocks to code visually, understand various programming constructs, and can think programmatically, we can push the boundaries by making more elaborate programs to do more complex operations. While not being as full featured as text-based languages, online block-based programming languages such as MakeCode also help bridge the gap between computers and electronic circuits. When we first started looking at introducing Python to our code club kids, we noticed some hesitancy after having used block-based programming until we explained things a bit more. Since it's inevitable that you'll be asked similar questions at your maker space or code club, I've included answers to some questions that you may encounter.

A few common questions from kids, and sometimes teachers, include

1. Why are we using Python instead of Scratch/ MakeCode?

2. Why is Python so hard?

3. Why is Python so boring?

4. Why can't we keep programming in Scratch/ MakeCode?

In case you're wondering, some answers to these questions could be as follows:

1. Python is more powerful than Scratch when modeling solutions to real-world problems. Scratch can really only let us do simple things, and MakeCode can interact with some microcontroller boards such as the BBC micro:bit, but Python has thousands of libraries full of new commands and can interact with many more electronic boards and devices and talk to systems, for example, connecting to computer networks, manipulation of complex data structures, and interaction with other systems at a very granular level, when required. Python also has many more ways of handling data than simple variables and lists that we have used in block-based programming. Although there are cases where Python is not fast enough, the concepts it teaches can ultimately take us further than block-based

coding, and there is also the ability to embed lower-
level (more granular) languages within Python or
import this functionality as a module.

2. Python is reasonably simple but has a lot of features
    that make it much easier than most other text-
    based programming languages. It still has a visual
    component due to the way indentation is enforced
    to describe program structure; this encourages more
    structured and therefore readable code. Python may
    have seemed a lot harder with the old Idle editor[1]
    and shell environment that came with it. These days,
    we have some great editors that are simple enough
    for kids to use while also allowing us to program
    electronic devices. As you program more in Python,
    you'll see that there's many tasks that are much
    easier in Python than in block-based programming.

3. Python can seem boring if we are only thinking of
    the visual aspect of block-based coding – making
    monkeys move around our screen or sounds come
    out of a drum icon can be easy wins that come from
    block-based coding. What about if we wanted to
    make something to talk to devices in our house
    and make them accessible from a web browser?
    What about all those devices or computers where
    your block-based code can't run? It's more than
    likely that something like Python will be more
    useful in those cases. What about if we wanted to
    connect to computers on the Internet and process

---

[1] https://docs.python.org/3/library/idle.html

live information that comes from them? What if we wanted to use Google Maps to track a device on a vehicle? All these things are possible with Python. Once we shift out of the limitations of just moving objects around our own screen, Python is very much more exciting than block-based coding!

4. It is completely possible to continue programming in Scratch/MakeCode since these block-based languages can be used on some robots and a handful of electronic microcontroller boards and accessories, including the PIC microcontroller boards[2] – however, this is still not as far-reaching as Python's large library of modules and does not allow programming on the many electronic microcontroller boards that support embedded versions of Python, for example, Adafruit boards, espresso boards such as the ESP8266 and ESP32, RP2040, STM32, and other reasonably inexpensive ARM-based processor boards. And since Python is also a scripting language, it allows automation in software tools, including 3D design tools such as Blender and OpenSCAD.

I've mentioned that there's a tipping point where programming starts to become difficult with block-based systems and easier with a text-based language like Python. If you never hit this point, then perhaps it's fine to keep using block-based programming, or perhaps it's worth pushing the boundaries *until* this happens. In some cases, kids may stagnate from swimming only in the Scratch/MakeCode pool, without ever venturing into

---

[2] https://en.wikipedia.org/wiki/PIC_microcontrollers

the wider scope of a language such as Python. Python is one of the most popular languages to learn since it is less wordy or complicated to use and can automatically figure out what data types[3] your variables or data structures require. When I say "types," this refers to how information can be stored, for example, integer, floating-point decimal, words, or a larger structure of these types, such as a list or array. It is also an interpreted language for most uses, which means you can make changes and rerun code immediately rather than waiting for the process of compiling your code into a form that can run. The former is less intimidating and falls nicely into our strategy of learning the basic concepts quickly. Python is quite efficient to write as it doesn't require encapsulating code sections between matching brackets as often as other languages and uses a simple format, a.k.a. "syntax." This means that there are less symbols such as trailing semicolons, curly brackets, and other things to worry about. Even on devices, running a cut-down version of Python known as MicroPython[4] allows us to debug quite easily and in a readable fashion.

Another reason for using Python early on is that kids just get used to it. When we apprehensively approached it as "hard" for kids to learn, they progressed much slower because of our attitudes.

When we encouraged kids to persevere and push toward completion on the Code Club lessons, we had them record their progress and have a volunteer or teacher ask them questions to confirm that they had indeed completed the projects. When we neglected to confirm completion or kids were allowed to stop and move on if they got "stuck," they would ultimately get much more frustrated in later workshops; so, this became something we worked hard to enforce and let them get the most out of more advanced projects. This was also a reason for ensuring kids have just enough help to make timely progress so they would not get discouraged or bored. In

---

[3] https://en.wikipedia.org/wiki/Data_type
[4] https://micropython.org

almost every year, there would be one or two kids who thought it was smart to look up solutions and cut and paste them. This always proved to be a pointless pursuit since they would invariably struggle to understand anything as we progressed to more advanced or hybrid projects that required a specific level of programming skills.

Tip   When going through the initial projects/lesson curriculum, encourage kids to complete each one before moving on to the next. It's OK for everyone to be at different stages, and it's OK to ask for someone to explain something again in a different way.

In practice, the quickest way to get started was using an online environment, such as https://trinket.io – this is used by the Code Club Australia projects, and after a few false starts, we learned that this was a good idea. This allows programming in the browser, but with the same debugging capabilities as we would have on the computer. On trinket.io, we can interact with online resources with enough scope to learn the basics.

For the project included in this chapter, I have used the Thonny editor, which runs on Mac, Windows, or Linux and comes already installed on Raspberry Pi OS. This gives us a nicely contained environment to use Python's Flask module for web application programming, which is not available on trinket.io at the time of writing. You can also use the Mu editor in much the same way, apart from the initial differences in configuration. In this chapter, we won't be programming any devices.

At some point, it may also be useful to install Python on your computers. To use the Python functionality in additional modules, you will need to be able to download these using Python's own pip installer – this will require some configuration if your Internet access is filtered through a proxy.

Note   A proxy is an intermediary computer through which schools route their Internet access. A proxy server holds a "cache" of previously requested online data to speed up access to commonly accessed information. Proxy servers can also protect us by filtering potentially dangerous content on the Internet. Although this is often invisibly set up on computers on a school or private network, sometimes certain software may require specific settings to use the proxy server and access the Internet.

Python Program Structure

A Friendly Python Environment on Your Computer

Trinket.io provides a beautifully simple environment to learn to write Python and learn the basics. The Code Club lessons manage to do a fine job of doing this with `https://trinket.io` (trinket), making all the lessons accessible to anyone with a browser. However, a free account has limitations, the main one being the restriction of not being able to `import` some built-in Python modules that include some very useful features. The point at which you will outgrow trinket.io is when you either want to run code that runs on and interacts with hardware devices or when you want to import modules that do not come built-in with Python. For example, the project in this chapter uses the Flask module, which is typically not a built-in module, but happens to come with certain Python editors.

Although it's not so hard to install Python to your computer, finding that elusive programming environment editor that satisfies our strategy to supply only what is required was previously difficult. There's a multitude of code editors and environments that cater for the more advanced programmers/developers, but until recent years, there was not really a very kid- or beginner-friendly editor.

The main issues with many editors, when teaching kids, were

- Too many distracting features that they would not need yet

- Confusing interfaces that did not distinguish between live programming and an editor

- Variations between operating systems

- Difficulty in maintaining the environment for less technical teachers or volunteers

The answers to these issues have been solved with the Thonny and Mu editors that were introduced in the last chapter. You will recall that we used the device programming mode for the BBC micro:bit microcontroller board. You'll be happy to hear that there is also another mode that allows you to run code on your computer – and yes, this solves all the preceding problems for us! All we require is a simple mode change. The initial configuration required for both editors is shown, after which only the Thonny screenshots are shown for brevity.

Thonny

To set up the Thonny editor for running Python on your computer, from the top menu go to Tools ➤ Options. In the Interpreter tab, select The same interpreter which runs Thonny (default), as shown in Figure 3-1.

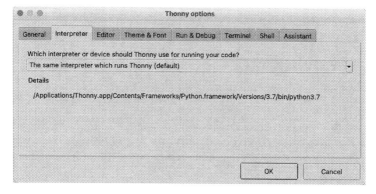

Figure 3-1. *Setting Python mode in Thonny*

Mu Editor

In the Mu editor, click the 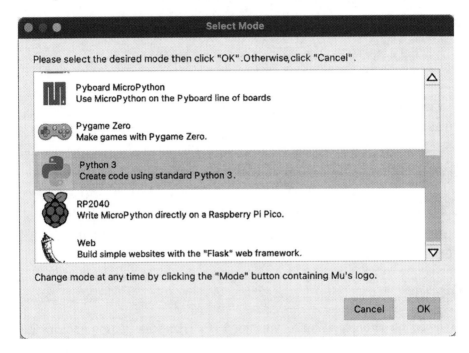 Mode button in the top-left corner, and select Python 3, as shown in Figure 3-2.

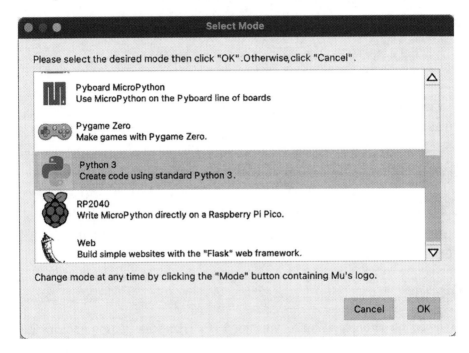

Figure 3-2. *Setting Python mode in the Mu editor*

Now that we've set our mode to Python 3, let's get coding (again)!

Test Our Environment

As with most languages, the simplest and first program anyone learns is often called "hello world." It essentially prints "hello world" on your screen. In Python, this can be done with one line (Listing 3-1).

Listing 3-1. Printing "hello world" using Python

```
print("hello world")
```

Open a new tab and type this into your editor. In both Thonny and Mu editors, when you click the run arrow button ▶ you'll see a save file window asking you where you want to save your script. Find somewhere logical such as "documents" and use the rather boring filename of hello_world.py. Once this is done, your program will run, and you'll see "hello world" printed out in your editor's console. Congratulations, this means your Python environment is set up correctly!

Since you can quite easily go through the Code Club or equivalent lessons, I'm not going to bore you too much with all the Python commands and rules. However, something that might be helpful now is to understand some common structures of Python scripts.

Installing Python Libraries in Thonny

You may recall my mentioning of the large number of Python modules or libraries that extend its capabilities. Although the Mu editor does come with Flask and few other useful libraries installed, Thonny does not – so it's worth showing you how to install these.

Note   As of version 1.0.2, the Mu editor does not easily allow adding of external Python libraries – however, it does include some libraries that fortunately cover those used in this chapter's project.

Run your Thonny editor and select Manage packages from the Tools drop-down menu (Figure 3-3).

87

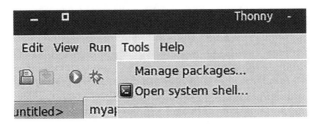

Figure 3-3. *"Manage packages" from the Tools drop-down menu*

From here, a window will open: Manage packages for <the location of your Python3>. You can now type in the name of any library and click Search on PyPi to find and click Install (Figure 3-4).

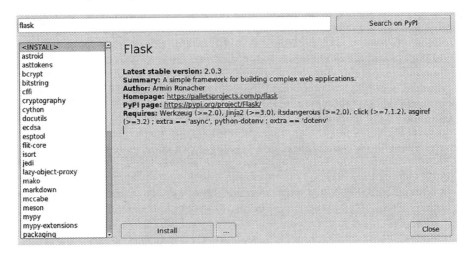

Figure 3-4. *Install package in Thonny*

Although the Mu editor already has the required packages needed for this chapter's project, adding packages in Mu is a similar process: click the cog in the bottom-right corner of the Mu editor, then type the package name under the Third-Party Packages tab.[5]

---

[5] https://codewith.mu/en/tutorials/1.1/pypi

MORE PROGRAMMING TERMINOLOGY AND CONCEPTS

Variables

Variables provide ways of storing data and should have meaningful names, for example, `counter`, `name`, `address`. Variables can be of a variety of types, for example, integers (`int`), decimal (`float`), words (`string`), etc.

Immutable/mutable

Variables can be mutable (changeable) or immutable (nonchangeable, also known as constants, e.g., `PI=3.142` or `GRAVITY=9.8`). Constants often use uppercase names to differentiate from mutable variables in Python.

Data structures

We can store data in structures that make it easier to manipulate and retrieve; these include the following:

- *Lists:* A list can contain a series of variables or other data structures and is mutable. We denote a list by separating its members with commas and surrounding a list with square brackets, that is, [and]. In addition to performing additions and deletions, we can also select sorted members or subgroups.

- *Sets:* Sets are like lists but only hold unique members. Set members are separated by commas and surrounded by curly brackets, that is, { and }. It can be useful to remove duplicates in a list by converting it to a set, for example, `mylist = set(oldlist)`.

- *Dictionaries:* This structure consists of associated keys and values and is immutable. Dictionary keys and values are separated with a colon, with each value pair being separated by a comma and the dictionary surrounded with curly brackets, that is, { and }. As with lists, the value part of the pair can hold other structures.

89

Loops/iteration

While loops are commonly used to repeat tasks until a condition is no longer set, for example, the following code will continue until a random value of x is generated that is larger than 4, whereas you can use `while True:` to repeat until an error occurs.

```
while x>4:
    print(x)
    x = randint(0,8)
```

For loops can set specific values to iterate (count) through and can also be useful to perform operations on each member of a data structure or from a file, for example:

```
mylist = ["a", "n", "d"]
for c in mylist:
    print(c)
```

This will print and vertically.

In some cases, for loops can also be used within other expressions.

Conditionals

`If..then..else` can use conditions, for example, `x>1`, to perform different commands depending on whether the condition is `True` or `False`.

Functions

Python has built-in functions such as `print()`, `set()`, or `ord()`. You can pass information to them via parameters that are variables or data structures in brackets (parentheses). One of the most powerful features of Python is being able to define our own functions.

Note   A function is defined by the form `def <function name>(<parameters separated by commas>):` followed by the code "inside" the function, indented. To return information back, you can use the `return` command followed by the information to be returned.

An example of defining a custom function is

```
def add_num(number_one, number_two):
    answer = number_one + number_two
    return answer
```

We could then call our function inside `print()`, for example, `print(add_num(5,6))` to print 11.

Local and global variables

This can get complicated, but it is easy enough to think of a global variable as being one that is able to be referenced from anywhere in your code, whereas a local variable is only used within a function. This can be confusing, but to prevent problems, you should pass values to functions via parameters rather than referencing a variable globally.

Object oriented

The way I describe this concept to primary-aged kids is that we have objects in Python to describe real-life things. These objects can have attributes, for example, an object type of animal could have an attribute called legs. Then methods are actions or functions that we can perform on instances of these object types. Although this is not something we have delved into in our code club, it has been useful to explain the idea when kids go through a project called "Turtles" from Code Club Australia's Python curriculum, because we create instances of turtles that are racing against one another.

Python Script Structure

Each year, our code club kids would work through their curriculums and then find themselves stuck when asked to write a script to solve a problem. To get them started, I would often describe a very simple program structure:

- Variables (a way to store values that we can modify, "mutable")

- Constants (variables that won't change, "immutable")

- Functions (custom commands that we define)

- Initialization (some code that we want to run once)

- Main loop or main function (where we put our code that we want to keep running repeatedly)

- Any code we want to run after our main loop ends

That is essentially the same basic program structure that can be used for most of your maker space or code club project scripts and is especially common for projects that use microcontroller boards such as the BBC micro:bit or even small single-board computers like the Raspberry Pi that run an operating system. The next project uses a similar repeating program structure and can be run as a workshop – typically, we have used this in our code club as two one-hour sessions.

WRITING A PYTHON FLASK WEB APPLICATION

In this project, we will build a website that uses Python to perform tasks in the background. Instead of displaying information with a text interface, we can send our output to the user's web browser. This kind of website is known as a web application because it can process information rather than just displaying it. We typically refer to the person using our web application as a "user." You may hear web programmers (developers) speaking about the user experience, which relates to how a user experiences a web application through their browser, for example, is it a smooth and flowing experience, or is it confusing and abrupt?

When the user visits the web application URL in their web browser, they will see the form in Figure 3-5, where they can enter a temperature in degrees Celsius and click **Submit**.

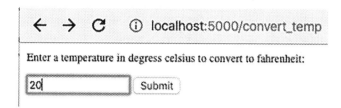

Figure 3-5. *Temperature input form in a web browser*

The application will then convert the temperature to degrees Fahrenheit as shown in Figure 3-6.

Figure 3-6. *Web application result in a web browser*

The *temperature* link allows the user to go back to the start and calculate another temperature.

What you will learn

- How to use the Python Flask module to create a website

- How to use web templates

- How to add web application pages (routes) with forms to allow data input, processing, and output in a web browser

What you will need

- A computer with a Thonny or Mu editor set to Python 3 mode.

- Another computer connected to the same network (optional for extended challenges).

- A basic understanding of HyperText Markup Language (HTML) – don't worry too much since I've included a cheat sheet.

Let's get started!

As described earlier, our environment is already set up by installing a Thonny or Mu editor and selecting Python 3 mode. We will save our script on the computer and run the script inside our editor environment.

From this point, the project tasks are exactly the same in both editors – so only Thonny screenshots have been included to keep things simple.

Step 1: Create some text in a website.

First, we need to create a flask object called app. You'll notice that this is like creating a variable, except that app will be a flask *object*.

In Python, just like how functions are used to perform actions on variables, methods perform actions on objects. Objects can also have attributes. Technically, in Python, all variables are actually objects and have types, for example, a variable of string type can hold the characters "fred" and an instance of a string that has this value could be first_name. A string attribute could be its length, and functions (which are actually methods) such as capitalize() or lower() can be performed on an instance of a string to change the capitalization of its value.

The Flask() object has a run() method. We can run our app by adding app.run() to the bottom of our program, as shown in Listing 3-2.

Listing 3-2. Our first Python Flask program

```
from flask import Flask
app = Flask(__name__)
app.run()
```

If we ran our script now, we would not see anything, but we have created an instance of a `Flask()` object called app. Our `Flask()` object has an attribute called `route()`. When we define routes in app, it tells our web application what code to run when a web browser requests a path, for example, in the URL https://mypage.com/about, "about" would be the path. Add these lines (**bolded** in Listing 3-3 for clarity) just *above* the `app.run()` line. The @ symbol indicates that `app.route('/')` is a *decorator* for the following function. We say that the route decorator is *wrapping* the `first_page()` function. This means that it extends extra functionality to that function, allowing the returned data to be sent to your web browser.

Listing 3-3. Adding a route at the path of '/'

```
from flask import Flask
app = Flask(__name__)

@app.route('/')
def first_page():
    return 'This is my first Flask page!'

app.run()
```

Save and run your project

You'll be prompted to save your web application program after clicking the run arrow button. Save it as `myapp-v1.py`.

If all goes well and your web application is running without errors, you should see the console output shown in Figure 3-7. If there's any errors, check that you have typed everything in correctly and try again. Note that the address in the URL is 127.0.0.1, which is our computer's loopback IP address. Although it is possible to allow other computers on your network by changing the app. run() command to app.run('0.0.0.0'), you should only do this if you're sure that you are on a closed network since this is just a test web server and not safe enough to expose it to the Internet directly.

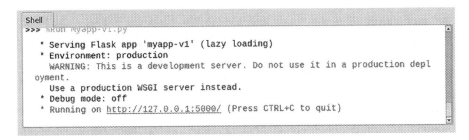

Figure 3-7. Console output when running myapp-v1.py

There is now a web server running on your computer. Open a web browser and type this URL in the address bar to visit your web application on port 5000 of your computer's loopback network interface: http://127.0.0.1:5000/. Alternatively, you could also type http://localhost:5000/, which is just another name for the loopback address.

Note   The loopback interface is not a physical network interface, but a separate virtual network interface which only allows your computer to connect to itself.

As shown in Figure 3-8, you should now see "**This is my first Flask page**" in your browser!

Figure 3-8. Viewing the web application output in your web browser

Back in your editor, you'll be able to see the raw requests that your browser is making to your Python web application in the console just below your program code, as shown in Figure 3-9.

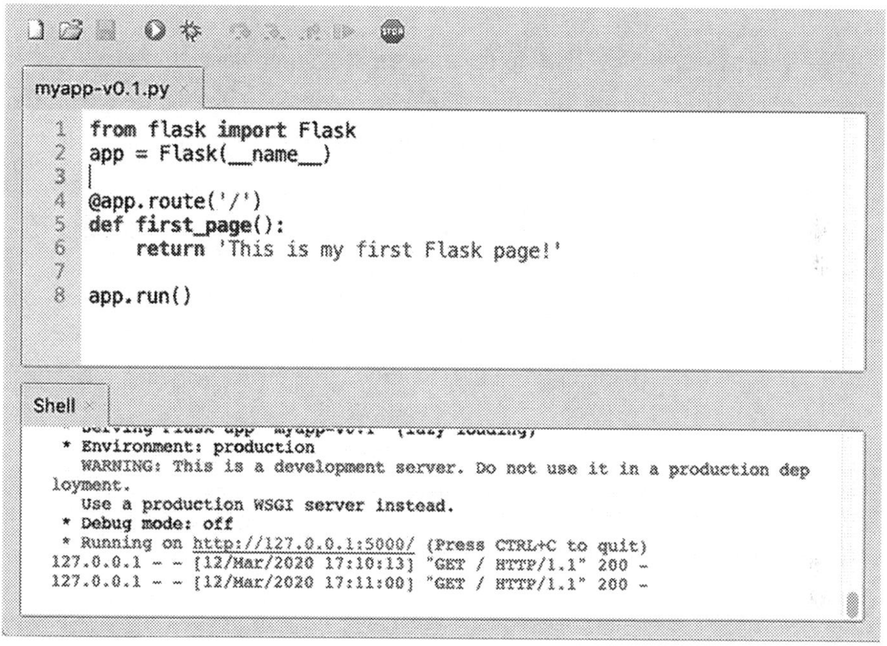

Figure 3-9. *Thonny console output*

The request made by your browser can be broken down as shown in Table 3-1. In this book, we will mostly be using GET and POST requests, the latter often being used for submitting data from a form on a web page. The response code is a number that is sent back to your browser. 200 means that the request was successful. If the browser requested a page that our web application did not recognize, it would have returned a 404 – not found response code.

Table 3-1. *Browser request components*

Type of Request	Path	Response Code
GET	/	200

Step 2: Create a form.

In this step, you'll learn how to create a form in HyperText Markup Language (HTML) and use it to send information to your web application, so it can be processed.

So far, we've just sent text back to our browser. It's rather plain, so we can use HTML to add some markup (formatting) tags to make it look better when displayed in your browser. HTML alone is static, meaning that it doesn't change, but by using Python with the Flask module, we can do tasks such as calculate or retrieve data from other locations, based on the information sent to our web application.

Press Ctrl+C in your editor to stop your Python script from running. Now try adding the <h1> HTML heading tags to the return line in your code (Listing 3-4).

Listing 3-4. Adding heading1 tags

```
from flask import Flask
app = Flask(__name__)

@app.route('/')
def first_page():
    return '<h1>This is my first Flask page!</h1>'

app.run()
```

Rerun your script and go to the same URL in your browser. You'll notice that your text is now a heading (Figure 3-10).

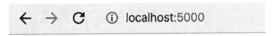

This is my first Flask page!

Figure 3-10. *Heading text displayed in your web browser*

We could send a whole HTML web page to the web browser – however, rather than adding lots of HTML tags and text to our script, we can use something called a *template*!

NAVIGATING YOUR COMPUTER'S FILESYSTEM

Your computer's operating system has a graphical file manager. In macOS, this is Finder; in Windows, it is File Explorer; and in Linux or Raspberry Pi OS, it can vary depending on which window manager you are using. However, in keeping with the theme of being a curious maker/hacker, I would really encourage you to explore using text-based command-line interfaces that exist on most desktop and laptop operating systems. There are many ways to access these interfaces, but on Windows you can press Windows Key + x; on macOS, you can search for "terminal" after pressing Cmd + space; and on Linux or Raspberry Pi, there are multiple ways, but often control + alt + t will open a command-line interface.

While running workshops, it's useful to include a cheat sheet limited to only the commands required. Here's one for some command-line interface (CLI) commands with the operating system listed in the left column (Table 3-2).

Table 3-2. *Some common command-line commands*

Operating System	Command	Usage Example	Description
macOS, Linux, including Raspberry Pi OS	`ls`	`ls Documents`	List contents of a directory
	`cd`	`cd Documents`	Change to directory
	`mkdir`	`mkdir test`	Create a directory
Windows	`dir`	`dir Documents`	List contents of a directory
	`cd`	`cd Documents`	Change to a directory
	`mkdir`	`mkdir test`	Create a directory

OK – back to creating our templates directory! Create a new directory where your `myapp-v1.py` file is saved and call it templates (all lowercase). In this directory, we will store our HTML templates for our application.

We are going to create .html files inside the `templates` directory. These files are going to include special tags that will allow us to populate them with our data and return them to the user's browser.

The eventual structure of our directory and files is shown in the screenshot in Figure 3-11. I've shown you this before we have created all the files because it's more useful to show you what we are going to do than to reveal it later.

Figure 3-11. *Our directory structure*

Now let's create an HTML form to read in a temperature value to be converted. Our Python editor likes to use `.py` files, so we will use the default text editor on our computer.

YOUR OPERATING SYSTEM'S DEFAULT TEXT EDITOR

Every operating system has at least one basic text editor that we can use to edit an .html file. Table 3-3 shows these for each operating system.

Table 3-3. *Table of text editors included in common operating systems*

Operating System	Editor Name	Location
macOS	textedit.app	/Applications/ Utilities/
Windows	notepad.exe	C:\Windows\system32\
Linux, Raspberry Pi OS	nano	Type nano from the CLI

Again, I would encourage you to investigate the command-line interface (CLI) options, but notepad can easily be found in the Windows program menu.

Create a new file in your operating system's text editor with the HTML content in Listing 3-5.

Listing 3-5. HTML template contents

```
<html>
    <body>
        <p>Enter a temperature in degrees celsius to convert to
        fahrenheit:</p>
        <form action = "/convert_result" method = "POST">
```

```
            <input type="text" name="value_entered">
            <input type="submit" value="Submit">
        </form>
    </body>
</html>
```

HTML CHEAT SHEET

HTML allows us to add markup to our text displayed in the browser. To get you started, I've included descriptions for the tags we are using (Table 3-4). The double dots indicate where we place our text that is to be marked up by the tags.

Table 3-4. *Some HTML tags and what they do*

HTML Tags	Description
<html>..</html>	The start and end of our web page. This can include other parts of our page, such as title, headings, body, and more
<body>..</body>	The main body of the web page to be displayed
<h1>..</h1>	Set the text to boldness and size for the top level, Heading 1
<form>..</form>	This creates a form and will include form elements such as buttons and areas where users can enter text input. This HTML element usually has added attributes in the first tag, which change the form's behavior

Save your template

Save your template into your previously created templates directory as convert.html.

Step 3: Add another route.

Now that we've made our HTML template file, let's add another route in our application to display the form we just created. You can think of routes as the paths that are at the end of URLs, for example:

```
http://application.com/convert_temp
```

Now we need to use the `render_template` function from Flask. Add this to the import statement at the top of your `myapp-v1.py` script (Listing 3-6).

Listing 3-6. Add the render_template import from the flask library

```
from flask import Flask, render_template
```

Add another route to your `myapp-v1.py` script just above the `app.run()` line (Listing 3-7).

Listing 3-7. Add another route at '/convert_temp'

```
from flask import Flask
app = Flask(__name__)

@app.route('/')
def first_page():
    return 'This is my first Flask page!'

@app.route('/convert_temp')
def convert_temp():
        return render_template('convert.html')

app.run()
```

Save your Python script

Save your `myapp-v1.py` script. You will notice that instead of returning text to the browser, we're telling our script to show our template by using `render_template('convert.html')`.

103

Run your web application, then view the /convert_temp path in your browser.

The URL will now be http://localhost:5000/convert_temp.

You should see our new form and a submit button. However, clicking Submit won't work until we tell our script where to send the form information!

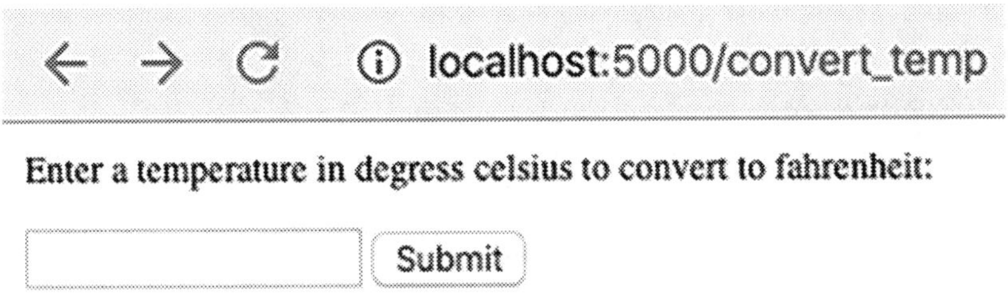

Enter a temperature in degress celsius to convert to fahrenheit:

[   ] Submit

Figure 3-12. *Temperature conversion form in a browser*

Step 4: Collect the form data.

In this step, we will create a destination to send the information entered in our HTML form. The action attribute in our HTML for template will point to a route/path called /convert_result. This will be a page where our calculated temperature will be displayed in the browser.

We will be using the request function from the Flask module, so add this to the first import line of your myapp-v1.py script (Listing 3-8).

Listing 3-8. Add the request import from the flask library

```
from flask import Flask, render_template, request
```

When we visit a URL in a web browser, a GET request is made by the browser to retrieve the web page. When we submit data in an HTML form, this creates a POST request that sends information to our Python script. In your script above the last route and above app.run(), add another route that allows POST and GET requests (Listing 3-9)

104

Listing 3-9. Add another route at '/convert_result'

```
@app.route('/convert_result', methods = ['POST', 'GET'])
```

Let's write a function to perform a calculation if data has been POSTed to our form (Listing 3-10). The data from our form needs to be converted to a float type of variable, because it will be a decimal number. We use a `float()` function to do this and store it in the value variable. Note that the backslash "\" indicates that the line continues, so you can leave it out and have a continuous line up to the closing bracket.

Listing 3-10. Defining a function to calculate a value for the '/convert_result' path

```
def converted():
    if request.method == 'POST':
        value = float(request.form['value_entered'])
        answer = (value * 1.8) + 32
        return render_template('conversion_result.html', \
value = value, answer = answer)
```

Make sure that the last return is all in one line. Again, a backslash is included to remind us, but you shouldn't need to include it. The answer is calculated and sent to a new HTML template called `conversion_result.html` (Listing 3-11).

Listing 3-11. Contents of conversion_result.html

```
<!doctype html>
<html>
    <body>
    <p>{{ value }} degrees celsius is {{ answer }} degrees in
    fahrenheit.</p>
    <p>Calculate another <a href='/convert_temp'>temperature?</a></p>
    </body>
</html>
```

<u>Save your project</u>

Click the save 💾 icon in your editor to save changes made to your file:
`myapp-v1.py`.
Listing 3-12 shows what our script should now look like with all three routes defined.

Listing 3-12. Three routes added

```
from flask import Flask, render_template, request

app = Flask(__name__)

@app.route('/')
def mypage():
    return 'This is my first flask app'

@app.route('/convert_temp')
def convert_temp():
    return render_template('convert.html')

@app.route('/convert_result', methods = ['POST', 'GET'])
def converted():
    if request.method == 'POST':
        value = float(request.form['value_entered'])
        answer = (value * 1.8) + 32
        return render_template('conversion_result.html', value =
value, answer = answer)

app.run
```

Notice that we send the `conversion_result.html` template to the browser to display the converted temperature – we need to write that next, but first we need to test that everything works as expected!

Test your project

Run your Python Flask project, then visit the URL `http://localhost:5000/convert_temp` in your web browser.

You should now be able to type in a temperature in degrees Celsius and hit submit to be taken to the `/convert_result` page, where the calculated Fahrenheit temperature will be displayed (Figure 3-13).

Troubleshooting

If your code doesn't work as expected, you can add `app.debug = True` above `app.run()`. This is OK to do since our web application is not exposed to the Internet.

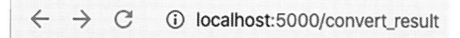

← → C   ⓘ localhost:5000/convert_result

11.0 degrees celsius is 51.8 degrees in fahrenheit.

Calculate another temperature?

Figure 3-13. *Convert_result page showing calculated temperature*

Note   You should understand that anything that is exposed to the Internet is available to everyone worldwide. The Python Flask server we are using for testing is not suitably strengthened (hardened) to be exposed to the Internet.

Congratulations! You just wrote your first web application in Python!

CHALLENGE: CREATE A DROP-DOWN SELECTOR TO CONVERT FAHRENHEIT TO CELSIUS

For this challenge, you need to add an option to allow the user to choose between "Celsius to Fahrenheit" and "Fahrenheit to Celsius." The user can use a drop-down selector to choose between the two calculation types in the form. You'll also need to assign the value entered in the form to a variable. Use if..elif to perform a different calculation depending on the selection in the form. An example of the changes you'll need in the form template, to add the selection box HTML, is included (Listing 3-13).

Listing 3-13. HTML template with a form to allow selection of two calculations

```
<html>
  <body>
    <p>Select units and a value to convert.</p>
    <form action = "/convert_result" id= "conversion_type" \
    method = "POST">
      <select name="conversion">
        <option value="c2f">Celsius to fahrenheit</option>
        <option value="f2c">Fahrenheit to celsius</option>
      </select>
      <input type="text" name="value_entered">
      <input type="submit" value="Submit">
    </form>
  </body>
</html>
```

Now add some code to the /convert_result route in your Python script. You can use if..elif again to perform different calculations based on the user's selection.

Just like how we got the `value` from the earlier form, you can get the `conversion` option using the following code:

```
calculation = request.form['conversion']
```

The other information you will need is the formula for calculating Fahrenheit to Celsius: `answer = (value = 32)/1.8`.

Happy coding!

Going Further: Internet and Other Devices

The Flask server we have been using is the easiest and safest way for you to immediately test your web application script. It restricts everything to the loopback interface and doesn't let anyone else connect.

On Your Private Network

Changing the `app.run()` command to include all interfaces with `app.run('0.0.0.0')` is only safe if you are on your own private network and you trust the other people on that network.

Using Your Mobile Device

Another variation on the local network scenario would be connecting your computer to your mobile phone's Wi-Fi access point – as long as this is the only network you are connected to at the time, this puts you on the internal network shared by your phone and your computer. Find your computer's IP address by looking at the network properties on your computer. In keeping with also using the CLI, you can also go into your terminal and type:

- `ipconfig /all` on Windows

- `ip a` on Linux or a Raspberry Pi

- `ifconfig` on macOS

You can then run your script and view your web application from your phone's web browser using `http://<your IP address>:5000/`.

The Internet

The obvious question would be, "How can we make our web application available to friends on the Internet?" Our little Flask web server will not handle more than one connection easily and is also not suitably hardened for exposure to somewhere as hostile as the Internet. The best way is therefore to use a web server such as NGINX (sounds like "engine-X") using something called uWSGI (sounds like "you whisky"). Technically, this is a topic itself, so rather than try to explain this here, I will point you to the page within the official online uWSGI documentation at `https://uwsgi-docs.readthedocs.io/en/latest/WSGIquickstart.html`. Note that although this is a step-by-step set of instructions, this is the time to leverage your technical support people and see if they can set up a server for you to host your scripts. Another online service can be found at `www.pythonanywhere.com/`, although at the time of writing, this does not allow members under the age of 13 years old but does offer a free plan. A good alternative may be that they can set up a server within your own network, for example, where other students at the school could see your applications, rather than everyone in the world.

Summary

- Programming with block-based languages, for example, Scratch and MakeCode, can reach a plateau due to limitations in data handling capabilities. The extensibility and more advanced data structures and commands supported by Python make it a viable alternative to block-based programming; it is supported on a wider range of microcontroller boards suitable for maker space and code club projects.

- Basic Python skills can be learned initially with browser-based platforms such as `https://trinket.io`. Using a set online curriculum such as code club or similar gave us an easy path to learning those skills on Trinket (around eight projects). Making the effort to see each project through to completion helped our code club kids to obtain invaluable debugging skills. This required active support from our teachers and volunteers, ensuring that our kids had everything they needed. The aim was to be efficient while keeping a focus on learning and seeing each project through to completion. To capitalize on learning, we applied these skills in small group workshops.

- The next step is to set up a convenient programming environment that allows us to extend Python further than Trinket.io. Thonny and Mu editors come with a Python 3 mode in addition to allowing programming on microcontroller boards (also known as embedded programming). The Mu editor comes with some additional libraries already installed and also allows adding of more. Thonny has a couple of advantages compared to the Mu editor:

  - It supports a wider range of embedded platforms.

  - It comes installed by default on the Raspberry Pi operating system (OS).

> **Note**   Leverage your IT support people to ensure you have the required Internet access; this may need a proxy server configured in the environment variables `https_proxy` and `http_proxy` for your operating system. Another useful setting for schools includes setting a network home drive as the working directory:
>
> In **Thonny**, set this in the `configuration.ini` file.[6]
>
> In **Mu**, set this in the `settings.json` file.[7]

- Outlining common Python program structure is useful when kids are tasked with creating their own scripts to solve a problem. An included project incorporates the Flask library to create a working web application to convert temperature from Celsius to Fahrenheit. We have a challenge to add the option for the user to select between the original functionality and from Fahrenheit to Celsius. This project includes relevant cheat sheets for limited HTML and operating system commands. The concepts we learn will allow us to create web interfaces for our programs, which can allow our Python programs to be used in browsers on computers and mobile devices. Interesting concepts learned from this project include

  - Creating an instance of a Flask object (object-oriented programming or OOP)

---

[6] https://github.com/thonny/thonny/wiki/MicroPython
[7] https://codewith.mu/en/tutorials/1.1/configuration

- Using HTML templates for input/output

- Adding debugging in a test environment and why this is not appropriate for exposure to the Internet

- Defining our own custom commands, known as functions

- Using Python decorators to add features to our defined functions

- Understanding the directory structure required for a Flask web application and how to edit .html files with common text editors

- Testing web applications on a mobile device

Chapter 3: Cheat Sheet

I have included cheat sheets throughout this chapter at the points where they are most relevant. These may be cut out and printed on a separate page if you are using these for a workshop at your own code club or maker space.

In summary

- Browser request types and browser response codes (Table 3-1)

- Common command-line commands (Table 3-2)

- Text editors found in common operating systems (Table 3-3)

- HTML tags used in our project (Table 3-4)

# CHAPTER 4

Getting Tactile with Python

Creativity is a wild mind and a disciplined eye.

—Dorothy Parker

Making things with your hands is engaging – one way to stop someone from fidgeting is to give them something to hold and play with. In this chapter, we add some crafty skills to the mix and leverage our other skills to tie everything together.

A Quick Tale: Keeping It Simple to Build Bigger

One of the earlier workshops we ran at our code club leveraged a couple of JoyLabz' Makey Makey[1] boards that we'd been given. By shorting copper arrows and circles on the Makey Makey circuit board to the ground, kids can trigger keypresses via a USB cable connected to a computer. At that point, we were still using Scratch, but I felt it was worth a mention as some valuable lessons were learned during that activity.

---

[1] `https://makeymakey.com/`

© Martin Tan 2023
M. Tan, *micro:bit Projects with Python and Single Board Computers*,
https://doi.org/10.1007/978-1-4842-9197-9_4

The initial objective was for our kids to draw an idea that would utilize the Makey Makey in creative and interesting ways. We provided some sticky tape, aluminum foil, corrugated cardboard, and some crocodile clip wires. After explaining how the Makey Makey worked, I suggested that the kids should draw a rectangle to represent the screen and then design a real-world object with cardboard and foil.

The first mistake we made when initially selecting participants was to let a few of the louder but not necessarily hardest-working kids do the activity. As they had not completed much of the Scratch curriculum activities, their grasp of programming was limited, resulting in them struggling to come up with viable ideas or a way to implement them. From this, we learned to qualify those who were ready to participate in the more freeform and complex workshops. We were to later discover that some of the louder kids were getting through just by copying projects from their friends or online. Intervening with these situations earlier turned out to be a better strategy as we could find where or why things went astray, and by reengaging many of the kids, this discouraged time wasting before it became a problem.

Another mistake was more nuanced – I suggested that the kids start off by keeping things simple, that is, design only the essential gameplay, but they ultimately overengineered their ideas and soon became overwhelmed. To kickstart things a bit, I hinted at a Whack-a-Mole game or musical instrument concept – due to our poor choices earlier, the latter did not materialize because we selected those without all the required skills.

Luckily, a code club kid named Ajay had a go at the Whack-a-Mole game. Checking in with him, it was clear that he was quite eager but like some of the others had rushed ahead and been overcome by complexity. Bringing things back to first principles, we took him aside and drew a rectangle on some paper. In the rectangle, Ajay drew a very basic concept of what the game would look like, that is, a circle to represent a hole and a small creature popping their head up. We then drew a hammer, and I started asking questions. Pointing to each item on the paper, I would ask simply, "what does this need to do?" and "when does this happen?" This established the basic events, and Ajay was then able to describe each event in simple terms. At that point, his eyes lit up, and he realized that he could visualize how the code would work. Every step of the way, we tested, and then he made foil-covered cardboard circles on a board and a foil-covered "hammer" with a wire to complete the circuit (pressing a key) when touched to the circles. From this rather clumsy foray into workshops, we learned to first qualify kids for future workshops and teach them to break down ideas into simple tasks. This allowed them to still think creatively but be able to produce something that worked, within time constraints. It also meant that kids started to get increased.

E-textiles: Building Circuits on Fabric and Cardboard

Growing up in Australia, my visual media was restricted to a limited diet of shows broadcast across five or so TV channels. While most of these served only to encourage passive consumption, one standout was *The Curiosity Show*. Comprised of science- and craft-related projects that could be made from everyday materials and objects available around the house, *The Curiosity Show* seemed to have that extra spark that got me thinking; luckily, much of this still exists on YouTube.[2] I fondly recall how the hosts, Dean and Rob, had a knack for inspiring me to start building things with everyday items, which I would not have otherwise considered. Similarly, there's a certain appeal with e-textiles and cardboard circuits that makes us look that little bit harder at how we can combine some common materials with inexpensive accessories to create some wonderfully interactive projects.

---

[2] www.youtube.com/@CuriosityShow

Starting with a Simple Circuit

Enough reminiscing! Here's a simple circuit (Figure 4-1). We have power flowing from the positive terminal (+) of our 3V power supply to its ground terminal. There is a light-emitting diode (LED), a resistor, and a switch. Resistors can reduce current flow and divide the voltage of the circuit so that other components will receive less power.

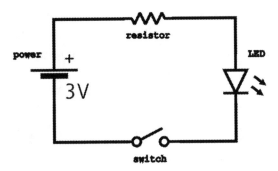

Figure 4-1. *A simple circuit*

Later, we can add sensor inputs, some microcontroller programming, and other outputs and many more things, but for now let's look at implementing our simple circuit in an e-textiles context – a wearable cap!

As I mentioned, the circuit in Figure 4-1 shows a resistor – this is because a standard circuit built with wires and a larger power supply will require a lower voltage to prevent damage to the LED. In practice, a conductive thread and copper tape that we will use have more resistance than copper wire, and this resistance increases with length. Some LEDs are also designed specifically for e-textile use and come with integrated resistors and larger holes for sewn connections (Figure 4-2).

Figure 4-2. *An e-textile LED with a built-in resistor on the left*

While we are on the topic of power, coin cell batteries were previously used to power e-textile and paper circuits; however, due to dangers to small children when swallowed, legislation in Australia now prevents the sale of coin cell devices without robust battery compartments and captive screws. After speaking with teachers, we agreed that we now require a safe and readily available alternative – so we will be working only with safer, cheaper, and longer-lasting dry cell batteries in this chapter.

Considerations for E-textile Projects

Washability

The first question I asked about e-textiles was, "Can I wash circuits?" The answer is "yes, but it depends." If your materials resist corrosion and moisture damage, your project will last for many washes. Stainless steel is the best – it won't rust or go black and lose its conductivity. How you wash and dry your projects will also make a difference. If you have less moisture-resistant materials, you will need to wash less and dry as quickly as possible to prevent corrosion. This is assuming that you make any nonwaterproof components such as batteries and circuit boards removable for washing – those components will generally not even survive one single wash without being damaged! The physical action of a washing machine can also damage parts, so hand washing is also a better way to look after delicate e-textiles.

E-textile components such as thread and crocodile clips will be labelled to indicate whether they are stainless steel – if they don't state that on the packaging or description, they will likely be tin-plated or similar and not last long. For large projects that are required to last over time, always go for stainless steel threads and components. If in doubt, ask or test them yourself. There's nothing worse than spending hours creating an awesome costume only for the thread to corrode and your circuit to stop working. If you're just doing a proof of concept to see if something works, or display something for a finite amount of time, then the cheapest components will do fine.

An easy way to increase the washability of your creations is to make some components removable. Metal press studs and conductive Velcro are a few ways to do this. I have even heard of people sewing conductive thread into standard Velcro to make it conductive. Possibly related, the same method works with sewing conductive thread into gloves so they can be used to operate mobile device touch screens!

Tools

The tools needed to get started with e-textiles are relatively simple and inexpensive.

Scissors: These just need to be sharp enough to cut accurately, but not necessarily of "the good scissors" standard.

Side cutters: These are just snips that will cut thin wire, like the wire in LEDs. They are readily available for under $10 AUD. Although you won't typically need these for all e-textiles or paper circuit projects, they are often useful if you have some solid wires that need to be trimmed.

Needles: It helps if the needles you use are slightly larger than the fine needles used for hand sewing, as fraying of conductive thread can make it more difficult to thread into a needle. Just make sure they are not so large that the thread pulls out of the holes your needle makes in the fabric. I have found that cheap hair wax or pomade from the supermarket works well to make the ends easier to thread. You can then just wipe it through your hair instead of on your clothes, as I would normally do. The best way I have found to thread these over and over again is by using a needle threader, which is a thin metal tool (shaped much like a soft drink can tab) and commonly comes with inexpensive sewing kits (Figure 4-3).

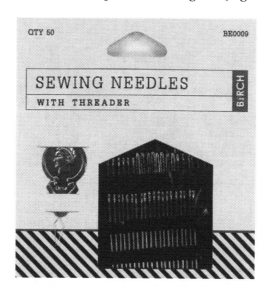

Figure 4-3. *Needle kits like this, with threaders, are available for less than $3 at Kmart*

Long-nose pliers: These are good for curling up the ends of LED wire legs to make them easier to sew onto fabric. They're not 100% essential, and if you're not using any components with wire legs, you probably won't miss not having this tool. Having said this, the first exercise in this chapter does require these!

Embroidery hoop: These are relatively cheap, that is, starting at around $5 AUD, and can be bought at $2 stores, sewing supply stores, Kmart, or even some supermarkets. The hoop stretches the fabric out giving you something solid to hold, making it easier to sew accurately and evenly (Figure 4-4).

Figure 4-4. *Fabric tensioned in a medium-sized embroidery hoop*

Threading Your Needle

Conductive thread can be finicky to thread as it unravels easier than standard threads. Put a very small amount of cheap hair wax or pomade on the tip of the thread to keep the strands together for threading. Wipe the rest through your hair or, alternatively, a hairier relative. A quicker and more reliable method is to use a needle threader to pull the thread through the needle (Figure 4-5); this also allows you to use a slightly smaller needle, which will make your stitches a bit more robust.

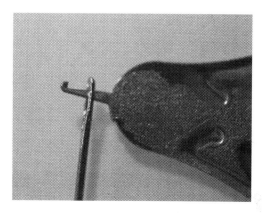

Figure 4-5. *Another style of needle threader*

What Type of Stitches Are Best?

Since not everyone will immediately have access to a class set or even a single sewing machine, it will be easier to get started by hand sewing e-textiles. Using a running stitch (over, under, over, under as shown in Figure 4-6) is the easiest but also can look quite plain with a dotted-line appearance. It is a great stitch if you are impatient, though.

Figure 4-6. *Running stitch (over, under, over, under)*

Backstitching (Figure 4-7) involves looping back and gives a neater appearance while using more thread. A variation on the backstitch is a zigzag stitch which is useful for allowing stretch fabric to stretch without breaking the stitches. To keep your e-textile projects accessible to even those without sewing experience, we can use a running stitch to demonstrate initially. Those with more sewing skills will undoubtedly end up making their own variations anyway.

Figure 4-7. *Backstitch (over, under, loop back)*

Fixing Sewing Mistakes

Sometimes, you will make mistakes and need to undo stitches. You can get an unpicking tool from sewing shops or with a sewing kit. This is simply a small tool that you can slide under stitches to pull them out.

Knots and Attaching Components

When you start sewing, you will need a knot to anchor the end of your thread in the fabric. The easiest way is to just form a loop at the end of the thread furthest from the needle and wind the thread through the loop a few times (Figure 4-8). Pull the knot tight (Figure 4-9) and snip the tail of the thread off as close as possible to the knot to prevent short circuits.

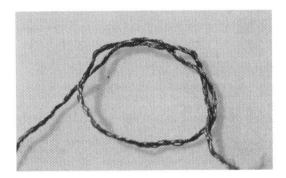

Figure 4-8. *Creating a knot to anchor your thread before you sew*

Figure 4-9. *Pull the knot tight and remember to trim the tail later*

When you finish sewing or need to keep stitches tight around components, leave a loop on one side of the fabric, and wind the thread around the needle a few times before pulling it through (Figure 4-10). The photo explains this much better (Figure 4-11). I usually do this twice so that you have thread tying against itself to prevent your sewing loosening. When attaching components to fabric, your thread should loop through the holes at least three times to ensure a good electrical connection - Figure 4-12 shows a socket for a battery holder, attached to fabric with conductive thread.

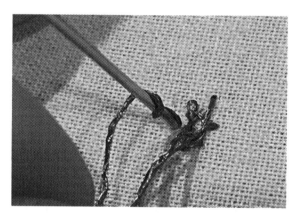

Figure 4-10. *Winding the thread around the needle to create a knot that stays put*

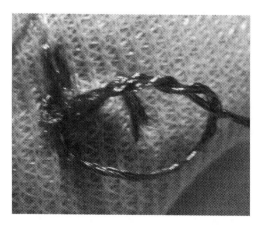

Figure 4-11. *Tying off, ready to tighten*

Figure 4-12. *Securing a component to the fabric with conductive thread*

Another consideration when sewing with conductive thread is the tails left from tying off your thread. Tying off is usually a matter of sewing three loops and making sure you run the thread underneath subsequent loops to make a knot (like the start of tying your shoelaces). Try to snip off the thread as close to the knot as possible without letting the thread come undone. Keeping the tail as short as possible will prevent short circuits – a dab of fabric glue can keep unruly tails secured and prevent knots from unravelling. Since this type of glue is designed to be washed, it can be more reliable than standard hot glue which melts easily. Alternatively, nail polish may be easier to come by than fabric glue, is washable, and works well to insulate conductive thread and prevent stray tails from connecting to other components accidentally (Figure 4-13).

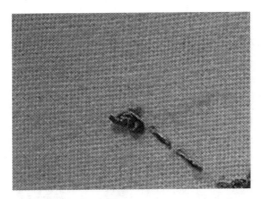

Figure 4-13. *Tie off your sewing and snip any tails to prevent them from touching other parts of the circuit, then use nail polish or glue to insulate them further*

126

OK – now that you have some basic guidelines for working with e-textiles, let's continue with the first project of the chapter!

A SIMPLE E-TEXTILE LED CIRCUIT

In this project, we will look at implementing a basic circuit that consists of a power supply, an LED, and a switch. This will consist of creating a test circuit in some fabric.

Things you will need

The materials you have available may vary; however, most online stores should have some sort of reference available to let you know how much power is required, for example, Kitronik has charts for LED power[3] or a calculator[4] to determine which resistors might be required in general circuits (not considering the extra resistance from longer runs of conductive thread). Note that LEDs designed specifically for e-textiles[5] will often have contacts shaped better for sewing, and for simplicity, this exercise uses e-textile LEDs with built-in resistors.

Materials

- A 50cm x 50cm square of nonstretch fabric, preferably the type that is reasonably easy to sew.

- Conductive thread – although stainless steel thread is recommended for long-lasting projects, you won't need it for this exercise, since we are just learning the basics.

---

[3] https://resources.kitronik.co.uk/pdf/leds.pdf
[4] https://kitronik.co.uk/blogs/resources/led-resistor-value-calculator
[5] https://kitronik.co.uk/collections/leds-for-e-textiles

- A 2xAAA or 2xAAAA battery holder with the wire ends stripped to expose the copper or alternatively a sewable JST PH 2.0 socket and matching battery holder with a matching plug.

- 5mm LED (sewable or standard) – try and get ones with built-in resistors (for this exercise, we will use built-in resistors with e-textile LEDs, but you can easily use standard through-hole LEDs with wire legs wound into loops to sew through).

Tools

- Needle-nose pliers to bend the wire legs if you are using standard through-hole LEDs.

- Scissors.

- Sewing needle suitable for your thread (you can use a slightly smaller needle if you have a needle threader, and this will make your stitches more stable in the fabric).

- Needle threader or some hair wax/pomade – hint: the needle threader makes life much easier!

- An embroidery ring to tension your fabric and make it easier to sew.

- An erasable fabric pen to mark your circuit; the ones that disappear in 48 hours or with a damp wipe are easiest.

- Some clear nail polish to seal the ends of your circuit and prevent short circuits from breaking your circuit (optional).

Threading the needle

Since you'll be repeatedly sewing, tying off, and rethreading your needle for e-textile circuits, a needle threader is highly recommended. These are a small flat metal tool with either a hook or wire loop that pushes through the eye of the sewing needle and pulls the conductive thread through, thereby threading your needle. An alternative is to use a small dab of hair pomade or wax to smooth the tip of the thread, so you can thread it easier. But since a needle threader is much cheaper than hair wax or pomade and comes with most sewing kits, for example, the ones available at department stores like Kmart, you'll save some frustration by getting one of these.

Step 1: Create a simple e-textile circuit.

In this step, we will create a circuit that connects the terminals of a light-emitting diode (LED) to a battery. We'll start off with an LED, a battery, and switch (optional) – the idea is to keep things simple so we can focus on our sewing skills.

You'll find it easier to sew the components into place first. Later, we can draw connections between components and sew along these lines to complete the circuit. Instead of using wires, we will be using conductive thread to connect our components. Your battery holder will have negative (–) and positive terminals (+) that can be attached to your fabric with conductive thread; alternatively, you can use an e-textile socket that allows a battery cage to be unplugged for washing (not critical since we are just doing a proof of concept, i.e., just making it work). The thread will also connect power to the LED.

- Start by clamping some fabric and stretching it tightly and uniformly in your embroidery hoop. Plan out the positions where you will to place your components and mark these with your fabric marker. The positive leg of the LED is the longer one and is called the anode, while the negative leg is called the cathode. Make sure that the negative leg of the LED is positioned so that you can sew a line back to the negative terminal of the battery holder.

- Thread your needle and tie a knot in one end of a 30cm length of conductive thread. Hold your battery holder against the top of the fabric and sew from underneath, threading upward through the positive hole of the battery holder. Repeat three to five loops tightly around the battery holder positive hole. You can add an extra loop across all the loops to hold things tighter. Do the same for each component of your circuit by following the circuit diagram. If you're including a switch, this should be on the positive side of your circuit (+).

Tip   If part of your circuit connects to another part of your circuit that it shouldn't, you may risk short-circuiting your battery which could damage it or in some cases make it burst. You can reduce the likelihood of this happening by keeping the tails from your knots short and covering the knots with a nonconductive glue or nail polish. This is known as insulation.

Step 2: Connect the LED.

We are now going to continue sewing with a running stitch (over-under-over-under) from the battery holder positive terminal to the positive leg of the LED. Your completed circuit should look something like the photo in Figure 4-14; the socket on the left is connected to a 2xAAA battery holder.

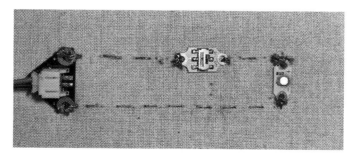

Figure 4-14. *The completed e-textile circuit with the positive terminal at the top*

Testing your project

1. Tie off the thread connecting the negative battery holder hole to the anode (−) of the LED. Remember to pass the thread underneath itself at least once. Snip off the tail as close to the knot as possible, then seal and insulate it with nail polish.

2. Now insert the battery into the battery holder and turn the switch on (Figure 4-15). Your LED should light up. Congratulations – you have created your first e-textile circuit! As you've seen, e-textile circuits are slightly different to standard circuits just due to requirements for flexibility, fit, and resistance of conductive thread.

Latching vs. momentary switches   A latching switch will stay on until you switch it off, whereas a momentary switch will only keep the circuit connected while it is being pressed, for example, a button switch that does not "click" or touch pads. You can use both: with a latching switch used to connect the battery to your circuit and a momentary switch to trigger a function quickly, for example, turning on or changing a light to a specific color when a section of clothing is touched.

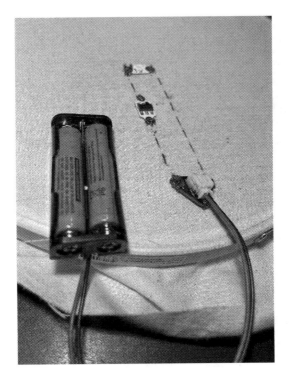

Figure 4-15. *Our circuit with the connected battery holder*

If your LED doesn't light up, check that your connections are sewn tight enough for a solid connection and that the battery is inserted correctly, that is, the positive side of the coin cell battery should line up with the positive side of the holder. Be careful that you don't wrinkle or fold the fabric as this can cause parts of the circuit to connect and create a short circuit – these can damage the batteries and if left too long could start heating up or catch fire!

BUILD A PROGRAMMABLE TOUCH CAP WITH LIGHTS

In this project, we will use our sewing skills to create a circuit around a piece of clothing – a cap. This project uses the Adafruit Gemma M0 microcontroller board, which allows us to use our Python skills and design some more complex functionality. To start, we will have some multicolored red-green-blue (RGB) LEDs turn different colors depending on where we touch our cap. The LEDs each require three connections:

- Power

- Ground

- A data connection

We can then daisy-chain the LEDs and individually control each using CircuitPython running on the Gemma M0 board. A cap is our chosen clothing platform since plain caps are cheap and readily available, and you may even have an old one you can use.

Materials required

- A cheap sports cap or hat like the ones available at Kmart.

- A computer running MacOS, Linux, or Windows, with a Thonny IDE installed.

- An Adafruit Gemma M0 board and suitable micro USB cable with the other end that can connect to your computer's USB port.

- Two e-textile RGB LEDs – most electronics hobby stores will have these with built-in resistors and big holes for sewing them into your project. I used the Kitronik ZIP Hex RGB LEDs.[6]

- About 6 meters or more of conductive thread; buy the stainless steel type if you want it to last longer.

- Two squares of conductive fabric.

- Fabric glue.

- Some clear nail polish to insulate your circuit and prevent short circuits.

- A portable rechargeable battery like the type you would use to charge your phone.

- Six metal press stud button pairs (optional – to make the Gemma removable for washing).

Tools required

- A sewing needle large enough to thread your conductive thread.

- A needle threader.

- An unpicking tool to unpick sewing mistakes (optional – you can improvise with a needle and stitches if required, but it will be slower).

- Scissors.

---

[6]https://kitronik.co.uk/products/35140-zip-hex-led-pack-of-5

- An embroidery hoop that is at least three times as big as the Gemma M0 board.

- 8 x 20cm long wires with crocodile clips on each end – we will use this for testing parts of our circuit.

  Step 1: Prepare the Gemma M0 board (Figure 4-16) with CircuitPython.

Figure 4-16. *The Adafruit Gemma M0 microcontroller board*

First, we should install the latest stable version of CircuitPython on our Gemma M0 microcontroller board (Figure 4-17). This is easy to do by loading up the latest version of the Thonny IDE on your computer and connecting the Gemma M0 via USB. From the bottom-right corner, click configure interpreter and select Install or Update CircuitPython. Check that the Target volume and version are correct, then press RESET on the Gemma M0 and click Install to update CircuitPython.

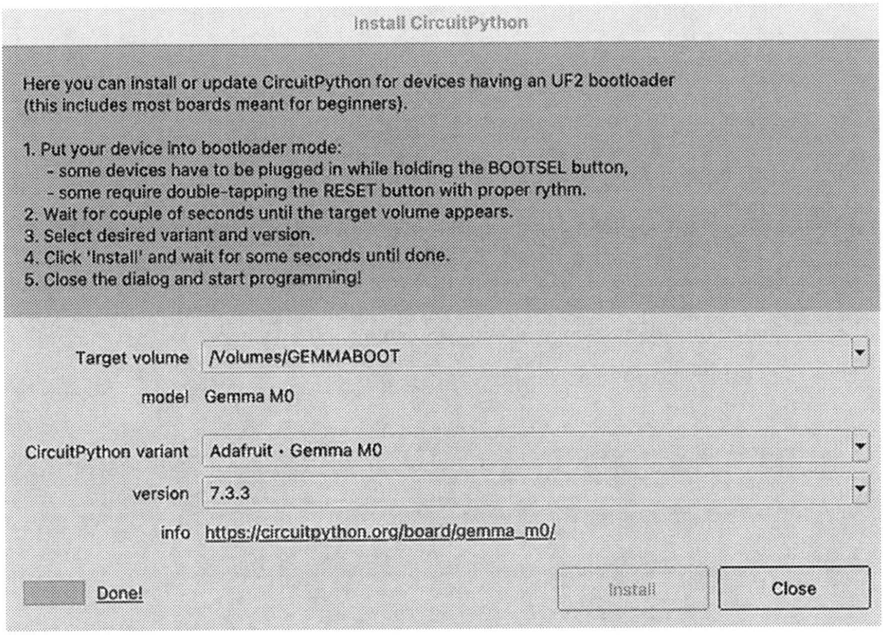

Figure 4-17. *Update CircuitPython on the Gemma M0 from Thonny*

Alternatively, for any Adafruit board, you can go to the CircuitPython page[7] and click your board to get the right firmware, press RESET twice, and drag the .U2F file across the GEMMABOOT folder that appears.

- Once CircuitPython is updated and restarted (disconnect and then reconnect the USB cable), you can use some simple Python code to flash the onboard LED and check that everything is working. Type the Python code from Listing 4-1 into Thonny and run it to make sure the LED blinks. As this is just to test that you can run Python code on the Gemma M0, don't bother saving it on your computer.

---

[7]https://circuitpython.org/downloads

Listing 4-1. Blink the onboard LED on the Gemma M0

```
import board
import digitalio
import time

led = digitalio.DigitalInOut(board.LED)
led.direction = digitalio.Direction.OUTPUT

while True:
    led.value = True
    time.sleep(0.5)
    led.value = False
    time.sleep(0.5)
```

Step 2: Create a test circuit and program.

Before we create an e-textile circuit, we will connect our circuit (Figure 4-18) using wires with crocodile clips and write some code to control individual RGB LEDs.

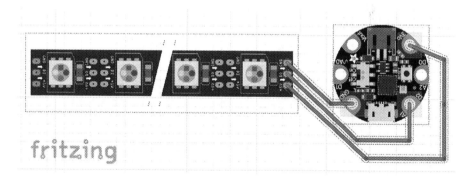

Figure 4-18. *Diagram showing connection from the Gemma M0 to RGB LEDs*

- Making sure power is disconnected from your Gemma M0 (you can move the slider switch to off), connect the crocodile clips to the RGB LEDs and the Gemma M0 as shown in Figures 4-19, 4-20, and 4-21. The second LED should have its in connected to the first LED's out terminal and the GND and +V to their corresponding terminals.

Figure 4-19. *Gemma crocodile clip connections*

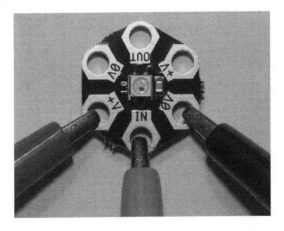

Figure 4-20. *First RGB LED crocodile clip connections*

Figure 4-21. *Adding a second RGB LED to the first*

- We will also need to download the CircuitPython libraries[8]—
  make sure you select the libraries that match the version of
  CircuitPython that you installed on your Gemma M0
  (Figure 4-22). Because the Gemma M0 storage is not huge,
  we will only copy across the NeoPixel libraries that we might
  need to control our RGB LEDs. This is as simple as unarchiving
  the `.ZIP` file (double-clicking will usually do this) and copying
  across the required files.

---

[8] https://github.com/adafruit/Adafruit_CircuitPython_Bundle/
releases/latest

The libraries in each release are compiled for all recent major versions of CircuitPython. Please download the one that matches the major version of your CircuitPython. For example, if you are running 7.0.0 you should download the 7.x bundle.

To install, simply download the matching zip file, unzip it, and selectively copy the libraries you would like to install into the lib folder on your CIRCUITPY drive. This is especially important for non-express boards with limited flash, such as the Trinket M0, Gemma M0 and Feather M0 Basic.

Contributors

makermelissa, adafruit-adabot, and tekktrik

▾ **Assets**   8

adafruit-circuitpython-bundle-20221119.json	88.4 KB	2 days ago
adafruit-circuitpython-bundle-7.x-mpy-20221119.zip	3.94 MB	2 days ago

Figure 4-22. *Downloading the CircuitPython library .ZIP file*

You will need to drag the library files across the `lib` folder of the `CircuitPython` drive on the Gemma M0 (Figure 4-23).

< > **lib**

Name ∧

adafruit_pixelbuf.mpy
neopixel.mpy

Figure 4-23. *Required NeoPixel (RGB LED) library files*

- Now connect the Gemma to your computer using the USB cable and type in the new code shown in Listing 4-2.

Listing 4-2. RGB LED color-changing Python code

```python
import board
import neopixel
import time

pixel_pin = board.A1
num_of_pixels = 2

pixels = neopixel.NeoPixel(pixel_pin, num_of_pixels)
```

```
while True:
    pixels[0] = (0,0,255) # red
    pixels[1] = (0,255,255)
    print("red")
    time.sleep(1)
    pixels[0] = (0,255,255) # blue
    pixels[1] = (0,0,255)
    print("blue")
    time.sleep(1)
```

Run the code and you should see the LEDs change as the code loops.

Step 3: Add capacitive touch.

Now that we have two LEDs controlled independently, we can add capacitive touch, which is supported by the Gemma M0. Since we have two spare capacitive terminals or pins, we will be able to connect these to two pieces of conductive fabric on either side of our cap. Update your code as shown in Listing 4-3.

Listing 4-3. Python to control LEDs using two capacitive touch pads

```
import board
import neopixel
import time
import touchio

pixel_pin = board.A1
num_of_pixels = 2

pixels = neopixel.NeoPixel(pixel_pin, num_of_pixels)

touch_pad_left = board.A0
touch_pad_right = board.A2
touch_left = touchio.TouchIn(touch_pad_left)
touch_right = touchio.TouchIn(touch_pad_right)
```

```
while True:
    if touch_left.value:
        pixels[0] = (0,0,255)
        pixels[1] = (0,0,255)
    elif touch_right.value:
        pixels[0] = (255,0,0)
        pixels[1] = (255,0,0)
    else:
        pixels[0] = (0,0,0) # off
        pixels[1] = (0,0,0)
```

Check your connections before connecting power and run your code with the Gemma M0 connected to the computer. Even without anything connected to A0 and A2, the Gemma will automatically adjust sensitivity when these are enabled – you can then touch the A0 or A2 terminal to control the LEDs, which will be turned off. Recheck your connections and code if it doesn't work. Once your code is working, we can transfer our circuit to the cap.

Step 4: Position and attach the two RGB LEDs.

- Decide where you want to locate your LEDs near the front of your cap with one on either side. Mark these with your fabric pen, then hold them in place and connect them using separate pieces of thread for the in and out pins. For the first LED, ensure that the out pin is angled along a seam and up to the top of the cap (Figure 4-24). The other LED should have the in pin angled toward the cap top (Figure 4-25). In the next step, we will be sewing along the inside of the cap to connect the out pin from the first LED to the in pin of the second LED.

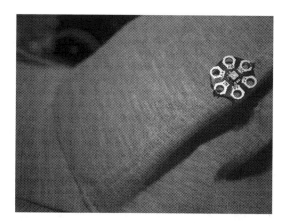

Figure 4-24. *Positioning and orientation of the first LED on cap seam*

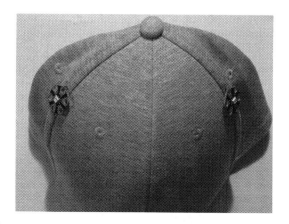

Figure 4-25. *Positioning and orientation of both LEDs*

Step 5: Connect the LEDs with conductive thread.

We will use a simple running stitch for all the connections in this project. Make sure that the connections to components are nice and tight. As with our previous circuit, every connection must be separate from other connections and not short circuit between positive and negative in the wrong places.

- Sew around the out pin on the first LED and then sew
  along one of the inside seams to the in pin on the second
  LED (Figure 4-26). This will allow us to control both LEDs
  individually.

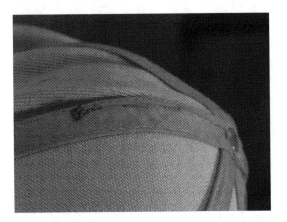

Figure 4-26. *Internal connection between LEDs (out to in)*

- Now use your fabric pen to draw some lines on the outside
  of the cap, connecting the ground (negative, "−") terminal
  to the ground terminal on the other LED, then sew along the
  line (Figure 4-27). Do the same for the positive ("+") power
  terminals and make sure that these do not cross (Figure 4-28).
  If they must cross, we can simply sew underneath the other
  connection, so that they do not short-circuit. Sew on the outside
  of the cap for these. Since these will be visible on the outside
  of our cap, you should make sure your lines look nice – so feel
  free to be a bit creative without making things too complicated.

Figure 4-27. *LED connection on the outside of a cap (gnd to gnd)*

Figure 4-28. *Both LEDs connected (two external connections and one internal connection)*

Note   A "short circuit" occurs when parts of a circuit are connected incorrectly due to one component accidentally touching another; this can sometimes result in damage to components or power supplies due to the resulting increase in electrical current.

145

- Now test your work by connecting three crocodile clips from the first LED to the Gemma M0 as we did previously (Figure 4-29). You can now also connect some conductive fabric to the conductive pins with a crocodile clip. Rerun your script from Thonny again and make sure that everything works as expected, that is, the LEDs should light up the same way they did previously when you touched the capacitive pins of the Gemma M0 board. If they don't, check that your sewing is secure and there are no short circuits and try again.

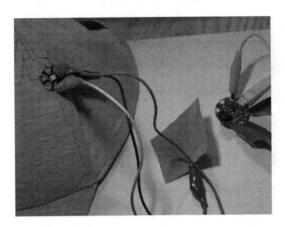

Figure 4-29. *Test your sewing, using crocodile wires to connect the Gemma*

Step 6: Position the Gemma M0 on the cap.

To make our cap washable, we are going to use metal press studs to connect the Gemma to our cap. This will let us remove the Gemma from the cap while still allowing connectivity to our circuit. Alternatively, to simplify this project, you can skip this step and sew the Gemma directly to the cap and skip ahead gluing on the conductive fabric squares.

- Put a new piece of fabric in your embroidery hoop and sew each pin of the Gemma board with separate pieces of conductive thread.

- Using running stitch, sew a line out for each pin and tie off as shown in Figure 4-30.

Figure 4-30. *Sewing the Gemma*

- Cut a square out of the fabric and sew press studs on the back of each tied off connection to the Gemma. Sew the opposite press studs to the back of your cap (Figure 4-31) so that they line up and you can connect your Gemma to the cap (Figure 4-32).

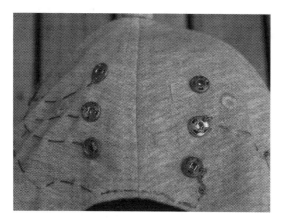

Figure 4-31. *Press studs also sewn to the cap*

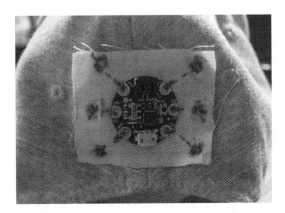

Figure 4-32. *Gemma connected to the cap via press studs*

- Using fabric glue sparingly, attach the conductive fabric squares to the sides of the cap (Figure 4-33). Take care to position them so that your ears won't accidentally touch them. Once the glue has dried, sew in all the connections to replace the crocodile clips from your earlier testing – where your sewing lines cross over, you will need to sew under existing lines (Figure 4-34), being careful that the thread does not touch (Figure 4-35).

Figure 4-33. *Conductive fabric square glued in place with conductive thread connection to Gemma*

Figure 4-34. *Sewing under another line to prevent short circuits*

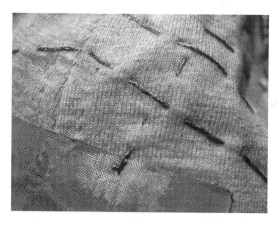

Figure 4-35. *The finished sewn lines, crossing without shorting*

- Once all the crocodile clips are replaced with sewn lines
  (Figure 4-36) and securely connected to the press studs
  (Figure 4-37) (or directly to the Gemma if you opted to connect
  the Gemma directly to the cap), double-check that your
  connections are correct, and with the Gemma connected to
  the cap, plug it into your computer to make sure everything
  works as expected. The lights should turn on when you touch

the conductive fabric squares. Fix any loose connections with tighter stitches. Be sure to save a copy of your Python code onto your computer as well. Now you can use a portable phone charging battery to power your cap – you may need a longer cable so that you can put the battery in a pocket.

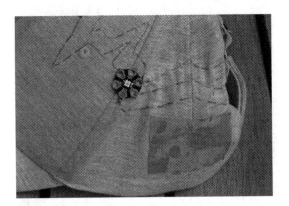

Figure 4-36. *All the connections replaced with sewn lines*

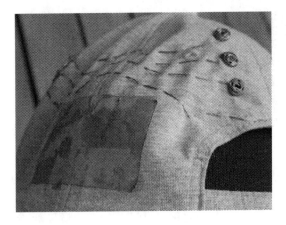

Figure 4-37. *Connecting to the press studs*

Step 7: Insulate internal sewing and next steps.

Congratulations, your cap is working with your code! Before you wear your cap, we will need to insulate all the internal stitches so that they don't short-circuit when they touch your head (remember, your skin and any moisture from sweat is conductive and will connect any parts of the circuit it touches!).

- Using some clear nail polish, take your time and carefully cover all the exposed conductive thread inside your cap. You can also do this on the outside, but keep in mind that if the metal parts get wet, your cap won't work. For a working cap in bad weather, you will need to work out a way to seal all the components from moisture, for example, it is possible that a water-proofing such as Scotchgard or similar may work, but I have not tested this.

- You can modify your code to perform more complex operations when both conductive fabric squares are touched together, trigger on double taps, etc.

Summary

E-textiles and copper adhesive tape circuits are a great way to mix in more creative crafts with your coding and electronics. For e-textile projects, start by isolating basic skillsets to reduce the number of variables when learning. This increases the likelihood of things working and prevents fault finding from becoming too complex and overwhelming. Later, you can design a circuit and test that it works with wires before transferring it to an e-textile environment. Once your circuit and code are working, only then should you push these to an e-textile environment. As with any other project, build separate parts and test as you go to make it easier to identify any issues. Fix any identified issues before progressing to the next step.

Trim any hanging conductive threads to prevent short circuits. Once your project is working correctly, your last step should be to insulate any exposed threads that may be touched. Microcontrollers using Python variants, for example, CircuitPython or MicroPython, can be incorporated into e-textiles to allow more complex functionality and interactivity. The programmable cap is a relatively inexpensive project which should help make e-textiles more accessible and is a good way to get kids started on the road to larger and more complex projects in the future.

Chapter 4: Cheat Sheet

Use stainless steel thread and parts for longer-lasting e-textile projects.

E-textiles can be a safe alternative to soldering circuits but may take slightly longer to implement.

Useful tools for e-textiles

- Scissors

- Needle and conductive thread

- Embroidery hoop

- Needle threader

- Unpicking tool

- Erasable fabric pen for marking where components go and where to sew

Workflow when building e-textile projects

- Design your circuit and test with crocodile clips first.

- Transfer to e-textile format.

  - Position components first.

  - Draw and sew connections.

- Test as you go.

- Make nonwashable components removable

Other tips

- Sew under conductive thread to cross lines.

- Use glue or nail polish to insulate bare conductive thread.

- Larger sections can be lined with material.

- RGB LEDs can be daisy-chained but operated independently.

- Try and use LEDs with built-in resistors to simplify your circuits and protect components.

- Consider differences between parallel and serial LEDs, the latter being like Christmas tree lights, where one defective component can prevent all the others from working.

# CHAPTER 5

Freestyling with Python: Going Off Map and Applying Skills

A Quick Tale: When Progress Levels Diverge

Something we learned over the year with our Code Club is that everyone finds their own pace and direction, but as volunteers, it's part of our job to try and stack the odds in the kids' favor by ensuring they collect enough skills and experience to make it worth their while. When the perceived return doesn't justify the investment of time and effort, kids get discouraged and lose interest.

The idea of having a curriculum for initial skill acquisition gives us some structure while we are running together – the reason this worked for us is that it is more efficient and almost guarantees that kids will gain some skills providing that they go to the effort of *completing* the lessons. This chapter will take you through some of the challenges we faced while trying to equip our code club kids with enough skills to prevent them

© Martin Tan 2023
M. Tan, *micro:bit Projects with Python and Single Board Computers*,
https://doi.org/10.1007/978-1-4842-9197-9_5

from plateauing, that is, so that they could continue to be challenged as the years progressed. You'll see how our students and volunteers graduated from simply following prepared lessons and began to develop our own projects using Python and other components. I've also included information on how a group of kids progressed from a simple drawing on a whiteboard to implementing a working project and ways in which you can then build on that project, scaling one feature at a time. The goal is to empower you to make this leap in your code club or maker space and push your skills further. During my journey with our code club, I've come across many parents and teachers who have enthusiastically jumped into similar pursuits only to find that kids soon lose interest or run into difficulties. Although there's lots of coding and electronic resources online, there's less information about keeping kids engaged and developing skills as an extracurricular activity outside of the classroom environment. For this reason, this chapter focuses on how we progressed our code club kids and overcame many of these challenges over the years and increased the value for everyone involved.

Since our code club was registered with Code Club Australia,[1] our first port of call was their Python curriculum (Figure 5-1) – these days, we aim to support the kids through at least most of the lessons in modules 1 and 2 and further, depending on progress. Code Club Australia's projects are built on the original Code Club UK[2] curriculum, which grew from Open Source[3] principles and encourages contributions from volunteers. Code Club World[4] represents the global link between these countries. These are backed by the Raspberry Pi Foundation. Having had firsthand experience at contributing to the curriculum and having had Code Club Australia

---

[1] www.codeclubau.org

[2] https://codeclub.org/en/regions/uk

[3] https://opensource.org/faq

[4] https://codeclub.org/en/

adopt some of my projects, I can highly recommend getting involved. Learning to code is great, and learning to help others is even better. For simplicity, I have referenced Code Club, since that is our personal experience – however, these references should be taken as pertaining to any of the available support resources that you deem suitable for your needs.

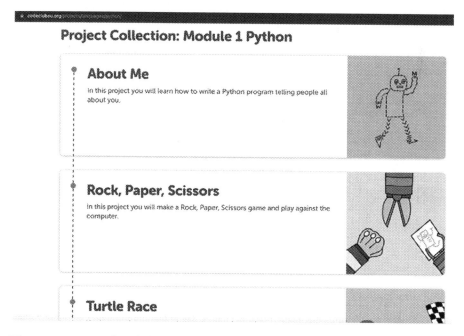

Figure 5-1. *Code Club Australia's Python curriculum*

While we were looking at ways to wean kids off Scratch, using the default command-line tools that came with Python was initially a little confusing for kids. The native editor that came with Python looked very similar to the runtime environment, and not everyone was familiar with interacting with the command line. While I do encourage everyone to jump into the command-line interface rather than just sticking with point and click user interfaces, it can be distracting to have so much power accessible to them, rather than being inside a dedicated editor like Mu or

Thonny. Earlier on, we had various challenges with getting any editors installed on the school computers, and since the Code Club exercises utilize https://Trinket.io, we found it to be a really good way to get kids started in Python. All you need is a modern browser, an Internet connection, and a free account. As part of each year's communications, we now send out an email to parents before code club commences, detailing how to set up required accounts online, one of which is Trinket.io. This puts the responsibility back to the parents and helps them understand what their kids will be doing. Doing this reduced the number of kids who would "forget" their Trinket credentials and opened communications, making it easier to keep parents aware of how things are going at code club. The Trinket.io Hour of Python also has some interesting starter tutorials, although we found that some guidance is required, and these were not as in depth as the Code Club Australia curriculum.

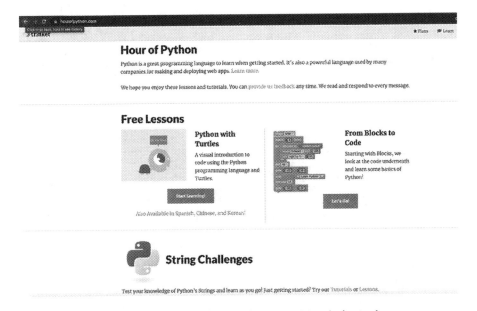

Figure 5-2. *Hour of Python, part of* https://trinket.io

Another useful resource that is used by many Australian schools is Grok Learning (Figure 5-3). This includes Python lessons and is also free for Australian school students from grades 5 to 12. CoderDojo[5] provides project-based learning for kids aged 7–17. Code.org[6] also has some great exercises; however, you'll need to pay for a subscription to use all of them.

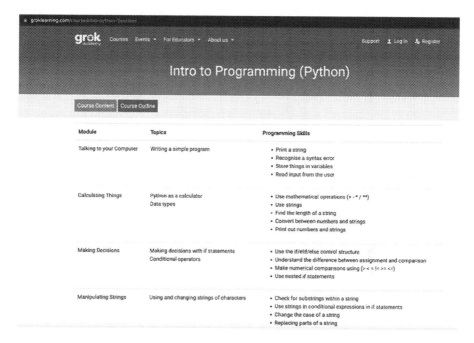

Figure 5-3. *Grok Learning Python curriculum*

All the listed curriculums are reasonably accessible due to the low or zero cost and are aligned with programming requirements in the Australian school curriculum.[7]

---

[5] https://coderdojo.com

[6] https://code.org

[7] https://v9.australiancurriculum.edu.au

In our earliest Code Club iterations, kids were putting in lots of time for a lower reward, that is, for all the time they spent, they would eventually plateau with their skills. Back then, one of our critical mistakes was that we kept kids engaged but didn't make sure that they were learning enough to empower them with any sort of vision that compelled them to continue pursuing programming as part of their future endeavors.

Once we managed to smooth out various bumps along the road, and kids were building momentum and completing each set project, it was natural to see some kids settling into a faster or slower pace. This presents some issues when there's only a few volunteers trying to help a group of around 20–30 kids to progress in learning so that they can have the tools to convert their ideas into real projects:

- How do we continue to reward those who put in extra work and legitimately complete the curriculum earlier?

- How do we also encourage those who are progressing slower but are working steadily and consistently?

As we fine-tuned our approach over the years, some of the solutions to the preceding two challenges include

- Obtaining a small number of micro:bit add-on kits that included Python components so that those who were able to complete initial curriculum lessons earlier were able to apply what they learned in a new context

- Writing some of our own projects to accommodate a variety of durations, from a single-hour session to a number of hours, that is, weekly sessions

- Continuously acknowledging progress by tracking completion of projects and seating those working on the same activities together, so they could compare notes and felt that they had some fellow travellers along for the journey

Finding Your Own Project – From Start to Finish

In 2018 Python, we selected a small group of kids from the main group that had been working with Scratch. It took a few tries to realize that those who were most vocal were not always the hardest workers of the group; we used a few methods of tracking progress, with initial results telling us who was best suited to moving on to Python programming. We ended up with a group of kids that understood programming concepts from Scratch, which we could then build on to learn additional features of the Python language. This was one of our first breakthroughs where we had a small group of kids who really started to understand Python and, as we were to find out, had gained some fluency! The previous groups we had selected often consisted of some fairly proficient programmers, but we also ended up with some of the louder yet less hardworking students; these kids would struggle with concepts that they had skipped over or not completed in the earlier curriculum. In contrast, our 2018 group consisted of only those who had been working hard to complete the earlier lessons, rather than those who were simply louder or said the projects were "too easy." This later led us to focus more on completion of projects, which meant that more kids could move on to the more interesting activities. Eventually, this included the whole group! But in 2018, we were still testing the waters, slightly apprehensive about transitioning to a text-based language after introducing the simple yet very limited drag-and-drop programming with Scratch. It is really all in the approach – if teachers and volunteers act like something is hard, then the kids will assume that it is!

Given that we'd brought across our group of Python learners, midway through the year, we had to leverage some efficiencies to give them a greater breadth of knowledge. I ended up leveraging a matrix from Code Club UK that cross-referenced lessons with the Python programming concepts to fill any skills gaps. This way, I was able to steer each code club kid through their own path to get good coverage of the concepts. This process would run something like this: once we looked at the lessons that had been completed, I would say, "OK, so it looks like you might like this one – it covers dictionaries, and you've already looked at lists, and dictionaries are pretty useful." Another volunteer and I would then work hard to answer any questions to help the kids keep up the momentum, and eventually they completed a good selection of the Code Club Python modules 1 and 2. They were eventually able to debug their code themselves after we verbalized our fault-finding thought processes with them, as we helped them through each lesson.

Beginning with Diagrams: The Self-Watering Plant Project

With our budding group of Pythoneers, we spent a couple of sessions playing with some robots and a Raspberry Pi with a Sense HAT. Although previous groups had been quite interested in making a robot move using Scratch, this group seemed much more interested in multicolored red-green-blue (RGB) LEDs than driving motors or creating autonomous robots. This was interesting and may have been hinting at a more sophisticated approach; rather than "move something left, right, forward," it was more about tweaking numbers to create different effects with an array of RGB LEDs. We had already completed a few projects, including the micro:bit Python emoticon communicator, so one day I brought in a moisture sensor for the micro:bit. I was interested to see how this group of Python kids would react to it – would they see the potential now that they had some computational skills?

The soil moisture sensor (Figure 5-4) that I'd brought along was inexpensive (around $6 AUD) and had three pins, two for power and ground which were + and -, respectively. The other pin sends a numeric value based on conductivity of anything touching both prongs. These are available online for under $10 and even cheaper if you look around online. At this price point, these sensors will corrode at some point, so if this is a concern you can spend a bit more for a longer-lasting version. Later, we did move to a different model that had some additional benefits – but I'll get to that soon.

Figure 5-4. *Moisture sensor*

On the whiteboard, I drew up a rough sketch to explain how the sensor was powered and how data was sent back to the micro:bit. It looked something like Figure 5-5.

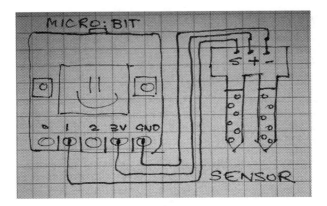

Figure 5-5. *Rough diagram of micro:bit and moisture sensor*

Once I had explained the drawing, I could tell from the expressions on their faces that these kids were now processing the possibilities. Straightaway someone saw how it worked and suggested, "ooh, we could have a water pump!" The essential information that I had provided was that the micro:bit pin1 was connected to the S pin on the sensor. So, to read the moisture content, they just needed to read this number from pin1. Using Google searches, they quickly found the Python command to read an analog value from a micro:bit pin.

As a quick recap, some important concepts that I had been repeating through the group's Python journey included

- *Initialization*: Setting up variables and structures.

- *A main loop that processes events*: This was typically a while True: loop that would always repeat and contained if..then conditions to manage events that occurred.

Once they understood the diagram I had drawn, it took around ten minutes for the kids to search for the command they needed and write their code.

To make things a little easier to connect, we also used an edge connector for the micro:bit and a mini breadboard that we could plug our wire ends into (Figure 5-6).

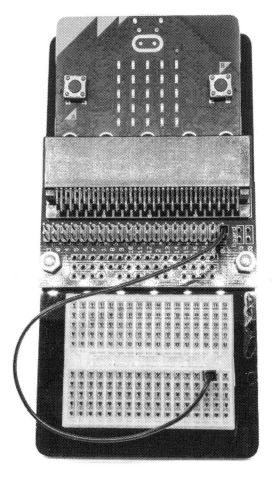

Figure 5-6. *Edge connector and breadboard mounted on an acrylic board*

This allowed us to use breadboard jumper wires to connect any of the 25 pins on the micro:bit to the breadboard. The breadboard holes are all connected vertically, allowing up to five wires to be connected on the top or bottom halves of the mini breadboard. In hindsight, this setup provided a more stable connection than alligator clips, because it reduced the movement of the micro:bit and the connected wires. In later iterations of this project, we were able to use improved sensors, but this did make our connections more precarious and prone to disconnecting or shorting; either would break our circuit and introduced more issues.

The initial script to check the moisture sensor was very simple (Listing 5-1).

Listing 5-1. Early moisture sensor code

```
from microbit import *
while True:
    soil = pin1.read_analog()
    print(soil)
```

Every time the while loop repeats, it reads the analog value on pin1. Our group had to compare the values of soil to determine the value that indicated the soil was sufficiently wet and which value range indicated that the soil was too dry. When using an editor such as Mu or Thonny, the print() statement will repeatedly print to the REPL console as the script runs.

Understanding the values at which the soil is too dry or too wet then allowed if..then to be used to perform appropriate actions. Initially, it was easiest to display a sad face on the micro:bit to indicate whether more water was required. If no water was required, the micro:bit would display a happy face (Listing 5-2).

Listing 5-2. Adding events

```
from microbit import *
while True:
    soil = pin1.read_analog()
    print(soil)
```

```python
if soil > 500:
    display.show(Image.HAPPY)
else:
    display.show(Image.SAD)
```

Note   Sometimes, it can be helpful to have multiple pot plants on hand to allow an easy comparison between dry and sufficiently wet soil.

Our proud Python coders were then tasked with writing up a simple explanation of how their code worked, and the plant was displayed at the front of the school (Figure 5-7).

Figure 5-7.   *The first micro:bit plant project from our Code Club*

This was a proud moment for both the kids and our volunteers – we had finally applied our knowledge to design our own project! We also showed that our coding skills could be used for something outside in the real world, outside of the computer.

You'll notice that this project was not written as a ready-made project as the earlier ones were – this hopefully remains true to the spirit of creating something from Scratch...I mean, in Python. As a small reward, I also bought a quantity of Python stickers from the "Talk Python to Me" podcast.[8] Each kid who completed all the Python modules got a sticker. I thought this was an appropriate thing to do as a percentage of the proceeds were being given to the Python Software Foundation[9] at the time. In terms of Python programming and hardware projects, this was a definite turning point for our code club.

Scaling Up Our Project: Understanding How Things Work and Adding One Thing at a Time

After completing this project, Code Club Australia invited my store to have a stand at a local library for Kid Inventor's Day. We took along some of our Code Club kids and did some demos. For the plant demo, I ended up implementing the pump idea and then explained it to the kids. It was basically just a simple extension of the micro:bit happy/sad display. We included a printout of the source code with a brief explanation and placed it next to the plant on the table. This was something we later implemented in the next year as one of our workshops in our code club.

For reference, I have included the source code, in Listing 5-3.

---

[8] https://talkpython.fm/home
[9] www.python.org/psf/

Listing 5-3. Adding a pump to the initial project

```
from microbit import *

pin16.write_digital(0)  # start with the pump off

while True:
    soil = pin1.read_analog()  # read moisture
    if soil > 500:
        display.show(Image.HAPPY)
        pin16.write_digital(0)  # turn off the pump
    else:
        display.show(Image.SAD)
        pin16.write_digital(1)  # turn on the pump
```

We connected pin16 to a relay, which is an electronic switch that controlled a submersible pump by sending a 1 (on) or 0 (off) from pin16 on the micro:bit. Later, this was simplified to use a directly connected moisture sensor and a relay switch connected to one of the micro:bit pins that is accessible without an edge connector (Figure 5-8).

Figure 5-8. *Direct connection bolt-on moisture sensor*

Our code club students' happy plant ended up the most popular project at Kid Inventor's Day, even more popular than the robot arena and fruit drum demos we had there for the store. Eventually, I was approached by Code Club Australia to write up the plant project for use in some New Zealand events. To make this more accessible, a version without the relay was used, which resulted in simpler project albeit less stable. Fortunately, I was asked to supply the relay and pump parts of my original project for a later public blog post by Code Club Australia.[10]

Pros and Cons of Simplifying Projects

As we have seen, sometimes simplifying a project can make it more difficult to successfully complete. This is not to say that we shouldn't optimize a design – just that there are other elements to consider.

Cost

By reducing the costs of materials and equipment, we can make a project accessible to a wider range of people and communities. In the first few years of our code club, we tried to leverage some of the existing equipment that the school had available. These included some educational robots, Sphero robots, drones, and a Lego Mindstorms set. Although some of these are potentially great for teaching, they are less likely to allow kids to create something unique and did not teach programming to a practical or useful skill level.

We ended up acquiring our first micro:bit microcontroller boards by contributing to a handful of 15-minute coding intro workshops for the school's open day. This was paid for by one of the parent groups tasked with setting up some activities for the day. Purchasing some low-cost

---

[10] https://medium.com/code-club-australia/micro-bit-for-moonhack-1f9626d94f47

microcontroller boards that supported Python and were very adaptable allowed us to create multiple workshops in the coming years and made a huge difference in productivity of our club. In this case, we were able to get more kids to try out programming and gained inexpensive tools to be used by more kids than a single expensive robot. In the case of the initial self-watering plant project designed for Code Club Australia, the lowest cost option was not as practical and made the project more complex.

Perception of Difficulty

Oftentimes, we would hesitate with seemingly "complex" or "difficult" ideas because one or more of the volunteers or teachers felt that something was difficult. What we didn't consider is that kids these days are quite adaptable and learn how to play new video games quickly and often. Something that may seem difficult or different to what we as adults might be used to may not be the same for kids. It may also discourage kids from attempting something if they have the expectation that it might be hard. When we began teaching Python from the start with new clubs, the kids would just accept that this was what programming was. We didn't hear any of the excuses that we encountered previously when we approached text-based programming this way. Keep in mind that I'm talking about a club or maker space, rather than formal teaching – our main goal for learning is to equip kids with immediate skills that they can apply and keep them engaged so they persist with their projects.

Reducing Challenges Can Limit What We Learn

When we started our code club, we were after easy wins – we would try to stack the cards in our favor so that kids could make *something*. As things began to plateau, we regretted not taking more risks and wished we had been more ambitious earlier. By the time we reached that plateau, the reward vs. time invested seemed less enticing to the kids. Once we attempted to be more effective in helping kids acquire practical skills, they were able to participate in more challenging workshops and activities much sooner. When I incorporated a relay switch into the self-watering plant project, I was thinking of the other uses of a relay switch. Removing that component limited the types of future projects that kids were prepared for.

Continuity

Limiting the scope of projects can make them easier to complete, but limiting things too much can also result in one-off projects that don't build on one another. Given the limitations of time that may impact your code club or maker group, you may be tempted to limit the scope of projects. However, having made this mistake previously resulted in kids being able to sample different activities but never gaining enough skills in any one area to be able to go beyond the basics. In contrast, when we started to set expectations and plan out a flexible but slightly ambitious path, these empowered kids to create. Journeying through an initial curriculum and then branching into multiple workshops and related activities equipped kids with a basic understanding with enough scope to be able to then apply their programming. This gave them a better chance at eventually becoming fluent in at least one programming language, which later can become transferrable. Our earlier efforts jumped around to different programming platforms for fear of kids becoming bored, but instead failed to increase their fluency in a single language. Through lack of planning, the kids in our earlier years also lacked a clear path or objectives. Once we set clear expectations of objectives and the path to those objectives, there was more of an understanding and vision about what we were trying to achieve, that is, working hard to gain some grasp of a single language that could be applied to workshops and other more advanced projects. Eventually, this led to some kids becoming self-reliant and progressing further than before and being able to debug and learn about other Python features or modules and apply them to their own projects.

Scaling Even Further

One of the weaknesses of the earlier v1.5 micro:bit models was a lack of storage and memory. This restricted the size of programs that could be stored and the amount of memory that could be used while running. Although the newer v2 micro:bit does have more memory and storage space, there are still limitations in the amount of pins that can be used and processing power. The micro:bit does support some communication standards (protocols) that can be used to talk to expansion boards and offload the work. These protocols include Inter-Integrated Circuit (I2C) and Serial Peripheral Interface (SPI). We'll look at these more in Chapter 7.

An easy way to expand your project with an existing fleet of micro:bits is to leverage the wireless abilities to make them work together. We looked at this functionality in the earlier micro:bit emoticon project, where we used code that would listen and send data to communicate by displaying different images on the LED array. For our plant project, one way to expand is to change the roles of half of your micro:bits, for example, if you have a class set or group; this way, you are using the same number of micro:bits but have different code running on some. So, in addition to having the sensor-connected micro:bit send signals to pins, it will send wireless data to another micro:bit.

There are a few different ways to leverage small microcontroller boards like the micro:bit to work together:

- Connect many-to-one to display activities of multiple units to one micro:bit and display results. This can put higher demands on that one micro:bit because it has to handle data from multiple micro:bits and may be slow to update information from each, or you can switch between monitoring each one.

173

- Add multiple peripherals to one micro:bit – you may run into limitations with storage space and memory, and connecting multiple components to one micro:bit will need additional electrical power and possibly custom wiring.

- Add expansion boards to a second micro:bit to take the load off one and keep programming simple. This is the same as programming a single micro:bit to work with a single expansion board but sending data wirelessly to the other.

As you can see, the last option is the easiest and most efficient use of the micro:bit's resources. When you're designing a project, it is often the case that you would look at your requirements and, based on those, pick a suitable microcontroller board to use. In this case, I'm looking at how we would get the most value out of a group or class set of micro:bits for kids. It also adds some variety since not every micro:bit will be programmed with the same code.

SCALING YOUR PROJECT: USE WIRELESS TO SPREAD THE LOAD

In this quick exercise, we will look at adding some lines to allow us to spread the load of our code across two or more micro:bits. This works by reading data from a sensor and sharing that data across more than one micro:bit so that you can implement other components as easily as you would on one micro:bit, for example, using a board that fits on the micro:bit pins for lighting up multicolored LEDs, driving motors or actuators, or simply displaying something on a second micro:bit display.

Radio code refresher

Taking the previous example of sending wireless data from a micro:bit, on a specific channel, you will recall these code lines to import the radio module and set the wireless channel to 10 (Listing 5-4).

Listing 5-4. Initializing radio communications on the sending micro:bit

```
import radio
radio.config(channel=10)
radio.on()
```

Adding this to a project such as our self-watering plant, we can send the moisture information wirelessly (Listing 5-5). Note that we are using str() to convert it into a string type for sending.

Listing 5-5. Sending moisture data to another micro:bit

```
while True:
    moisture = pin1.read_analog()
    radio.send(str(moisture))
...
```

Now that we've sent data wirelessly on channel 10, we need to receive it at the other end. We will also need to convert it back from a string type (characters) into an integer type (whole numbers). I've shown this in Listing 5-6 with bolded lines showing how to receive data into the received_data variable and convert it back to an integer type with int().

Listing 5-6. Receiving moisture data on another micro:bit

```
from microbit import *
import radio

radio.config(channel=1)
radio.on()
while True:
```

175

```
received_data = radio.receive()
if received_data:
    print(int(received_data))
```
. . .

The print() statement is just there for checking that it works, using the REPL console. You can replace that with an action, which could be to display an icon on the micro:bit LED display, light up an external LED display, play a sound, or even operate a servo motor to lift a flag. Remember to reset it to something else when data is not received; you may also need to add a sleep() delay to prevent it from double triggering, a.k.a. "debouncing." So, in plain English, this would be described as follows:

1. Collect the moisture data on the first micro:bit.

2. Send the moisture data wirelessly.

3. If the moisture is under or over a certain threshold, or within certain bounds, do something on any of the micro:bits.

4. Repeat.

There are multiple online resources with examples showing how to run a servo[11] or LED[12] connected directly to a micro:bit. Look at brands such as Adafruit, Kitronik, MonkMakes, and Pimoroni for add-on boards that can scale up even more and operate multiple servo motors or lights. These boards typically use I2C or SPI protocols I mentioned earlier but provide you with prewritten modules and code examples to make them easier to operate. Because you're not sharing your micro:bit with any other hardware, using wireless communications to share data makes it easy to connect and control additional hardware to your original project.

---

[11] https://support.microbit.org/support/solutions/articles/19000101864-using-a-servo-with-the-micro-bit

[12] https://support.microbit.org/support/solutions/articles/19000101863-connecting-an-led-to-the-micro-bit

The challenge here was finding a way to scale up a simple project within the confines of the hardware that we used. Trying to connect and power more than two components would ordinarily have resulted in running out of storage and memory on our humble micro:bit – however, due to leveraging one of the features, that is, wireless, we were able to easily expand our project much further!

Code Club Alumni

As you may recall, our first code club consisted of David (a teacher at the school who initially registered the club), Jay (a previous school student), and myself. Once our club began to grow, we were lucky enough to have parents of kids at the school volunteer to support the club. As with most school extracurricular activities, there are sometimes biases where parents may try to "fix" or steer these activities, which unfortunately can spoil things for kids. In the past years, we had parents come in, and rather than learning to code themselves, they would raise issues such as "the kids need mice instead of trackpads" or "we should teach them <insert other programming language here>" or would proceed to tell us why everything was "too difficult." We also had the parent who worked in the video game industry and would suggest that everything else was "boring" for kids except, of course, video games, which prompted other volunteers to point out the reasons that had led to the choices we had made. Funnily enough, many of these issues are solved when the kids themselves volunteered more in later years. Currently, there's three students from multiple years back at our code club. The fact that kids are enthusiastic enough to come back and help others learn gives me hope that this will help our code club persist for at least several more years!

Typically, we would have younger kids attending when a parent or sibling volunteered for code club. My son ended up attending in grade one and seemed to light a bit of a fire under our code club back in the first year when he showed the club a game that we had been working on. Later on, he would get involved with some of the things I was prototyping for code club workshops and also create his own variations on code club projects. One that was particularly memorable was "Draw your own adventure" which took elements from the prewritten code club Scratch project called "Paintbox"[13] and mixed these with a platform-style game, where a cat character would be able to run and jump on levels drawn by the player.

Ethan, one of current volunteers, came into our club early on because his sister had attended code club and ended up pushing herself a bit further with Python. Eventually, she came back for a few years as a volunteer and would bring her younger brother. In some ways, Ethan is a second-generation code club volunteer – he ended up becoming one of the school leaders for his contributions to our code club. While attending code club, Ethan worked hard to finish every prewritten module we had, including all the workshops. This was a great effort as he was also quite busy with sports, such as field hockey, in his personal life. He also attended a bunch of code club events such as Moonhack.

After I was asked to write the first Moonhack projects back in 2014, our club was able to have some kids attend the live Moonhack event for a few years. Although one of the teachers at code club pointed out that it might be hard for parents to get into the Melbourne CBD on a school night – talking to other parents revealed that they would often drive their kids across town for sports – what they said was, "Why should code club be any different?" Thinking about this, it made a lot of sense, and hopefully it made a difference to some of these kids with some good memories of those times. So, we ended up getting kids and parents to the event, and no one complained and many mentioned that they were thrilled to have the opportunity. A couple of days before Moonhack one year, Nicola from Code Club Australia called about an opportunity to be on *That Startup Show* – unfortunately, most families had already shuffled around activities

---

[13] www.codeclubau.org/projects/paint-box/

to be able to attend the live Moonhack event that week, including myself. However, as luck would have it, Ethan and his sister were happy to be involved, and their parents managed to shuttle them down to be in the filming. They did a great job after having to wait around the set quite a bit, and it was yet another exciting event to discuss at code club that week.

Adapting Our Skills: An API Project in Python with Trinket.io

During various code clubs, I would try to regularly remind the kids that it was good to ask questions after first attempting to solve any problems on their own. I would say that the ideal situation is that they work hard enough that it would push us to struggle to come up with more and more interesting things to do. Prior to becoming a returning volunteer, Ethan found himself having completed all the workshops and all the projects from the existing two Python modules from Code Club Australia (currently, there are three in addition to a bunch of extra projects related to various events run by Code Club Australia).

What were we to do? After some pondering as to what we could do, it occurred to me that it should be possible for someone like Ethan to leverage skills from the previous projects and perhaps write his own project. From the prewritten code club projects and workshops, a few of the Python/programming concepts we could draw from included

- *Application programming interfaces (APIs)*: An online interface that allows programmatic retrieval and submission of stored data

- *Dictionary structures*: Storing values indexed with keys

- *JavaScript Object Notation (JSON)*: A way of serializing data when retrieved from APIs

One of the Code Club projects involves retrieving the current coordinates of the NASA International Space Station (ISS) and plotting them on a world map.[14] I remembered how much some of the kids enjoyed this project, so this and other projects that involved the preceding concepts were what we drew on to create Ethan's new project.

Since this chapter is focused on the process of taking skills learned and applying them to create something new, I will include insight into the thought process and actions we used to develop the project. The objective is to allow you to follow this process and apply our learnings to create your own projects, hopefully accelerating the growth of your own code club or maker group for kids. Although this project is not as scalable as the self-watering plant, it is solely Python and runs on a computer, interacting with free Internet resources – so I felt it was worth including as a second example of the process of building something from the bottom up using skills gained from prewritten examples. This exercise documents the rough steps performed by a grade 6 student at the time. Although I've included some code, it is more the discovery process and application of learned concepts that is important here.

CREATE A PROJECT THAT USES API DATA

Background

Using their own accounts on `https://trinket.io`, the kids at our club had worked through the Code Club Australia Python modules prior to this process. This allowed them to reference working code that they had written, which helped reinforce their prior learning and improve Python fluency by applying the code in slightly different contexts.

---

[14] `https://codeclubau.org/projects/where-is-the-iss/`

Objectives

Start with an objective that can be broken down into steps. For this example, we decided to get online content from an API and present it to the end user in a question/answer format that was displayed on the screen.

For example, breaking this description into smaller steps gave us

- Search for a suitable public API

- Requirements for the API

  - Free

  - Must be kid-friendly

  - Does not require authentication

  - Interesting and entertaining information

- Read and understand documentation and examples for the chosen API

- Make live requests the same way we did with the Code Club ISS project and break the information into components

- Write code to present this to the end user and give feedback

- Repeat this multiple times using a loop

Find a suitable API

Search online for free APIs and pick a few to try. Typically, the API information page will supply example requests and show the expected format of the returned information. We wanted to use a data in JSON format because that format was used in a prewritten project that we had completed earlier.

After looking through a few APIs, the Open Trivia API was selected due to these features:

- Easy to interact with without authentication.

- Free to use.

- Data was in a familiar format for us, and the multiple-choice format suited our objective well.

The information about using The Trivia API was found at `https://the-trivia-api.com/docs/` and uses a Creative Commons attribution license: `https://creativecommons.org/licenses/by-sa/4.0/`.

Make some live requests

Using the documentation, we generated a URL required to retrieve a single question with multiple-choice answers in JSON format (Figure 5-9).

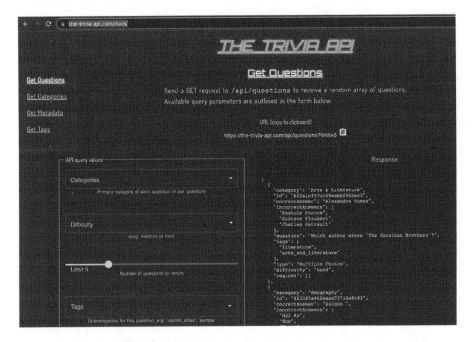

Figure 5-9. *The Trivia API URL generator*

Referring to the Python documentation for the requests module, we can usually find example code. Use knowledge from projects that you have already completed. Saving all your previous code is useful here because it can make it easier to program next time. You can also create snippets of generic code to reuse – this is known as boilerplate code. Here is some simple code that was written to make a GET request to the API endpoint (Listing 5-7) in our example.

Listing 5-7. Requesting data from the API endpoint

```
#!/bin/python3

import urllib.request as ur
import json

url = 'https://the-trivia-\
api.com/api/questions?limit=1'

    response = ur.urlopen(url).read()
    print(response)
```

Response:

```
[{"category":"Film & TV","id":"625fd6f3dc0dd3b72da64d17","correc
tAnswer":"1989","incorrectAnswers":["1977","1981","1985"],"ques
tion":"Indiana Jones and the Last Crusade was released in which
year?","tags":["film","film_and_tv"],"type":"Multiple Choice","d
ifficulty":"hard","regions":[]}]
Indiana Jones and the Last Crusade was released in which year?
```

OK – this works! The next step will be to extract information from the returned JSON format.

Extract the information

Looking through earlier working projects and doing online searches such as "python3 list shuffle" can help us understand how to extract some of the information we will need.

For example, we can comment out the `print(response)` command by placing a hash (#) in front. This is a handy way to delete the command without deleting it, so we can remove the # and add the **bolded** lines shown in Listing 5-8.

Listing 5-8. Extracting the question from the JSON data

```
#!/bin/python3

import urllib.request as ur
import json

url = 'https://the-trivia-\
api.com/api/questions?limit=1'

response = ur.urlopen(url).read()
# print(response)
json_response = json.loads(response)
print(json_response[0]['question'])
```

We will also need to extract incorrect and correct answers from our JSON array and into a list. Then we need to use `random.shuffle()` so that we can later display a multiple-choice question to the user (Listing 5-9).

Listing 5-9. Extracting the multiple-choice answers and shuffling

```
#!/bin/python3

import urllib.request as ur
import json
from random import shuffle

url = 'https://the-trivia-\
api.com/api/questions?limit=1'

response = ur.urlopen(url).read()
# print(response)
json_response = json.loads(response)
```

```
print(json_response[0]['question'])
mylist = json_response[0]['incorrectAnswers']
mylist.append(json_response[0]['correctAnswer'])
shuffle(mylist)
print(mylist)
```

This nicely pulls out the required information that can be presented to the end user and have them input an answer. We would then compare the answer to correctAnswer. This can be repeated in a loop – I recall that in this example the end user had the option to answer with "q" to quit out of the program.

From that point, things were straightforward, and Ethan was able to carry on and implement those last few features quite easily.

Summary

Developing a new project can potentially be a natural progression from guided projects for those able to implement basic Python concepts without help. Once an idea is put forward, and objectives determined, all that remains is learning to consult and interpret the documentation relevant to required hardware and extra Python functions or modules. For an extra challenge, kids with the appropriate communication skills could learn to document such a project to be reused as a workshop or even contributed as a community project. Open source contributions are a great way for kids to learn about coding and collaborating[15] with more experienced developers; it also provides a much broader perception of the value of resources than simply profit.

---

[15] https://opensource.guide/how-to-contribute/

Chapter 5: Cheat Sheet

- Show context of creating own project (hand-drawn if possible).

- Curriculums to use include Code Club, Grok Learning, Code.org, Trinket.

- Completion of lessons/prewritten projects helps to standardize a minimum skill level required to progress to more advanced activities.

- A higher cost vs. reward over time can discourage kids, so prepare adequately to maximize efficiency from the beginning and minimize time spent waiting around.

- Find your own project (start to finish):

  - Diagrams are a quick way of showing projects that use hardware.

  - Leverage known event-driven iterative structures as a start.

  - Breadboards with edge connectors (for micro:bits) can offer more stability than alligator clips for more complex designs.

  - Understand, then add one element at a time.

- Beware of oversimplification or cost-cutting:

  - *Perception of difficulty*: Sometimes, we need to lead with confidence and enthusiasm, rather than aprehension, to instil confidence in others.

  - Reducing challenges can introduce needless complexity and limit useful learning.

  - Continuity lets us build upon our previous triumphs.

- Scale up:

  - Know the limitations of your hardware.

  - Spread the load of resources across multiple micro:bits.

  - *Many-to-one*: Display output of many micro:bits on one micro:bit.

  - Add multiple peripherals to one micro:bit; it might be more difficult, and there are resource limits.

  - Use additional micro:bits for simpler code and wiring.

- *Code club alumni*: Leverage participants to give back by volunteering.

  - Lots of benefits with the preceding model

- Adapt our skills:

  - Build on previous prewritten projects.

  - Reuse code and create boilerplate snippets.

  - Add another level after prewritten projects and workshops and apply learned skills and concept knowledge.

  - Look at improving more by applying coding skills to help with contributions and collaboration on community open source projects, or volunteering to give back by providing materials or time to code club/maker groups.

CHAPTER 6

Collaboration: Working with Others

A Quick Tale: Devs and Testers

One year, when we were still doing Scratch programming, we ended up with a couple of weeks where there was a group of kids who had already finished their projects. I had been considering an idea for collaboration, so we took a small group of kids through this activity which I called "Devs and Testers." This is short for "Developers and Testers" – since programmers are referred to as "developers" or "devs" in commercial software teams.

Before this point, everybody had been working independently of one another. The only collaboration had been to have the kids walk around the room and look at what their peers had created. Sometimes, they would play various games and ask questions or suggest improvements, but that was it. The Devs and Testers activity takes this quite a bit further, teaching kids about collaborating with a team on an existing project. This can easily be applied to any type of project, regardless of whether it involves hardware, and using any programming language. The workshop activity I have outlined here is adapted from that earlier activity.

© Martin Tan 2023
M. Tan, *micro:bit Projects with Python and Single Board Computers*,
https://doi.org/10.1007/978-1-4842-9197-9_6

DEVS AND TESTERS

Introduction

This is a group activity where two teams will be working together to improve some software.

These teams are

- *Testers*: They run the software and test it for things that don't work properly (bugs) and suggest improvements (features).

- *Developers*: They change the code to fix bugs and write code to add features.

Prerequisites

You should have at least done some coding projects or have written your own programs.

You will also need one large whiteboard and some cards (20 or more) to write on, or you could use large butcher's paper stuck to the wall. Of course, you'll need some whiteboard markers for the whiteboard, normal pens for the cards or butcher's paper, and tape or magnets to stick cards to the whiteboard or a wall.

Step 1: Choose teams and a project.

In this step, we will choose a Python project and decide who is on the Developers team and who is on the Testers team.

Activity Checklist

- Decide who will be in the Developers team. It doesn't matter who goes first as people can swap teams later. If you are using a project written by a student in your Code Club, they should be on this team.

- Now decide who will be in the Testers team. The testers need to be able to test the project, find bugs, and suggest new features to improve the project. There must be at least two people in the Testers team, with more people in the Developers team.

- Your teams must first pick a project to use. Make sure it is one that everyone knows well enough to add to. It could be a Code Club project, like Clone Wars or Create Your Own World, or one that a student/maker has written.

Step 2: Share the code.

In this step, we need to make sure that both teams have the same version of the code.

Activity Checklist

- Once your teams have decided which project to use, members of both teams will need a copy of the code. If you have an online `Trinket.io` account, just share your project and tell the rest of the team the link, so they can remix. To do this, log in and click the `Remix` button in the upper top-right corner of the Trinket page.

- If your Code Club or Maker group uses Python offline, you'll need to share the `.py` file(s) and folders with your other team members. If you work off a shared drive or a cloud-based shared drive, decide on a folder to use, copy your code there, and invite your team to access that folder with read/write access.

Step 3: Prepare the issue tracker board.

In this step, we need to set up a way to keep track of bugs that the Testers team find and features that they suggest. The Developers will need a way to record the changes they made to the code and allow the Testers to test any changes before they are marked as *completed*.

Activity Checklist

Draw two lines down the whiteboard, so that it is divided into three columns.

At the top of the board, label the first column from the left TO DO, label the middle column WORK IN PROGRESS, and label the last column COMPLETED. It should look like the image in Figure 6-1.

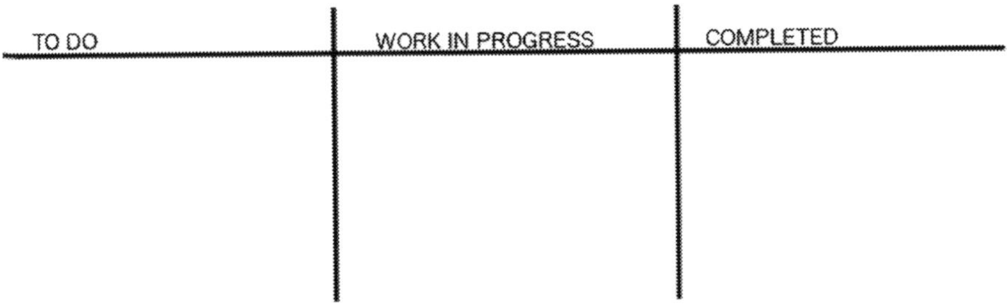

Figure 6-1. *Issue tracker board example*

Take the cards and put them near the Testers team. The Testers team will use these to let the Developers team know when they have found a bug or have a new feature suggestion. This method of tracking progress and managing workflow is called *Kanban*, and the board is called a *Kanban board*. Years ago, I did some work at Toyota and remember that they ran Kanban servers – interestingly, this was because the Kanban system actually originated from the Toyota Production System (TPS).[1]

Ready to start

With your teams chosen and your Kanban board set up, you are ready to begin improving your project!

---

[1] https://global.toyota/en/company/vision-and-philosophy/production-system/

Step 4: Begin the process.

This is where the real fun begins. The Testers team get to test the project and start giving the Developers bugs to fix and features to add. Remember to use *one card per bug or feature*.

Activity Checklist

- The Testers should run the project by pressing the green flag and start looking for bugs. When a tester finds a bug, they will need to grab a card and write a description of the bug and their name. The description should include how to find the bug and what is going wrong. It should be as clear as possible for the Developers to understand.
  An example bug card could be

  ```
  BUG:
  The sprites end up in the wrong places when the game
  restarts
  How to See the Bug:
  Re-start the game and after the first run, the balloon
  sprite is always stuck at the right side of the screen.
  The position of the balloon stops the player from being
  able to play the game without using the mouse to move it
  back before running.

  FIX:
  Set the sprite position at the start of every game.
  ```

- The Testers should also look for ways that the project can be improved with new features. When they think of a good feature, they should grab a card and write a description of the new feature, adding their name to the card. If they know how, they can suggest how it could be done.

An example of a feature card could be

```
FEATURE:
Convert a single player game to double player

DESCRIPTION:
Add another balloon with different controls, so 2 players
can race each other at the same time.

HOW TO IMPLEMENT IT:
Duplicate the balloon sprite and scripts, then change the
keys to control the second sprite. Change the 2nd sprite
to another color. If player 1 gets to the end first, end
the game and display "Player 1 wins!" or if player 2 gets
to the end first display "Player 2 wins!".
```

- Once a bug or a feature card is written up, stick it in the TO DO column. The Developers choose a card each and move it to the WORK IN PROGRESS column. They should talk to the Tester who created the card to get more information. The developer should take notes in point form.

- Then the developer needs to work on fixing the bug or adding the feature. Before moving the card to the COMPLETED column, it must be tested by the tester. If the tester is happy, then the card is completed, and the developer can grab another card to work with. The whole process is shown in Figure 6-2.

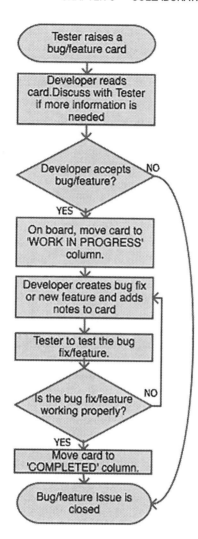

Figure 6-2. *Bugfix/feature workflow*

Challenge: Release the new version of your software

Once a few bugs and features have been completed, create a new version of the project, and add all the fixes and features. You can call it "version 2" if the first was version 1. Once this is done and the Testers team is happy with it, try swapping people across to different teams and do it again!

If you are interested in using a more realistic versioning system, you can use minor versions for the nonstable, more buggy versions, for example, 0.1, 0.2, 0.3, etc., and use major versions for the stable releases of your software, for example, 1.0, 2.0, 3.0, and so on.

Other options

While running this activity, we organically came up with some variations, which included implementing a team leader role to develop a criterion for triaging bugs/enhancements to reject or accept them and prioritize the more important items. The team leader could also assign developers with the appropriate skills to specific issues. Other options included rotating kids through each team to give them an opportunity to try different roles and challenges.

What Is Open Source Software?

According to Red Hat, Inc.,[2] "The term 'open source' refers to something people can modify and share because its design is publicly accessible." As outlined on the Open Source Initiative website, open source also refers to licensing and distribution, and these licenses can flow down to derivative works, too.[3] There are many different open source licenses,[4] and these vary

---

[2] https://opensource.com/resources/what-open-source
[3] https://opensource.org/osd
[4] https://opensource.org/licenses

broadly in the areas of attribution, distribution, collaboration, and the way they affect derivative works. From its early beginnings in the late 1990s, open source has now become widespread with millions of open source projects today.[5]

No discussion of collaboration is complete without talking about open source software, which encourages collaboration and contributions in the form of feedback, bugs/fixes, and code enhancements. I originally became interested in contributing to open source after using open source software and working with friends who were developers on some significant open source projects. What struck me about these people was that they mentioned improving their programming skills and learned from others while contributing fixes to issues opened by users.

My own initial open source contributions started with the Fwknop project, which was created by Michael Rash. The Fwknop project uses Single Packet Authorization to use a network packet with an encrypted payload to modify firewall rules to allow specific connections to an online server. While using the software with some friends, we needed some additional features, one of which included allowing access to some online web applications that included a wiki, pastebin, and bug tracker. This feature would maintain access to a user only while they were connected to an online chat server. Part of my contributions required that I understood more about the Perl language. After talking to other friends who initially said they "knew a bit of Perl," I found that they didn't know enough to help me – so I went through the original code and taught myself what I needed to know with the help of the Internet. The other aspect of contributing code was to look at the programming style used by the original programmer and contributors as Perl is less strict in how things are done than a more structured language like Java.

Although slightly more involved than our simplified workflow we used with the Devs and Testers activity, open source projects have their own preferred workflow for opening an issue on their bug tracker website,

---

[5] www.statista.com/statistics/1268650/worldwide-open-source-projects-versions-ecosystems/

engaging in discussion about the bug or enhancement, and eventually creating a patch to implement the update to the software. A patch for collaborating is typically created by comparing versions of the source code with and without your code updates. Examples of tools that will generate a patch like this are diff (Mac and Linux) and fc (Windows), which are run from a command-line interface, for example, `diff file1 file2 > file.patch` will output a patch file called `file.patch`.

Another reason for applying an open source license to a project is to prevent a profit-focused company from "owning" a project and restricting future development or access to it, when it fails to meet profit targets. In contrast, an open source project can be passed over to new volunteers and will often persist where closed source proprietary may not. The result of applying an open source license can be much more long-lived innovation than might be seen in a more limited closed source product. A license that is attached to a software project dictates the conditions under which the software can be used, modified, and distributed. The benefits vary depending on the type of software, and there are pros and cons to be considered with each license. You should always take the time to ensure that the license you choose is appropriate for the requirements of the software and userbase. It should also be noted that many commercial companies also contribute to community- and volunteer-based open source projects to give back, or demonstrate good will, to the community. Examples of some well-known companies that contribute to open source include Adafruit,[6] Pimoroni,[7] IBM,[8] and Microsoft.[9] Contributing to open source is also a great way for kids and volunteers to gain more experience in collaboration on software and hardware projects.

---

[6] https://blog.adafruit.com/2022/02/07/500-adafruit-projects-have-been-certified-as-open-source-by-oshwa/

[7] https://github.com/pimoroni

[8] www.ibm.com/opensource/

[9] https://opensource.microsoft.com

Working Online: Collaborating with Online Tools

Online tools can be used for everything from communicating with your teammates and friends to implementing workflows for tracking code changes and issues and even brainstorming on a virtual whiteboard. In our code club, we used several different tools to facilitate communications between volunteers and teachers, create and distribute resources for kids to reference, track progress, and even keep parents updated on code club happenings.

Code Collaboration Tools

Although we never utilized code collaboration tools with the code club kids, I would often use these when submitting updates to the code club curriculum during the earlier years of volunteering. Nonetheless, I'm adding some explanation of such tools in the hopes that your code club or maker space will progress further due to standing on our shoulders, or you are lucky enough to have a professional developer as one of your volunteers. I also regularly utilize code repositories whenever any code I write progresses past the point of being run a few times and needs to be maintained in a controlled way. Understanding the basics of collaboration with these tools is useful if you or your code club/maker group volunteers or kids want to contribute to any public open source projects.

The idea here is to simply give you a simplified overview of how these tools are used by developers and how they might be useful for your code club or maker space. It is also useful to understand the workflow and tools so that you can collaborate and learn from other developers online – since one of the best ways to encourage kids to learn and build is to do it yourself!

Code Collaboration Terminology

In the spirit of teaching kids to collaborate, we should learn some universal terminology regardless of which languages or programming frameworks we are using. These code collaboration tools can also be used to collaborate on open source electronic hardware projects and supporting software libraries. This section is intended to give you a simplified understanding of what these tools do and some basic terminology to get started interacting with open source projects and their maintainers. I've included some footnotes with links to tutorials that will get you started.

Issue Tracker: An issue tracker is a web application that helps us raise issues such as code bugs or enhancements, just like in our Devs and Testers activity. Opening an issue in an issue tracker is the first step to contributing to open source – this can be in the form of a bug report or a suggested enhancement. Most online code repository services also include an issue tracker that you can use for your project or when contributing to other people's projects. It is important to read through existing issues to ensure that you don't create duplicate issues or issues that waste the developers' time, especially on very large public open source projects. Projects will often have some rules or a code of conduct to follow, and failing to follow these can sometimes get your issues closed or ignored.

Code Repository: A code repository is a place to store your code, either online or on your computer. The advantages of storing your code in a code repository include the following:

- It is easier to collaborate with others, control, track, and reverse changes.

- You can make use of more secure authentication (people identifying who they are) and authorization (what they can do).

- If you use an online repository, it is easier to make your code available to people in remote geographic locations.

- Often, you can manage your code using software tools such as the open source tool, `git`.

Examples of online code repository services include GitHub,[10] Bitbucket,[11] and GitLab.[12] Most of these have pricing that starts with free plans up to subscriptions for more features and scale. Online code repositories can be private where only people you specify can read and write or public where anyone online can see your code. You can also set up git repositories using software on your own computer.

Branch: A branch is a separate version of a repository that is still treated as a part of the repository. By default, we will have a main branch which is often called...main. A branch can be maintained in parallel and then merged back into the main branch. Sometimes, other branches are used to denote when code is not stable, for example, a branch called dev or test.

Fork: A fork is a copy of a whole code repository that we can create and work on without affecting the original project. Depending on the licensing of the original project, we may still be bound by some restrictions that the original programmer (developer, or dev) has specified. The time when we would create a fork is if we wanted to add our own updates that may or may not be submitted back to the original project as a potential contribution. Other times, we might want to privately use our own version and develop some features that would not be useful to others. However, if you make something that may be useful for the community, it is good form to contribute back, especially when dealing with open source. Even if your additions aren't ready for direct integration with the original project, it's worth talking to the devs about whether it would be appropriate, or they

---

[10] https://docs.github.com/en/get-started/quickstart/hello-world
[11] www.atlassian.com/git/tutorials/learn-git-with-bitbucket-cloud
[12] https://docs.gitlab.com/ee/tutorials/

might be able to modify your changes to make it viable for adding to the project. If we only forked a project to create a patch, then we would usually destroy the fork once the patch has been approved and merged into the original project.

Merge: Merging some new code into a repository will require that any conflict with existing code is resolved. For this reason, it is important to try and work with the most up-to-date version of the repository possible.

Clone: Cloning a repository is where you make a copy of it on your computer. This is known as a *local repository*. Often, you'll do this after making a fork of a code repository and want to add or make your own modifications to the code.

Add: Adding a file or folder to a repository means that it will be recognized and controlled to record changes to that file or folder. You need to be careful about what files you add to a repository, especially when it is public.

Commit: Once you have added or modified files in your local repository, you can create a commit, which prepares the files to be merged to the original project.

Push/Pull: Merging your locally edited code to your repository is usually done with a *push*, for example, you can push a commit to your online repository branch. A *pull request* is a request to have your code updates merged into a repository. You can also do a pull from the online repository to update your cloned local repository, to keep your local repository up to date with the online repository. You should do this before creating a commit so that you are always working with the latest version of the code.

Readme: Most online public code repositories will include a file named README.md e.g., Figure 6-3. This is a text file written in Markdown,[13] providing a simple way of documenting information about a code repository; including how to use it, how to install any required libraries that it depends

---

[13] https://www.markdownguide.org/

on (dependencies), and sometimes information about how to contribute or if they welcome contributions at all. For example, some projects will say "pull requests welcome," which means that they want contributions to help the project grow.

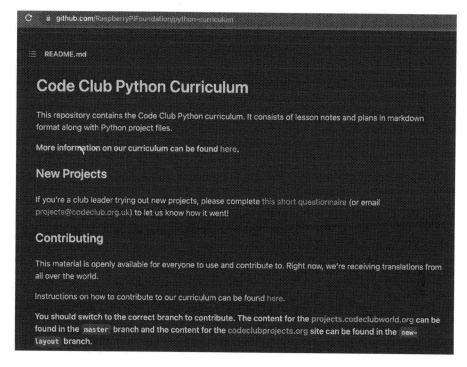

Figure 6-3. *The Code Club UK Python Curriculum Readme.md file*

Although these are the basic operations used for when collaborating with code online, this only just scrapes the surface of what can be done with these tools – there are complete books dedicated to documenting code collaboration tools. As with any online communication medium, it is important for kids to take precautions by not revealing any personal or identifying information to others when collaborating online. Use pseudonyms and be careful to ensure that no sensitive information, such as passwords, is put into any public repositories. Currently, all code repositories are continually scanned by third parties – this means that as soon as any credentials or sensitive personal information is uploaded, it will be copied and so should be treated as compromised.

Other Collaborative Tools

If the Kanban approach to managing tasks appealed to you, Trello[14] is a tool which allows a similar style of collaboration to be used online. It has a free option that you can use straightaway, and in conjunction with a private video conference, it would allow you to run an online version of the Devs and Testers activity. As mentioned earlier, remember to state the code of conduct expectations right at the start for any communication platforms you use for your code club or maker group.

Using Programming Terminology to Communicate When Collaborating

In Chapter 3, we talked about introducing programming terminology while learning Python. This becomes valuable as kids progress and need to describe the techniques and features that they are using when writing code. One important objective is to eventually become fluent enough with a single programming language to enable kids to prototype their creative ideas. Another bonus of using correct terminology is that it enables collaboration as their skills grow. Being able to suggest a well-known data structure or specific way of doing something and providing solid reasoning to justify decisions in code or when building hardware projects is of great benefit to facilitate rapid progress in larger projects. By learning the correct terminology, your code club or maker group can scale their projects more easily since they can then understand online documentation. Essentially, being able to debug their projects, they will also be able to teach themselves to learn on their own, using online resources and books.

---

[14]https://trello.com/home

One of the best ways to develop this type of collaborative skillset is for kids to work on a project with a programming partner. In our club, we used a prewritten micro:bit traffic light lesson programmed in MicroPython, which the kids would follow. The second part of the traffic light lesson was to modify the code and set up another traffic light to have a specific state, depending on the first one. This required referencing a state table – this proved complex enough that I found myself referring to the table while I was writing the project myself! Writing code that would make two devices work together required communications and a way of managing who was using which wireless channel.

Testing Yourself: Creating Your Own Game Writing Workshops with What You've Learned

Over the years, we had some students who would excel in code club, creating interesting projects that they could scale, for example, a game with an increasingly large number of levels. One of our code club kids, Jamie, eventually came back as a volunteer for a few years and was particularly persistent at writing games in Scratch that he would scale up quite well. What we'll look at now is how to break this down into components and create a workshop that will teach others how to design a scalable rather than closed-ended game.

CREATE A WORKSHOP FOR WRITING SCALABLE GAMES

Objective

The objective of this exercise is to analyze the thought process and workflow used to build scalable games and attempt to create a workshop that allows others to replicate the skill, for example, so participants can write their own scalable games. We will use the game idea for this exercise.

Analysis

Sometimes, we see prodigious kids in code club who can create something great but may not yet have the skills to show others how to replicate their efforts. By asking questions about their methodology, we can help piece together the information and present it in a form that others can learn from.

Questions can include the following:

1. What happens when the player reaches the next level? *This will tell you how the game scales.*

2. What are the basic elements of your game engine that control gameplay? *This will give you an idea of how the gameplay is controlled (usually a loop that updates variables, based on events).*

3. How do you keep track of score, number of lives, health, or player inventory? *This will show you some of the event functions that are called from the main loop.*

4. What is the process used when you create a new game? *This will reveal the methodology used to design games and should be communicated as a point of difference, since most beginner programmers don't consider the scalability of their software until later in the writing process. By that time, they have probably already written their code in such a way that makes scaling more difficult.*

Structure of workshop instructions

Once the main elements are described, we can provide a lesson/workshop template using something that you are familiar with, for example, Word, LibreOffice, or if you have something else that you like to use to present for training.

The structure that I use is something like this:

Introduction: State the objectives and what everyone will achieve by the end of the workshop. In the game example, this could be "Create a multilevel game that is scalable."

What you will learn: This will be a breakdown of the main skill components that will translate into steps. Later, we will break these down further into individual tasks under each step. Mentally, this is a good way to make the overall project less overwhelming for the participants, structuring the project logically. A logical structure makes things easier to remember and visualize.

What you need: Put any requirements in this section, especially if specific hardware or tools are required. In the game writing example, we could talk about the software that needs to be installed, including any software dependencies such as code libraries that may need to be downloaded beforehand.

Steps and tasks: A good number of steps would be three to four, and then you can have four to five tasks under each step. Use screenshots or pictures when you need to show something visually, and make sure that it is clear which part of the picture is important. Crop out anything that is not relevant. If you can describe something in one line more effectively than three screenshots, just use the line of text.

Challenges and stretch goals: Always include a challenge to keep those who finish early busy. For the game example, this could be to create additional features once the main game is finished and tested. For a micro:bit activity, it could be to scale up the project to allow the use of multiple micro:bits simultaneously.

Troubleshooting: It can be helpful to show what to do if things don't work and give participants an idea of where to start looking and give them a checklist for reducing things that can create confusion when trying to fix something that isn't working.

The next steps here would be to list preparation steps to deliver the new workshop. If the original author or volunteer is a bit nervous, offer to assist them with delivering the workshop, just to get comfortable with things the first time. If all goes smoothly, you will have helped someone create a workshop that can help others create bigger and better projects – and maybe even create their own workshops.

That's it for this chapter – we've covered some of the key concepts in collaboration and creating your own workshops and helping others take that extra step toward sharing their skills with others. Although I've covered the tools that we have found useful over the years, there's plenty more out there, and these change over time – this chapter should at least give you an idea of what features may be useful for your group and give you some ideas of how to evaluate what you need. The security and privacy areas were topics that I feel go hand in hand with collaboration and sharing, and hopefully this should give you an idea of what principles to apply when setting up your tools.

Communications

Email was the first method of communication we used, since the school where our code club was using email to communicate to parents. This was fine at the beginning of our code club since communications were limited to the following:

- What are we doing this week?
- Whether there has been a room change for code club.
- When someone will be away sick.

Soon enough, our email started to branch into other threads, with such topics as

- Hardware purchases

- Discussion of using school-owned items such as Sphero[15] and Lego Mindstorms[16]

- Discussing potential solutions to issues of forgotten passwords, where to save work, and so on

In subsequent years, we also ended up with more volunteers, and keeping everyone updated resulted in larger numbers of emails. Coming from a background of using communications recreationally and for community projects, I eventually created a Slack space (Figure 6-4), which is typically used by developers to chat online.

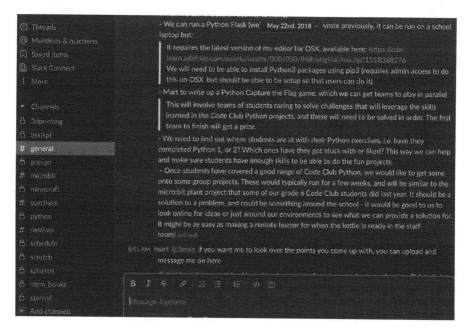

Figure 6-4. *Chatting in Slack for volunteers*

---

[15] https://edu.sphero.com
[16] http://hackeducation.com/2015/04/10/mindstorms

This allowed us to organize communications into separate channels that reflected various activities and subjects. We could also look at code snippets and images, and everyone could respond whenever they had a spare moment, without it being overly intrusive to our busy day-to-day routines outside of code club. One of the limitations of Slack is that for long-term storage of chats, it requires a subscription. Since the idea of code club is that it is free, anything we used was due to donations or fundraising or resources that were also used by the school. I later migrated our chats to Discord, which is like Slack in appearance but essentially free and lets us keep track of past chats more easily. Discord was more familiar to our alumni volunteers, so this worked well. It also offers voice and video chat, but we never ended up having everyone online at the same time to utilize these. Our planning meetings at the start of each semester were typically just a smaller subset of the volunteers and teachers, which made sense since many were happy to just turn up and help with whatever we needed at the time.

Another useful tool when you need to extrapolate reference information from your chats is a wiki. This is like your own private website with all the information easily available for new volunteers, for example, code of conduct, processes for doing things, notes on workshops, and other useful information required to get started quickly and consistently. Ensuring that your wiki supports Markdown[17] can make it much easier to edit. For the reasons discussed in the next section, I would recommend that you refrain from storing anything sensitive in a wiki. Wikis can be run on a server that is on your private network or online – if you are doing the former, your IT person can likely set this up for you, and for the latter, please read the section in this chapter on security and privacy.

The advantages of a live chat were that we could discuss more things in depth and organize our topics in an easily searchable fashion. This was also a good way to send nonsensitive information that we might need

---

[17]`www.markdownguide.org`

urgently for an upcoming session. There were multiple instances where documentation sent in our chat a few minutes before code club was able to be received by volunteers on their mobile devices, while at code club. As mentioned earlier, we never graduated to holding full meetings over Discord, but I can't help but think it would have been great if we had been able to get everyone free at the same time. One thing that did work was to be able to organize multiple workshops in parallel, by sending the required information into each workshop channel. This was convenient for volunteers to just look in the relevant channel for any discussion or documentation that they needed. As things quietened down during the early pandemic years, we stopped using Discord as we seemed to settle into what we knew worked and just focused on discussing the scheduling for these during the year. With more volunteers in the future, we may use Discord again.

Security and Privacy When Working Online

When we started to collaborate online, we had a mix of parents and high school–aged volunteers, most of whom were already on the same or similar chat systems that I set up for our code club. For our code club kids, earlier Scratch accounts always used a pseudonym, and they practiced online safety rules that they learned at school regarding no personal information online. As we graduated to Trinket.io and TinkerCAD, the same rules applied, except that we had parents more involved in preparing their accounts and making sure that kids knew how to log in. This reduced a lot of time that was wasted in earlier years when kids would frequently forget passwords and lose saved or unsaved work repeatedly.

So that sounds all fine, right? I once tried to turn my back on security, and it turns out that you can't do that. If you're online at all, you run into scammers, dodgy folk will try and trick you, and even from an opportunistic perspective, people will just try and get your things. It's just how things are on the Internet. At the end of the day, having one thing in place to protect you just doesn't work – a single point of failure is just that one point where failure means everything is compromised, for example, just have a look at the haveIbeenpwned.com list of websites[18] that have been compromised at least once. There's a whole lot there, right?

Yes, the tone here has changed slightly – that's because this is just me talking to you, frankly, because this part is important, not just for your code club or maker group, but in general. It is also now part of the Australian curriculum for schools. Security does not mean "use this specific antivirus" or "subscribe to this service because it is the best," it really means that you need to increase the cost for someone attacking you and reducing the reward vs. the effort required. Sometimes, this just means you should not put the information out there in the first place, if you don't need to or it is avoidable.

So now that we understand that we need to be careful, how do we do that? When I am asked about this by family and friends, instead of just saying "yes, this is secure and this isn't," I also talk about principles to apply. Here are some principles for you to apply.

Separate Your Things

- Use different passwords for each service you sign up to. You can use a password manager that is appropriate for what you want to do. Look at the features for different password managers. An important feature is being able to generate strong passwords or, as they should be now, passphrases.

---

[18] https://haveibeenpwned.com/PwnedWebsites

- If you can use different emails for some things, do that. Some services offer a pseudonym feature. Be aware that some of these do not hide the real email address to a human but might fool an automated system, so you can at least track down which service might be responsible for a compromised account or putting you on an annoying email list.

- Don't use your work email for your social or code club communications or online accounts. This limits cross-contamination. Likewise, don't use your work computer for social or code club things, and vice versa. Even having a cheap computer for home use is better than risking problems.

Use Layered Defenses

Layered defenses include turning on disk encryption on your computer, using multifactor authentication whenever it is available, and making your computer autolock in case you forget when working at a café. There's a trick to making these things work for you – you need to consider context. So, if you are somewhere that you might be observed putting in a password, use biometric logins such as fingerprints or face recognition. Use multifactor authentication (MFA) in a way that works for you, for example, most services let you use an app on your phone with a one-time code that you can put in every so often rather than every time (checking "trust this device" usually does this). Use your chosen login method as an extra layer, where you can. This might mean that you use facial recognition authentication to get your multifactor code from your phone. Although these can be frustrating if used incorrectly, a little bit of thought can tell you which method is most appropriate for a given context in which you use your devices.

Be Careful with What Software You Use

Do some effective research on how secure something might be. Be aware that anyone can post on the Internet. So, finding one comment on a forum may not mean much, but reputable sources have a lot more clout. And although you might not be able to tell whether a service is safe or not, it's still possible to do some research. An easy way to do this can be to search for the service or software followed by the word "vulnerability." This will show you vulnerabilities rated as a combination of impact and likelihood. You will also see how the vendor or author of the software has responded to vulnerabilities. Did they fix them, did they ignore them, and how long did they take? If there's no information on these, sometimes you will at least see whether the vendor addresses security problems in their product at all because there will be a notice detailing the process for when people find security issues.

Be Careful What You Trust

Does this mean you shouldn't trust anything? In a way, yes. However, a good way to put it would be as in the old proverb, "Trust but verify." For instance, if you receive communications from someone you don't know or over a channel where you can't verify that it is from a particular person, check on another communication channel. Although there's a lot of attacks and scams out there, just taking a minute to verify something can often reduce your chances of getting scammed. Even checking the Australian government scamwatch.gov.au[19] website takes just a minute but might prevent a lot of stress later. Other useful resources include esafety.gov. au[20] in Australia, cert.nz in New Zealand, or for a more global and more detailed source, www.cisa.gov.[21]

---

[19] www.scamwatch.gov.au

[20] www.esafety.gov.au

[21] www.cisa.gov/uscert/ncas/current-activity

These principles should be a good start for you to investigate being careful online, in addition to policies and processes that may be in place at the school, library, or wherever you host your code club or maker group. Please do not take this as discouraging hacking – hacking to break things with permission or innovate and create has been an important way of learning, creating new things, and discovering serious problems in the technology we use.

Chapter 6: Cheat Sheet

Devs and Testers Activity (2 x 1-Hour Blocks)

- Choose two teams – developers (programmers) and testers (find bugs and suggest improvements).

- You will need a whiteboard and sticky notes for tracking your bugs and enhancements with a Kanban board. See Figure 6-2 for the activity workflow.

- Work out a method for sharing code within the teams. The workshop can also be performed online with collaborative tools.

Open Source Software

- Open source software has source code available and allows you to collaborate with modifying and improving the software, for example, bug reports, feedback, fixes, and even becoming a permanent team member in some cases.

- Licensing is important for open source software as it helps keep it accessible for all and can also affect derivative works. There are many different licenses – all with their own requirements for attribution, commercial or noncommercial use, and contribution.

- Open source can also apply to hardware designs with many companies embracing both, for example, Adafruit, Pimoroni, IBM, and Microsoft.

Collaborating with Online Tools

- Online tools are available for communications between your volunteers.

- Email is fine to get started but can get unwieldy quickly and make it hard to find things.

- Using a collaborative tool like Discord is free, and you can easily set up a private server and include voice, video, and audio chat in addition to text-based chat with images. These types of tools have the advantage of allowing multiple channels/rooms so you can manage information for multiple activities in parallel while having it more easily accessible.

- To make things even easier to reference for new and existing volunteers, you can also have a wiki. Some overhead is required to add content, but if you choose a wiki that is easy to edit, it can be worth a bit of extra time compared to that saved by having easily accessible content.

Security and Privacy When Working Online

The main principles to remember in this area are as follows:

- Separate things, for example, use different emails for work vs. private.

- Layered defenses, for example, use MFA and add controls on mobile devices that are contextually appropriate, that is, biometrics can be easier if you are in a public place.

- Be careful with software that you use – look at the big picture and determine what the vendor's focus is; are they actively fixing security and privacy issues?

- Be careful what you trust – double-check with a trusted source when dealing with communications from unknown sources.

Code Collaboration Terminology

- *Issue tracker*: A web application that tracks code issues raised for a project.

- *Code repository*: An online repository to track versioning and changes to your code.

- *Branch*: A separate version of a repository stored with the repository.

- *Fork*: A copy of the whole code repository that is separate from the original; used to work on the code without affecting the main repository, for example, for contributing code patches.

- *Merge*: Adding new code to a repository.

- *Add*: Add code or files to be later merged into the repository.

217

- *Commit*: An update that contains files and a comment to be merged into a repository for tracking.

- *Push/pull*: A pull request is a request to have your code merged to a project; a push is when you send a commit from a local repository to the online repository.

- *Readme*: A file, usually formatted with Markdown, that has information for a repository that includes how to install and use the software and how to contribute to the project.

Creating Your Own Workshops

- Creating a workshop is a good way to enable others to achieve more by leveraging their existing skills and applying them in a smart way.

- Helping one of your volunteers or code club kids to create a workshop can be that next step from being a solo programmer to enabling a group to learn how to do something.

- Using a template can make creating a workshop easier by helping to structure the information. The main parts of a template could include

  - Introduction

  - What you will learn

  - What you need

  - Steps and tasks

  - Challenges for once you have completed the main steps

  - Troubleshooting

CHAPTER 7

Electronics: Basic Skills and Tools

With the introduction of microcontroller boards, it is possible to program a large portion of the logic for projects in high-level languages such as Python or Arduino. These languages use modules and libraries that can make it easier to program hardware. Low-level languages such as the assembly language can be embedded in higher-level languages like MicroPython. Libraries can sometimes be used to offload heavy lifting tasks while keeping the main logic readable and easy to update. This chapter is an introduction to the skills required to get started with kits and prototyping your own projects.

In this chapter, we will look at designing hardware projects, starting with an idea and selecting the hardware and parts, and incorporating a microcontroller board that can be programmed with a version of MicroPython. We will cover some of the concepts and skills involved when integrating additional components and building the required circuitry in an electronic badge prototype built on a reusable circuit board known as a breadboard.

© Martin Tan 2023
M. Tan, *micro:bit Projects with Python and Single Board Computers*,
https://doi.org/10.1007/978-1-4842-9197-9_7

A Quick Tale: Getting the Burn for Electronic Projects

As a kid, I remember a friend, Andrew, showing me small speaker amps and other electronic kits that he had made. Given my fascination with music, radio, and audio, the fact that he had made these really impressed me at the time. He also showed me an FM bug and some other kits that came from a local magazine called *Talking Electronics* written by Colin Mitchell. Incidently, I recently came across an online interview with Colin, found his website, and ended up buying a bunch of the original kits from him.[1] Just prior to being introduced to *Talking Electronics*, a school friend and I had been catching the tram down to a local Dick Smith electronics store in Richmond, Victoria, to buy some of their kits – although they were good for learning to solder and how not to solder, they just weren't up to the standard of the clear explanations and elegance of the *Talking Electronics* designs. My dad's unwieldy fixed temperature soldering iron seemed too clumsy for the work, and eventually I bought a tiny, pencil-sized 12-volt soldering iron. The smaller soldering iron, although cheap and still not adjustable, seemed to be closer to the right temperature and was much more forgiving for the small kits I was building. Eventually, I started reading more of the *Talking Electronics* articles and began to understand a bit more about why the circuits worked better and even got better at the "how" part, too. In later years, I built a bunch of kits from various sources, including a karaoke box, small stereo amplifiers, FM bugs, and various LED-based projects that would light up to sounds or play simple games. Eventually, we did a very short electronics subject at school, and I recall it as memorable as one of a few rare times where a personal interest had intersected with a school topic.

---

[1] www.talkingelectronics.com

These days, most of the logic can be programmed onto microcontroller chips which can also control other smaller expansion boards and breakout boards to perform tasks such as reading input from sensors or sending commands to motors and output to small screens or arrays of light-emitting diodes (LEDs). In contrast to the older circuits that still exist, microcontrollers and their circuits are mostly digital these days. However, you'll still need to understand a few basics about electronic components and what they are used for. I've included a primer to get you started – we'll talk about some basic electronic components and how they are used when programming microcontroller boards like the micro:bit and others. Given that we will be looking at using some components with microcontroller boards, we will primarily be looking at digital circuits that use high and low values to represent binary 1s and 0s and chips composed of logic gates. In contrast, analog circuits rely on variances in voltage. Within the context of microcontrollers, analog signals may come from sensors, for example, measuring heat, light, sound, and other variations in the environment. To allow microcontrollers to process these signals, they are first converted into digital forms using an analog-to-digital converter, which may be part of a microcontroller chip. To output analog signals, for example, sound, these are converted from digital into analog signals or sometimes use digital signals to mimic something that looks analog, for example, flashing LEDs very quickly to make them seem less bright, or apply the same principles to change the speed of motors. At the time of writing this, there's a global chip shortage with some components no longer being made and the factories that produced them closing during the COVID-19 pandemic. Some effects of this are finite lives for certain equipment and what seems like an increase in perceived value of some.

Basic Electronic Component Primer

This primer will provide an introduction to some of the electronic components which you may come across in soldering kits and when integrating with various microcontroller boards like the micro:bit and Adafruit's CircuitPython boards. These are all based around electrical current – electrons are negatively charged subatomic particles, which travel from the negative terminal to the positive terminal of an electrical source, that is, electrons move in the opposite direction to the electrical current. I like to think of this as "Negative is attracted to positive." I proudly recall my school physics teacher saying, "you did pretty well for someone who didn't do any work." I like to think that he was referring to my keen interest in electronics outside of school, but he was probably just saying something akin to "you could have done much better (in the specific curriculum topics, if I had focused more on them)." You can find the electronic symbols used in this chapter at `https://github.com/PanderMusubi/inkscape-open-symbols`. These symbols are under a GNU General Public License (GPLv3).[2] As there are too many different types of each component to cover in a single chapter, we will only cover some common uses for various forms of these components – to give you an idea of what you can use when creating projects. This information, although far from complete, should at least get you started. And something I have learned as someone who is paid to hack things is that sometimes you must take the most efficient path to what you want to achieve within a given time.

---

[2] `www.gnu.org/licenses/gpl-3.0.en.html`

Electronic Schematics and Datasheets

A schematic is a diagram used to document an electronic circuit, representing connected components with symbols. By reading an electronic schematic, you should be able to recreate the same circuit. Datasheets are documents that detail the feature requirements of an electronic component or integrated circuit chip in your circuit. These include information such as the expected voltages and current required to power components or chips and how to program more complex chips, including microcontroller chips. Any areas that need to be considered are included in a datasheet, including security and environmental considerations.

Breadboards and Circuit Boards

Breadboards allow you to create an easily modifiable circuit by allowing components and connecting wire to be placed on a board with holes connected in rows. Some breadboards also have sections that run alongside the main circuit to allow power to be connected. Once your circuit is working as expected, you can either transfer it to a printed prototype circuit board (sometimes called protoboard) or design a custom printed circuit board. The latter will allow you to reduce the size of your finished circuit since it can use multiple layers of circuitry and optimize the positioning of components and the copper tracks that connect them. This will result in a more compact footprint.

Through-Hole vs. Surface-Mount Components

Many components come in both through-hole and surface-mount versions. Surface-mount components are smaller and attach to the surface of a circuit board (PCB), whereas through-hole components have legs that are seating in holes and soldered to the circuit board.

Resistors

Resistors create electrical resistance in a circuit and are the most common component we will use in a circuit because their main job is to prevent too much power from being absorbed by other components. Through-hole resistors are identified using the International Electrotechnical Commission (IEC) standard 60062 RKM codes; these read from left to right with three or two bands of color codes, another optional band to the right is a multiplier, and a metallic-colored band on the rightmost end indicates tolerance as a percentage. The way I remember the number of the color codes is starting with black (0) and brown (1), then going through red (2), orange (3), yellow (4), green (5), blue (6), violet (7), and then gray (8) and white (9). Put simply, you have black (0) and brown (1) and then the colors of the rainbow less indigo, ROYGBIV, then gray (8) and white (9). The multiplier band uses the same order of colors to represent the multiplier as 0, 10, 100, 1k (1000), 10k, 100k, 1M (1,000,000), 10M. Using these codes, you can calculate the value of a through-hole resistor by reading the color codes from left to right, then applying the multiplier band to the right (see Figure 7-1).

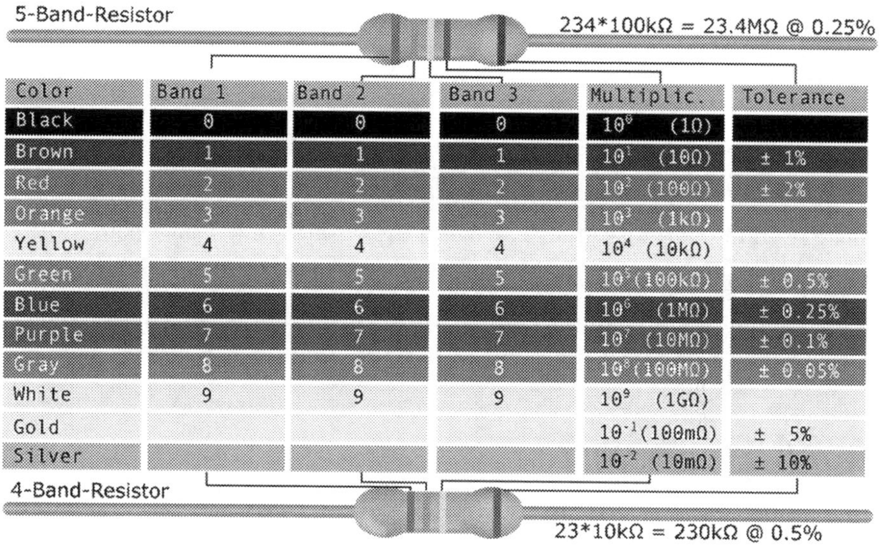

5-Band-Resistor   234*100kΩ = 23.4MΩ @ 0.25%

Color	Band 1	Band 2	Band 3	Multiplic.	Tolerance
Black	0	0	0	10^0 (1Ω)	
Brown	1	1	1	10^1 (10Ω)	± 1%
Red	2	2	2	10^2 (100Ω)	± 2%
Orange	3	3	3	10^3 (1kΩ)	
Yellow	4	4	4	10^4 (10kΩ)	
Green	5	5	5	10^5(100kΩ)	± 0.5%
Blue	6	6	6	10^6 (1MΩ)	± 0.25%
Purple	7	7	7	10^7 (10MΩ)	± 0.1%
Gray	8	8	8	10^8(100MΩ)	± 0.05%
White	9	9	9	10^9 (1GΩ)	
Gold				10^{-1}(100mΩ)	± 5%
Silver				10^{-2} (10mΩ)	± 10%

4-Band-Resistor

23*10kΩ = 230kΩ @ 0.5%

Figure 7-1. *Resistor color codes*[3]

Ohm's Law

I like to think of voltage as being the size of an electrical charge, with current being how fast it is moving, and resistance being an amount that both decrease when traveling through something. You can find more accurate descriptions in any number of technical websites or textbooks, but hopefully my description will help you enough to get started.

As I recall from my high school days, the equation for Ohm's law as it relates to electrical circuits is

V = I x R

---

[3] This image is from https://openclipart.org and reproduced under a CC0 1.0 license: https://creativecommons.org/publicdomain/zero/1.0/

or

I = V/R

where V = voltage, I = current, and R = resistance.

This means that when electricity travels through a resistor, it can affect the voltage or current as shown in the equation. For an easier method to calculating the required resistor for LEDs, there are multiple online calculators, for example, the Kitronik online store provides such a calculator to match up resistors with the LEDs that they stock.[4]

Symbol for Resistors

The symbols for a resistor are shown in Figure 7-2. For the record, I've seen both used in Australia. The Ohm value is usually written above the symbol, and a variable resistor, also known as a potentiometer (pot), is similar with an additional vertical arrow pointing to, and touching, the symbol.

Figure 7-2. *Resistor symbols (EU version on the left, US/Japan version on the right)*

Transistors

Transistors come in many different types and forms – two very useful circuit applications for transistors include amplifying a signal and acting as a switch. In digital circuits, they are predominantly used as a switch. Amplification may still be relevant for raising a signal to a required level for

---

[4]https://kitronik.co.uk/blogs/resources/led-resistor-value-calculator

digital processing or if you would like to make analog circuits for e-textile and analog audio projects. These types of circuits are also great fun when learning the basics of soldering. Personally, I remember learning about transistors being heat sensitive while learning to solder them (badly) in FM bug projects that converted sound from a microphone and amplified it for broadcasting, using variations in radio frequency, hence the "FM" part, which stands for "frequency modulation." One type of transistor used in analog amplification circuits is the PNP transistor, so-called because of the order of the layers of silicon that they are constructed from.

A commonly used switching type of transistor is known as NPN. Both types of transistors have three legs to connect to circuits, known as the collector, emitter, and base. These are typically labeled as C, E, and B, respectively. Other types of transistors vary in how much power they can handle and how various environmental factors affect their performance. Transistors can also be found in chips, which makes them much smaller, and sometimes are used in pairs, for example, "Darlington pairs." For switching, an electrical current is applied to the base, which then allows electrical current to flow from the collector through to the emitter wire.

Symbols for Transistors

The symbols for NPN and PNP transistors are shown in Figure 7-3. You will notice the base wire on the left of each symbol, with the emitter having an arrow and the collector being the wire without the arrow. These symbols are sometimes shown with a circle around them, with the base, collector, and emitter denoted by B, C, E, respectively.

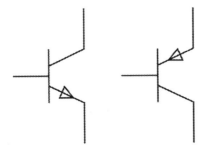

Figure 7-3. *Transistor symbols (NPN on the left, PNP on the right)*

Capacitors

Capacitors store electrical charge between two plates, which is then released. This has the effect of buffering current and is used to keep power supplied to components, such as microcontroller chips, cleaner and more constant, preventing power interruptions or spikes that could result in less consistent behavior. Capacitors come in a variety of different sizes, shapes, tolerances, and ratings; they also vary in the type of material they are constructed from, depending on the qualities required, for example, guitar effects pedals typically use film capacitors because other types of capacitors exhibit increased microphonic properties that can color the audio signal. Ceramic capacitors are often used to smooth power supplied to microcontroller and other chips, and additional features include less electromagnetic or radiofrequency leakages – such side-channel leakage may be exploited to compromise data in circuits with a requirement for confidentiality of data. There are also polarized and nonpolarized capacitors available, the former usable only for current flowing a specific direction.

Symbol for Capacitor

The symbol for a capacitor is shown in Figure 7-4.

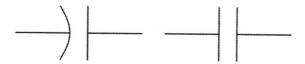

Figure 7-4. *Capacitor symbols (polarized on the left, nonpolarized on the right)*

Diodes

Diodes only allow electrical current to flow in one direction. Although there are many reasons why we might require directional flow, one of the simplest reasons why a diode might be used is to protect circuitry or components that may otherwise be damaged if electrical current were to be delivered to them. Diodes are also arranged specifically in logic circuits to set specific pins as being either high (1) or low (0) based on the state of other wires supplying current.

Symbol for Diode

The symbol for a diode is shown in Figure 7-5. Notice that the arrow points toward the negative end of the diode, which is the same direction that the diode allows the current to flow.

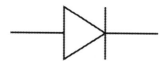

Figure 7-5. *Diode symbol (anode "+" on the left, cathode "-" on the right)*

Light-Emitting Diodes (LEDs)

LEDs are like diodes in that they only allow current to flow from the anode to the cathode, but also give off light when current flows through them. The color of light depends on the material used. RGB LEDs can generate 16.7 million colors because they contain three smaller LEDs which can each be adjusted in brightness in increments from 0 to 255. RGB LEDs have two wires for power (positive and negative) and one for data. Although a single-color LED can be lit by simply supplying the right amount of power by using resistors to limit the supplied voltage, RGB LEDs require a microcontroller to send the right signal to change color, and they can be addressable, allowing individual RGB LEDs to be controlled.

Symbol for LED

The symbol for a single LED is shown in Figure 7-6.

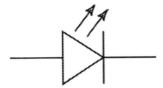

Figure 7-6. *Symbol for a light-emitting diode (LED)*

RGB LEDs can be represented as three LEDs, sometimes labeled with red (R), green (G), and blue (B) – these are often pictured as a block that also encloses a driver chip that is connected to each of the individual LEDs. Brand names for RGB LEDs are NeoPixel and ZIP LEDs, and these usually have four external pins, that is, DC power in, ground, control data input, and control data output. The output lets you chain multiple RGB LEDs, for example, in a strip, ring, or matrix. Single-color addressable LEDs also come in these types of arrangements.

Integrated Circuit (IC) Chips

In addition to the smaller footprint of surface-mount technology (SMT) components, complete complex circuits are also available in miniature form on a chip. This reduces the number of larger components that need to be included in a circuit that involves chips. It is not uncommon for a project to consist of a chip that comes premounted on a printed circuit board (PCB) which in turn is connected to a "breakout board," which allows easy connection of external components or boards. Something to remember when using integrated circuit (IC) chips is that the first of the number pins is typically marked with an indicator, for example, a dot.

Soldering!

Soldering involves melting solder to create a robust conductive connection between components and a circuit board or even to one another. This is useful when you want to make your breadboard circuit permanent, portable, and more compact. You may even want to mount it inside a case so you can attach other operating controls such as buttons, knobs, sockets, and so on. With the right precautions and equipment, your code club or maker group kids can begin soldering from around the age of 11. Supervision will be required since the tip of the soldering iron is hot enough to melt fingers and other flesh at the 450 degrees Celsius temperature required for lead-free solder. If you've never soldered before, or not soldered circuits, we will be looking at that basics so you can also teach your maker kids! Keeping with the theme of eventually scaling up our activities, these instructions intentionally consider budget and practicality, rather than recommending the highest quality or most expensive top end gear.

Tools You Will Need for Soldering

This section outlines a minimal set of tools required to get started putting together electronic kits or prototyping your circuits on printed circuit boards.

Soldering Iron/Station

The essential features for circuit board soldering are stable temperature control and the ability to change tips. If you don't want to spend money on digital temperature control, you can figure out the best temperature by trial and error and make a mark on the dial to remind you. For lead-free solder, look for around 450 degrees Celsius and around 400 degrees Celsius for leaded solder. Bonus points for a soldering station that also has a holder for your soldering iron so that you don't burn yourself while it is sitting on the bench. A pen-like but usable quality soldering iron is the Miniware TS80P[5] which runs from a USB-C power supply, like the type used to charge a laptop. The Pinecil[6] is a similar and slightly cheaper version of the TS80P, and both can be reprogrammed with custom open source firmware, for example, IronOS,[7] allowing you the option to modify and enable features in the future.

Solder

Solder is a thin wire that is melted by the soldering iron to create a solid and conductive connection between electronic components and small copper circles (pads) on the printed circuit board (PCB). As mentioned earlier, solder comes in a nonleaded and leaded form with the latter

---

[5] www.miniware.com.cn/product/ts80p-soldering-iron-main/

[6] www.pine64.org/pinecil/

[7] https://github.com/Ralim/IronOS

melting a little easier. However, I've talked to tradespeople who need to use nonleaded for work, and they have no complaints. The thicker the solder wire, the faster the rate of solder flowing, and the thinner it is, the more accurate you can be but at a slower rate. A good place to start could be 0.5mm for through-hole components. Surface-mount components usually use a paste with a lower melting temperature and a special oven or plate, but for a small one-off quantity, they can be soldered in small with reasonably fine solder and a hand soldering iron. A core of flux that comes with most solder is a paste that will help the solder flow to the right places as it melts.

Tip Cleaner

Before soldering, I've learned to always poke the hot tip of the soldering iron into what resembles as curly steel wool scouring pad, also known as a soldering iron tip cleaner. It will keep contaminants out of your solder joints which will result in better conductivity and a stronger solder joint.

Helping Hands/Mini Vise

Helping hands are simply sets of crocodile clips mounted on bendy wire or interlocking plastic arms that are anchored in a metal or timber base. They are handy for holding things in place while you solder. As I discovered early on when I accidentally destroyed transistors with too much heat, the crocodile clips can assist with soldering components that are more sensitive to heat, for example, transistors, by acting as a heat sink to draw away the heat during soldering. If you're reasonably quick with your soldering, this shouldn't be too much of an issue – or at least after some practice! Another method I use quite often is to just grab a piece of Blu Tack, which can hold components while you're soldering – often, this is a much more flexible method of holding things, except that you can only hold things to a surface (or like me, a small piece of timber), and it won't act as a heat sink. A mini hobby vise consists of a pair of jaws coated with a soft rubber or similar material to protect your PCBs. Vises either come with a clamp to mount on the edge of a bench or have a flat base that sits on the table. You can pick up some inexpensive vises from hardware, hobby, or electronics stores. The Panavise junior is a nice smooth vise with an articulating head that may be worth looking into.

Cutters/Side Cutters

Cutters are basically a scissor-type tool that resemble pliers – you use them to cut wires or trim the legs of through-hole components after they are soldered to the PCB. At a pinch, you can also use them to strip the insulation off flexible wires instead of using wire strippers.

Wire Strippers

These are like cutters but have an indentation to allow a more controlled way of stripping the insulation off wires to expose the copper below, so you can solder it. They're convenient to have, but you can get away with using a hobby knife, scissors, or cutters. One of the handiest tools I managed to get is the Leatherman Squirt ES4 Electrician's tool – it folds up small enough to put on your keyring and has wire strippers for a range of wire thicknesses. Sadly, the ES4 has now been discontinued. If this looks good to you, I suggest looking for it secondhand or trying to find an equivalent "electrician's" mini multitool.

Heat-Proof Mat

For this one, you can just use an old piece of timber, heat-resistant cutting board. Otherwise, for a reasonably low price, for example, $20 AUD, you can get flexible heat-proof mats, many with built-in areas where you can organize small components or tiny screws as you build or tear down your projects.

Solder Sucker/Desoldering Braid

At some point after either soldering the wrong component or needing to change a component value or even just when grabbing components from old equipment, you will likely find yourself needing to remove solder. The key to this is to add some solder first and then use either some braid to absorb the solder from the PCB or use a suction pump, known as a solder sucker, to remove the solder quickly. Although you may not need this tool at first, at some point you will – it's up to you whether you buy it now or at a later stage. Just remember that when you need it, you'll be glad if you bought the tool beforehand, rather than having to go off to the store in the middle of building something!

Other Useful Things to Have

Protective safety equipment: Protective eyeglasses should always be used to prevent any solder from spitting into eyes.

Soldering fan with carbon filter: An inexpensive fan which can house some carbon impregnated foam can be purchased. The purpose of this is to draw any solder fumes away from you with toxins absorbed by the carbon in the foam. The foam can be changed once it no longer works.

Magnifying light: I've seen these for much more than a simple lamp but also found a cheaper and lighter version that runs off a USB port. Put simply, these are made of a ring of bright LEDs with a magnifying glass in the middle, mounted on a flexible arm, allowing you to illuminate and magnify whatever you're soldering or desoldering, with the bonus of being hands-free. Sometimes, you may find these with a clamp for a desk or bench.

Veroboard: This is simply a board made from the same material as PCBs, lined with small holes and copper strips or pads. I've mentioned this as it is a great way to practice your soldering of through-hole components. Also, grab a bunch of resistors or LEDs to solder.

How to Solder

The main idea when soldering is to melt the solder to both the component wire and circuit board. This requires heating both quickly and evenly, then applying solder at the intersection of the component and the board until it becomes shiny. A good solder joint will look shiny and be slightly convex, with no cracks. A great way to practice is to use a type of generic circuit board known as Veroboard – this is just a rectangular printed circuit board with copper pads for soldering, which are connected in strips; Veroboard is inexpensive and comes in both surface-mount and through-hole versions.

Now for the how-to part: Making sure you are in a well-ventilated area, plug in your soldering iron and set the temperature to 450 degrees Celsius for lead-free solder or 400 for leaded solder. You can adjust this as you go, so that the solder flows quickly and smoothly. While you're waiting for the soldering iron to heat up, make sure you have some Veroboard, a few through-hole components to practice, and some Blutak[8] or helping hands. If you happen to have a small vise handy, you can put your Veroboard between the jaws, with the edges against the jaws. Place your practice component legs in neighboring holes in the Veroboard, with the component body on the opposite side to the copper tracks. Bend the legs out slightly so that the component stays in the holes and have your Veroboard with the copper side facing toward you. This is where you will be soldering the component legs to the copper pads.

Depending on which soldering iron you bought, it is probably now heated to the set temperature, so clean the tip of the soldering iron and grab the handle, being very careful to ignore those weird stock photos that show people holding the hot part. This is serious – soldering irons can melt skin, so make sure you hold the handle correctly. In your nondominant hand, grab your solder, making sure that at least 10cm of solder wire is protruding. Now, place the hot tip of your soldering iron so that it is

---

[8] https://diy.bostik.com/en-AU/products/stationery/blu-tack

touching and heating both the copper pad and the leg of the component, on the side where the end of the component leg sticks out. Count to one and touch the end of the solder to where the component leg touches the copper pad; it should melt onto both the component and the pad. Feed the solder until the solder flows into the pad and count to two. Pull the solder wire away and then the soldering iron. If you've done everything right, your solder joint should look shiny and uniform and be slightly dip inward rather than bulging outward. A good way to learn the timing and amount of solder required is to watch a video.

Teaching Kids to Solder

Given the dangers involved, the youngest age for soldering should at least be 11 years with supervision. Have kids well separated and ensure that there is somewhere safe to place the hot tip of the soldering iron. Set up a bench and have kids stand rather than sit, to reduce the chances of dropping a hot soldering iron in their laps. If a soldering iron drops, they can step back to avoid it.

To be safe, assign one volunteer to at most two kids, when they are learning. Ensure that you are familiar with first aid processes for the location before starting, so that you know who to call for and where to go if any accidents occur. In the event of an accident, no kids should be left alone with hot soldering irons. Set up strict rules and processes and have these displayed where they are easily visible at the soldering bench.

Handy Software Tools

There's a variety of software tools available for all manner of electronic design, calculation, and simulation. Both old and new, they vary in usability and features. I've included some that have been useful both in my experience and that primary and secondary school teachers who visited our code club have mentioned were useful.

TinkerCAD

Although we predominantly used this online web-based tool over the years to give our code club kids an easy platform to get started with 3D design, it now has a drag-and-drop interface for building and simulating circuits for the Arduino microcontroller board and the BBC micro:bit. It also supports a version of Python on the micro:bit. Although the coding aspect is geared around initially using a drag-and-drop interface, you can toggle between block-based coding and the C programming language (Arduino) and MicroPython (micro:bit). If you write a program using the drag-and-drop interface, the resulting text-based interpretation will often be slightly less readable and is structured differently than if you started out text based. That said, during the COVID-19 lockdown, TinkerCAD (Figure 7-7) was a useful way for primary and secondary students to learn about circuits and programming microcontrollers, when working remotely. TinkerCAD is made by Autodesk, the same company that makes more advanced professional 3D design software like (in order of difficulty) Fusion 360 (Figure 7-8), Inventor, and AutoCAD; however, be aware that, due to the difference in interfaces, jumping from TinkerCAD to Fusion 360 will be a much steeper learning curve than going from Fusion 360 to Inventor. The key here is that once kids reach the point where TinkerCAD starts making it harder to do something than Fusion 360, for example, fillets (rounding on edges or adjacent surfaces), then it is time to move to Fusion 360 or a similar tool with a more CAD-based interface. Delaying the move can either create frustration or result in a learning plateau. Moving to Fusion 360 presents the following challenges:

- Licensing is costly for primary schools, but high schools have an educational license available. There is a free startup license that may work for clubs and maker groups not affiliated with a school.

- Fusion 360 requires software to be installed, so it depends on your IT support and environment.

Once you outgrow TinkerCAD, there are more options out there. FreeCAD is less intuitive but does allow Python scripting to automate building which may appeal to those who wishing to apply their Python skills, or want to create designs that lend themselves to this approach. Blender is free and open source but focuses more on modeling than structural design. It is also covered in the Code Club curriculum and other tutorial series, so it might be another viable option, depending on your requirements.

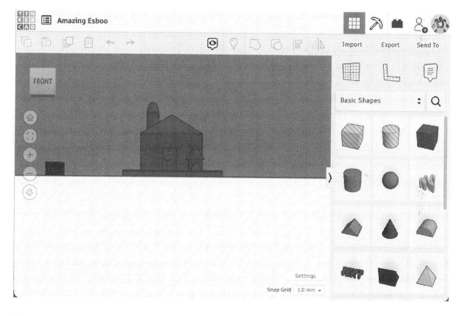

Figure 7-7. *TinkerCAD runs in a web browser, making it easy to get started designing*

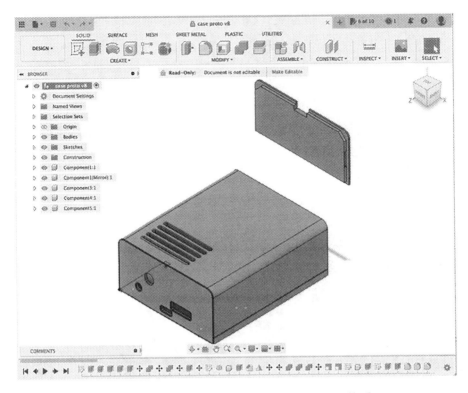

Figure 7-8. *Fusion 360 requires software to be installed on a computer, but is easier once designs become more complex*

To get started in TinkerCAD, we include it in the list of online services for which code club parents need to register accounts for their kids. The other advantage of this is that kids can continue working on their projects outside of a code club or maker group. This reinforces the idea of ownership of maker skills rather than something learned and then immediately discarded. As with programming skills, the easiest way to get started in the 3D design aspect has been to let kids progress through the initial dozen lessons that you are presented with upon creating a TinkerCAD account. Our code club kids ramped their skills up much faster when we put them through the introductory lessons, rather than letting them loose to find their own way. Some of the 3D prints designed by our code club kids for a city project are shown in Figure 7-9. For the circuit-building and microcontroller programming component, the same is true; going through the initial exercises lets kids reach a practical fluency level much quicker and is less frustrating. Written instructions to get started in the basics are also available through TinkerCAD's documentation and blog posts.[9]

Figure 7-9. *3D prints designed by our Code Club kids in TinkerCAD for our city project*

If you're keen on looking at how analog circuits work, tools like CircuitLab[10] (online) and the slightly dated LTspice[11] (installable for Mac, Windows, and Linux) can be useful to show how signals are modified by circuitry, for example, if you are interested in looking at audio effects circuits such as amplifiers or waveform modifiers such as distortion or signal modulation.

---

[9] www.tinkercad.com/blog/official-guide-to-tinkercad-circuits
[10] www.circuitlab.com/
[11] www.analog.com/en/design-center/design-tools-and-calculators/ltspice-simulator.html

Embedded Programming

So how does all this talk of electronics tie in with our investment into Python? A growing number of microcontroller boards (also known as "embedded devices") are now using a compact version of Python known as MicroPython that can be loaded on the device and runs when the board is switched on (booted up). MicroPython is an easy way to get started for programming microcontrollers (also known as *embedded programming*). Other variants of MicroPython include the cut-down version of MicroPython we used on the micro:bit and Adafruit's fork of MicroPython (CircuitPython) that runs on their boards and also some other manufacturer's boards. CircuitPython[12] was a way to provide support for Adafruit boards without increasing the load on the MicroPython developers at the time and has now evolved into a well-supported and capable option for supported microcontrollers. Although the Raspberry Pi Pico W is supported at the time of writing, there were a few features being worked on which made MicroPython an easier choice at this time. However, you should be aware that some modules for Adafruit components have stopped continuing development (deprecated) to allow for better continued support in CircuitPython – so you will need to look at the support for the hardware components you are using to decide which type of embedded Python is best for your projects.

Some Useful Concepts to Understand

As this is not a textbook, or anything even close to a complete reference source, you'll notice that I'm zeroing in on the most important and useful concepts with directions on where to find further information. I believe that this approach of determining which skills are most relevant to your objectives is the quickest and easiest way to get active with making things.

---

[12] https://learn.adafruit.com/welcome-to-circuitpython/what-is-circuitpython

Microcontroller Breakout Board

A breakout board allows programmable microcontroller circuits on a silicon chip to be connected to external interfaces, for example, organic light-emitting diode (OLED) screens for output and sensors or buttons for input. These boards come with a programmable microcontroller soldered to them and include various component circuitry with the required diodes and capacitors to ensure a smooth and safe power supply is provided to the microcontroller. Often, ground and power pins are present to draw from the board's power supply to power external components, in addition to general-purpose input/output (GPIO) connections and other specialized connectors that allow the use of interface features in the microcontroller.

Common Communication Protocols

To communicate with components that are connected to the microcontroller board, rules are used for communications, known as protocols. Three common protocols used include Inter-Integrated Circuit (I2C), Serial Peripheral Interface (SPI), and Inter-IC Sound (I2S), for example. In digital microcontroller systems, support for various protocols and mathematical functions e.g., encryption to protect data that is being stored or transferred, can be implemented using code that is built-in to microcontrollers, or alternatively by using firmware which can be updated and modified (bit banging). The latter method allows better upgradeability and flexibility at the cost of being slower. From a security perspective, this can be an issue since it may be difficult to ensure that electronic hardware built to a specific cost can be upgraded when built-in protocol support becomes outdated. In this chapter, we will be using the implementations supported by MicroPython on the microcontroller we choose. From a practical perspective, I2C is slower but simpler to get started with than SPI; so, we will start by using I2C. Although you don't yet need to understand the very low-level details of these protocols when using MicroPython, you can read more about how to use SPI and I2C in the MicroPython documentation.[13,14]

Approaching a New Microcontroller Electronic Project (Digital)

Let's look at building our own electronic badge project, which will give us plenty of flexibility and can be as simple or complex as we like. For this, we'll use the Raspberry Pi Pico W, since it supports MicroPython which is familiar to us. The Pico W also incorporates wireless and Bluetooth features for communicating with other devices, and allows loading our code via USB. The Pico W supports the I2C and SPI protocols and is compatible with the Thonny IDE with which we are already familiar. At the time of writing, a search on `https://digikey.com.au`, a popular parts store, reveals the rp2040 microcontroller to be one of the most readily available and cheapest. This ticks most boxes for us:

- Supports a programming language that we are familiar with

- Has good community support which makes integration with other components easier

- Supports features that we require

- Has an easy method for loading our code

- Is readily available and more likely to be available in the future

- Is not overly expensive to buy which allows us to spend more money on add-ons

---

[13] `https://docs.micropython.org/en/latest/library/machine.SPI.html`
[14] `https://docs.micropython.org/en/latest/library/machine.I2C.html`

You can read about the technical details and find descriptions for input/output pins in the Raspberry Pi Pico W datasheet.[15]

Software and Hardware Support for Proposed Components

Initially, it would be good to support some sort of display, some buttons, LEDs, and an interface for some other add-ons. With I2C, SPI, and GPIO support, we should be able to find common components that use these protocols. Electronic supply companies such as Adafruit and SparkFun are known to contribute to open source and provide active support which will make it easier to make things do the tasks we require. I do still love that I can go online and talk to Lady Ada, the CEO of Adafruit, and she will often have written some of the supporting code for the products herself or employ dedicated and helpful people who contribute to open source, whether that be their own CircuitPython, Arduino, or MicroPython. Cheaper parts can be sourced from marketplaces such as AliExpress but are less likely to have as good support from the seller – in this case, it is important to check whether a part is widely used by the community, as this will be a more reliable source of support outside of the basic examples that the seller may provide, if any.

Support for Languages We Are Proficient In

Since we are already getting familiar with MicroPython or close variants, we'll be looking for support for this language in the microcontrollers and parts from which we will be building our project. Depending on the bootloader, we may need to use some programmer hardware to connect to our device, or it may be as simple as being able to drag files to a filesystem accessible over USB. For the latter, the Raspberry Pi RP2040 Pico W allows

---

[15] https://datasheets.raspberrypi.com/picow/pico-w-datasheet.pdf

this, which means we don't need separate programmer hardware. If you're using Windows, Mac, or Linux, this microcontroller board won't require additional driver software, which simplifies things even more.

Availability of Parts to Scale Things Up

Given the good availability of the RP2040 chip used in the Raspberry Pi Pico boards and corresponding cheaper cost (around $10 AUD or less), we know that buying a bulk order will be easier for our code club or maker group. Since this chip is so readily available, it is also used in other microcontroller boards, which is great in case the Raspberry Pi version is ever out of stock. This will also allow us to improve and repeat our project for successive years, which means we can spend less time and effort in rewriting for a different platform and spend more time adding near features and fine-tuning our existing project.

Draw a Diagram, Create a Schematic

To conceptualize our project, we can draw up a simple schematic and start designing before we even spend any money at all. We can research the required components and add-on boards until we find those which are best suited for our project. You can either draw the schematic physically on some graph paper or use free software such as Fritzing or something similar. Since most components have datasheets available online, we can study these to ensure that they are likely to work with our project.

Breadboard Prototype

Once we have our design roughed out with a schematic and know that our components are compatible with one another, we need to build a prototype. A prototype is a test version of our project that will enable us to test whether our design works in the real world. Using a breadboard for this allows us flexibility to swap out parts until everything works when our code is loaded. As this is a predominantly digital project that is driven by our code, it will be somewhat easier to see what is happening. However, we may still need our multimeter or perhaps even a logic analyzer to troubleshoot at this stage. A multimeter allows us to check voltages and current at various stages – this lets us check that our electrical circuit is working as expected. A logic analyzer can connect into our digital circuit to capture the numbers that represent our I2C or SPI instructions and convert these back into something that will be readable to us.

Going Further

Once we have our project working in a breadboard prototype, we can go even further and have our own custom printed circuit board (PCB) fabricated. This is a way of converting our breadboard prototype into a more robust prototype. Since all the features we require are in the Pico board, the easiest way to incorporate this will be to add sockets for the header pins, so that the microcontroller board will be connected into the circuits. Although it is possible to obtain the raw RP2040 chip and mount it directly onto a PCB, this will require additional components to both protect the microcontroller and supply the required power. So, to start off, it makes sense to connect the Pico board to our PCB.

Introducing the Raspberry Pi Pico

The Raspberry Pi Pico is a reasonably bare-bone microcontroller board that can run Python scripts to interact with devices using various communication methods (protocols). Unlike previous Raspberry Pi single-board computers, the Pico does not run a fully fledged operating system. Although most datasheets can be very detailed because they need to communicate all the features of a microcontroller or device, the Raspberry Pi Pico W is refreshingly simple in comparison.[16] Don't worry about reading this completely, as I will be giving you the necessary details as we progress. From there, you can read about specific areas in the datasheet, as required, for example, when selecting the GPIO pins we will be using or which pins we use for I2C and powering our components.

UPDATING MICROPYTHON ON THE RASPBERRY PI PICO

To make sure you have the best compatibility with devices, it's useful to have the latest firmware on your Raspberry Pi Pico. Thankfully, the bootloader on the Pico provides two very easy ways to do this. First, you'll need to put the Pico into update mode by holding down the bootsel button on the Pico while plugging it into your computer via the micro USB cable.

Updating firmware via the USB filesystem

The first way to update the firmware is by dragging the .u2f file to a USB drive that will appear in your computer's file manager. The drive should come up named as RPI-RP2 in your file manager (Finder on Mac, Explorer on Windows, and whichever file manager you may be using on Linux/Raspberry Desktop).

Updating firmware over USB with Thonny

The second method of updating the firmware is from within the Thonny editor. From the Thonny menu, select Tools ➤ Options ➤ Install Firmware, or click in the bottom corner to access the same options (Figure 7-10).

---

[16] https://datasheets.raspberrypi.com/picow/pico-w-datasheet.pdf

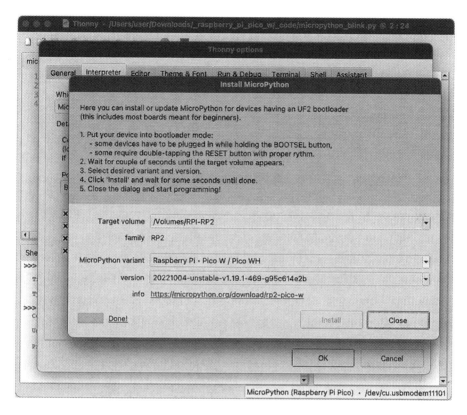

Figure 7-10. *Thonny MicroPython firmware install*

For more details about updating firmware on the Pico, there's also instructions on the official Raspberry Pi site.[17] Do not disconnect the Pico while the firmware is writing as there is a slight chance of making the Pico unbootable. Once complete, you can restart the Pico and check the Python version in the Thonny REPL.

---

[17] www.raspberrypi.com/documentation/microcontrollers/micropython.html

The Raspberry Pi Pico comes in a few different forms, designated by "H," "W," and "WH"; these indicate soldered headers, wireless+Bluetooth, and wireless+Bluetooth with soldered headers, respectively. The Raspberry Pi Pico microcontroller board supports the I2C and SPI protocols in addition to UART, pulse-width modulation (PWM), and GPIO pins. Although we will be debugging our Python code in Thonny's REPL, there is also the option to use an Serial Wire Debug (SWD) interface to debug at the much lower microcontroller level.

A major difference to other microcontrollers is that the Pico is designed with education in mind, so it does not have extensive security features that, for example, the STM32Fx microcontrollers have. This is something to keep in mind if someone in your code club or maker group wants to design a project that requires controls to prevent tampering or other security requirements. For such an application, you will need to look at a different microcontroller. But for now, let's move on to this chapter's project which uses libraries to integrate external devices with a Raspberry Pi Pico!

Note   I used the SparkFun tool, Fritzing, to draw the breadboard diagrams in this chapter's project. You can use this tool to design your circuit as a schematic diagram and then display it as a breadboard diagram like the ones I have included. Fritzing is an open source software, but you can pay a small fee to get the precompiled version that is ready to install on your computer. This is a handy tool that may be useful when explaining things in your Code Club or Maker group, so I'd recommend considering it. Fritzing also allows you to add more third-party parts as they become available.

PROJECT: PROTOTYPING AN ELECTRONIC BADGE

Here's an electronic badge project that includes a display, some buttons, a sensor, and LEDs. This should give you a good base to continue adding to and runs MicroPython code written in our Thonny IDE that we used previously. The badge is based around the Raspberry Pi Pico board, driven by the RP2040 microcontroller.

What you will learn

- How to use the Raspberry Pi Pico bootloader to upload firmware and Python code

- How to program a more feature-filled version of MicroPython on a more powerful microcontroller

- How to set up MicroPython libraries to easily enable multiple I2C and GPIO input and output devices

- How to use a breadboard for prototyping

What you will need

- A computer with the latest version of Thonny IDE installed. This could also be a Raspberry Pi 3B or 4B+ model running a current version of Raspberry Pi operating system[18] (OS) or another Ubuntu-based OS. Note: The Raspberry Pi Pico that we will be programming does not run an OS but only runs a MicroPython firmware that interprets our MicroPython code.

---

[18] Instructions for installing Raspberry Pi OS: www.raspberrypi.com/software/

251

- A Raspberry Pi Pico (a base version is fine but will require soldering of header pins to connect to your breadboard – the "H" version includes these presoldered. The "W" version includes wireless capability – this is optional but will give you the ability to expand your project later to connect to wireless networks).

- A ¾-sized breadboard and a mini-sized breadboard.

- Some breadboard jumper wires and small connector wires with pin ends rather than socket ends. You may also find it useful to have some solid wire U-shaped jumpers[19] as these will make it simpler to make small connections on the breadboard, for example, connecting ground or 3.3V to the breadboard power rails, marked as "–" and "+".

- A micro USB cable to connect from your computer to the Pico board. Make sure the other end has a compatible plug to fit your computer.

- An SSD1306 OLED 128x32 display (these come in larger sizes which will be fine too, e.g., 128x64, 128x128 pixels).

- A DHT11 temperature and humidity sensor with a 10K resistor (it usually comes with this resistor).

- Some standard low voltage 3.3V LEDs.

- Soldering tools if you need to solder the GPIO header pins, that is, temperature-adjustable soldering iron set to around 450 degrees Celsius and lead-free solder as a minimum.

---

[19] https://au.rs-online.com/web/p/breadboard-jumper-wires/6348651

Let's get started!

Let's get our development/programming environment set up first. Ensure that you have the very latest version of Thonny that is available. Version 4.0.1[20] was the latest at the time of writing. This will be more important for compatibility with the "W" model of the Raspberry Pi Pico, and it also pulls in newer MicroPython firmware versions if you need to update the Pico.

Step 1: Run Thonny and plug your Pico into your computer via the micro USB cable. Click in the bottom-right corner and select Configure Interpreter (Figure 7-11).

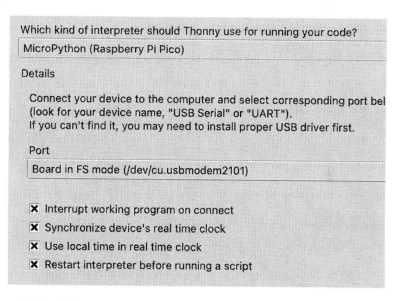

Figure 7-11. Thonny options pop-up

---

[20] https://github.com/thonny/thonny/releases/tag/v4.0.1

You should see the Thonny options pop-up – use the drop-downs to select the following:

- Interpreter as MicroPython (Raspberry Pi Pico)

- The Port – on my Mac, it comes up as /dev/cu.usbmodem2101, but on Windows you would see "Com1" or similar. A hint is that it will come up when your Pico is plugged in.

If you've just received your Pico or updated the firmware, you should see the Python prompt, showing the MicroPython version in the REPL window at the bottom of Thonny (Figure 7-12).

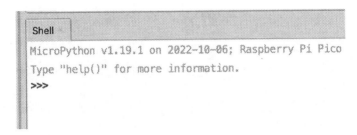

Figure 7-12. *Pico MicroPython version displayed in Thonny REPL*

Test that you can run code by typing in a simple while loop (Listing 7-1); you should see "hello" printed repeatedly in the REPL (Figure 7-13).

Listing 7-1. "Hello" loop

```
while True:
        print("hello")
```

```
 Shell ×
    hello
    hello
    hello
    hello
    hello
    hello
    hello
    hello
    hello
```

Figure 7-13. *"Hello" printed in Thonny REPL*

I decided not to do the usual "Blink" code since the design of the Raspberry Pi Pico and the "W" models vary, that is, the "W" version has the built-in LED connected to the wireless chip, whereas the standard model is connected to an internal pin.

This way, there was just one piece of code for everyone!

Step 2: Since we missed out on some bright lights in the first step, let's set up the OLED display. To connect the display easily and not have it wobbling around everywhere, we'll use a breadboard with some jumper wires (Figure 7-14).

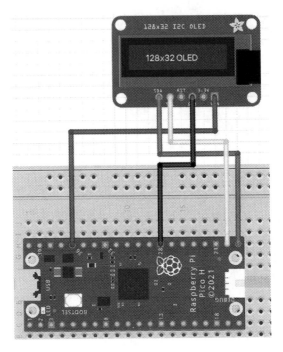

Figure 7-14. *128x32 OLED connected to I2C pins, power, and ground*

Note   With the breadboard held sideways as shown in Figure 7-14, the holes are connected vertically. They do not connect across the middle gap which is why the vertically aligned Pico GPIO pins are not shorting together. The two rows at the top of the breadboard are power rails that are connected horizontally, so you can connect ground (GND) and 3.3V to the + and − rails, respectively, to make power connections simpler and cleaner for your prototype circuit.

This makes more sense after seeing the Pico pins from the Raspberry Pi Pico W datasheet (Figure 7-15).

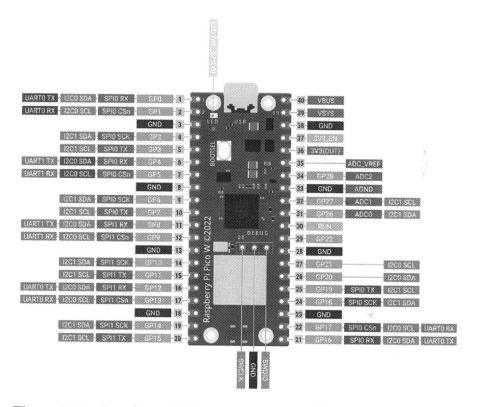

Figure 7-15. *Raspberry Pi Pico W pinout from https://datasheets.raspberrypi.com/picow/pico-w-datasheet.pdf*

If you have a Raspberry Pi Pico standard or H model, you can find an equivalent datasheet on the Raspberry Pi site.[21] Connect your OLED display to the Raspberry Pi Pico as shown in Table 7-1.

---

[21] https://datasheets.raspberrypi.com/pico/Pico-R3-A4-Pinout.pdf

Note   As the OLED device can use 3.3V and that is also the Pico's GPIO input/output level, the device is compatible – if they were different, we would need to use a *signal level converter* board between the Pico and the device to convert signals from 5V to 3.3V and back again.

Table 7-1. *Connections between the Pico and OLED display*

Raspberry Pi Pico Pin	128x32 OLED Display Pin
SDA(GP16)	SDA
SCL(GP17)	SCL
3.3V(OUT)	VIN
GND	GND

Check your connections, making sure that you're using the GP numbers on the Pico. Because we are programming in MicroPython, connecting to the OLED display is easy – we just need to install a module onto our Pico and write some test code.

Installing a MicroPython library from Thonny

Our 128x32 OLED display uses the SSD1306 chip – we will need both the SSD1306 and OLED MicroPython modules for our project. These will abstract us from some of the low-level code that does all the I2C communications. To search for modules, go to the Thonny menu: Tools ➤ Manage Packages.

Now you can type in "ssd1306" and click Search on PyPi[22] (Figure 7-16).

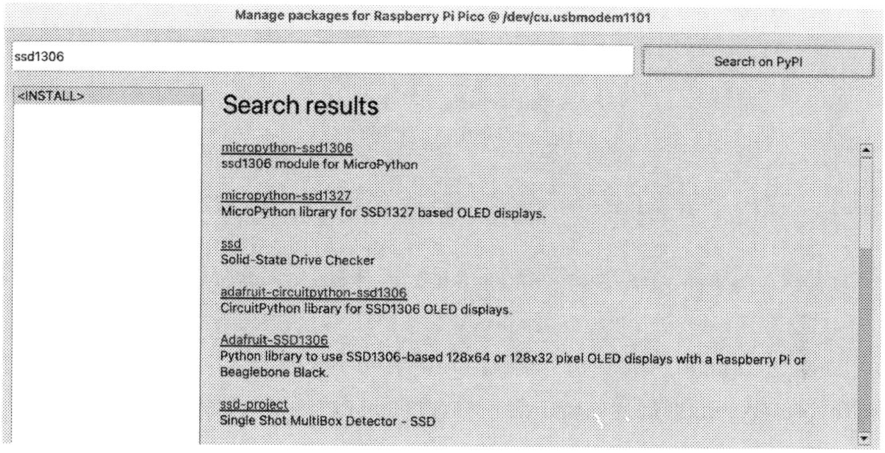

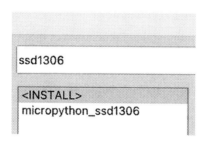

Figure 7-16. *Searching for a module on PyPi in Thonny*

Since we're using MicroPython, we need to click the first result, micropython-ssd1306, and then click Install to install it on our Pico. You will then see that the module name will appear under <INSTALL> (Figure 7-17).

Figure 7-17. *ssd1306 module is installed on the Pico*

---

[22] https://pypi.org

Now repeat this process to install the oled driver. Once both modules are installed, you'll see both listed (Figure 7-18).

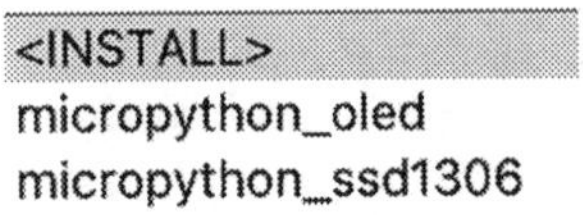

<INSTALL>
micropython_oled
micropython_ssd1306

Figure 7-18. *MicroPython oled and ssd1306 modules installed*

Click Close and you'll see the module files in Thonny's bottom-left corner (Figure 7-19) – yes, the modules are also written in Python! This means you can click on them to view the code so you can understand how they work. I highly recommend doing this, as it will make it easier to understand when something is not working as expected – it's also a great way to learn more about how things work.

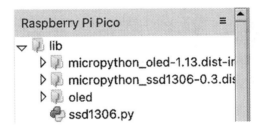

Figure 7-19. *Module files and folders on the Pico, displayed in Thonny file manager*

Phew! OK, now that we know how to install MicroPython modules in Thonny, we can do this for any device with a chip that is supported. Now let's write some code – under the Thonny programming tab, start entering your Python code.

First, let's import the built-in machine module so that we can access the GPIO pins and I2C capabilities on the Pico (Listing 7-2).

Listing 7-2. Importing Pin and I2C support from a built-in module

```
from machine import Pin, I2C
```

> We will need to import the required functions from the external modules that
> we installed (Listing 7-3) and call them to set the pins for our I2C display
> device. *I've commented the code to show what each section of code does –*
> *comment lines are denoted by a hash (#) at the start of the line.*

Listing 7-3. Add function imports and set up the OLED display

```
from machine import Pin, I2C
from ssd1306 import SSD1306_I2C
from oled import Write, GFX, SSD1306_I2C

# set up I2C pins connected to OLED
i2c = I2C(0, sda=Pin(16), scl=Pin(17), freq=200000)

# create OLED object
oled = SSD1306_I2C(128, 32, i2c)
```

> Looking at the code, you can see that we specify the device number 0, the
> pins we are using, and which frequency to use when communicating. This
> creates an `i2c` Python object, and we use that to create an `oled` object that
> specifies the resolution of our screen, that is, 128 pixels wide by 32 pixels
> high. I included some extra OLED functionality just in case we want to get a bit
> fancy later.

> Now we can use the `.text()` method on the `oled` object to tell it where we
> want to write text, that is, at position 0 pixels across and 20 down, then use
> the `.show()` method to write it to the display (Listing 7-4). A method is just a
> function for an object.

Listing 7-4. Adding text to the display with .text() and
.show() methods

```
from machine import Pin, I2C
from ssd1306 import SSD1306_I2C
from oled import Write, GFX, SSD1306_I2C

# set up I2C pins connected to OLED
i2c = I2C(0, sda=Pin(16), scl=Pin(17), freq=200000)
# create OLED object
oled = SSD1306_I2C(128, 32, i2c)

# write something on the OLED and wait 1 second
oled.text("It works!", 0, 20)
oled.show()
time.sleep(1)
```

Run your code on the Pico by clicking the run button in Thonny. You should see the text displayed on the OLED screen (Figure 7-20). Notice the way that the U-shaped solid jumper wires really clean up the breadboard circuit. If your code doesn't work, look in the REPL for an error and check your code, working upward from the last line number referenced.

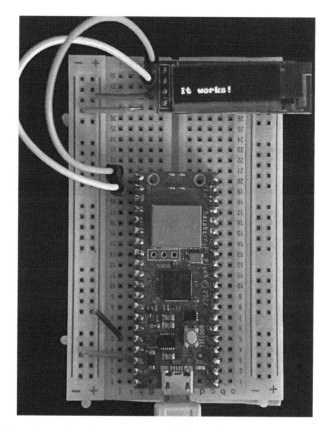

Figure 7-20. *Text displayed on the OLED display*

Congratulations! You have successfully set up and written code to interact with an I2C device. At this point, you should also save your working MicroPython code to your computer. Use the Save option from the File menu or click the save 💾 icon in Thonny. You can then select whether to save to your computer or the Pico.

Step 3: Now that we have the beginnings of an electronic badge circuit, it's time to add some button switches! You can think of a switch as completing a circuit. For our Pico microcontroller board, we will simply be connecting an input pin to a ground, that is, setting it to low or 0 (both low and 0 are the same). Fortunately, the Pico board has a built-in resistor, so we don't need to add one to adjust voltages and only require a wire to connect the right pins. If we were to connect the pin to 3.3V, then we would be setting it to high or 1. Here is the circuit – I have shown the jumper wires connecting to the breadboard as this is how it will really be set up (Figure 7-21). You'll see that there is a common ground wire for all of the buttons. Whenever you have a ground in your circuits, they should all be a *common ground*, that is, connected to one another and to the ground.

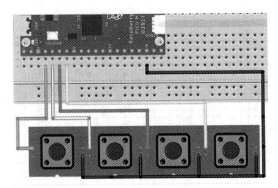

Figure 7-21. *Connecting four buttons to the Pico*

Buttons are simple, so we can leverage Pin() from the built-in machine module to set up a pin and pull it high (make it 1 by default and do something when it connects to the ground). Here is a photo of how your circuit should look with the buttons connected on the second breadboard (Figure 7-22).

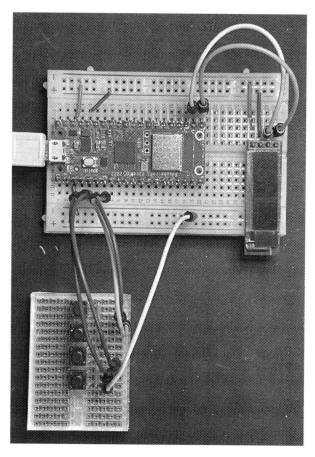

Figure 7-22. *Our circuit with buttons connected*

This is an example of the type of code we will use to create a button object, named `button`, in Python (don't add it to your code just yet as we'll use a more elegant way to set up all four buttons). The `Pin()` function uses three parameters in the brackets here; the pin number (e.g., 5), the pin mode (i.e., INput or OUTput), and the default state (e.g., PULL_UP) mean that it is set to high by default:

```
button = Pin(5, Pin.IN, Pin.PULL_UP)
```

To check whether the button has been pressed, we use an `if..then` command within a loop, as shown in Listing 7-5 (still don't add this yet).

Listing 7-5. Print "button pressed" when pin 5 connects to the ground (low)

```
while True:
    if button.value() == 0:
    print("button pressed")
endif
```

We will also need to "debounce" the button, so that we don't accidentally detect multiple presses each time it is pressed. Since humans are not very precise, a single press duration can vary, and so "debouncing" makes it easier for the machine to identify varying durations as one press. To do this, we just use a `time.sleep(1)` command to wait for a second. OK, now add these lines to your code (Listing 7-6).

Listing 7-6. Adding four buttons and a debounce

```
from machine import Pin, I2C
from ssd1306 import SSD1306_I2C
from oled import Write, GFX, SSD1306_I2C
import time

# write something on the OLED and wait 1 second
oled.text("It works!", 0, 0)
oled.show()
time.sleep(1)

# create dictionary to set up pins
buttons = {
    "button1": Pin(5, Pin.IN, Pin.PULL_UP),
    "button2": Pin(4, Pin.IN, Pin.PULL_UP),
    "button3": Pin(3, Pin.IN, Pin.PULL_UP),
```

```
    "button4": Pin(2, Pin.IN, Pin.PULL_UP)
    }
while True:
    # Clear the screen
    oled.fill(0)

    if buttons['button1'].value() == 0:
        oled.text("Button 1 pressed", 0, 0)
    elif buttons['button2'].value() == 0:
        oled.text("Button 2 pressed", 0, 0)
    elif buttons["button3"].value() == 0:
        oled.text("Button 3 pressed", 0,0)
    elif buttons['button4'].value() == 0:
        oled.text('Button 4 pressed', 0, 0)

    # update the display
    oled.show()
    time.sleep(1)
```

Run and save your code, then click each button to see the button shown on the display. So now we have input and output devices connected to our electronic badge.

A reminder about Python dictionaries   Dictionaries are like a list of key and value pairs. You can reference a key by using <dictionary name>["<key>"] so in the code we are just creating a dictionary of Pin objects to make our code more efficient and elegant.

Step 4: The DHT11 is a reasonably inexpensive temperature and humidity sensor. It's not super accurate but is an easy example to add to our project. The sensor has four pins but only uses three. Those we will use are 3.3V, GND, and data. We can read information from the data pin at one-second intervals.

If we try to read any faster, it will fail – that's just a quirk of this sensor we must consider and teach our code to account for it. The DHT11 comes with a resistor that needs to connect between the data pin and 3.3V. Let's connect it to our circuit (Figure 7-23).

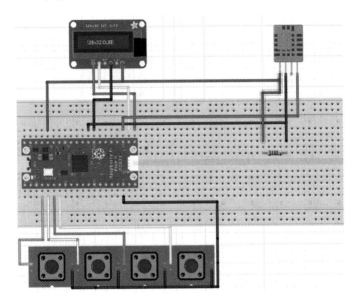

Figure 7-23. *Connecting the DHT11 sensor*

We also need to install another module. In Tools ➤ Manage Packages, search for "dht" and select the MicroPython DHT12 module (Figure 7-24).

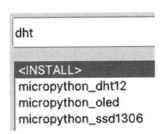

Figure 7-24. *Installed DHT12 module*

You will notice that there are URLs with documentation displayed when you install a module in Thonny – usually, I scroll to the bottom to get the examples because they seem to help me get it working quicker. Although I have tried to make it easier to build this circuit with pictures, it is important to see how this circuit is represented as a schematic diagram with symbols, which I used in Fritzing to generate these images. Although our circuit is digital and mostly boxes connected with wires (or tracks on a PCB), you will at least recognize the wiggly line as the resistor symbol (Figure 7-25).

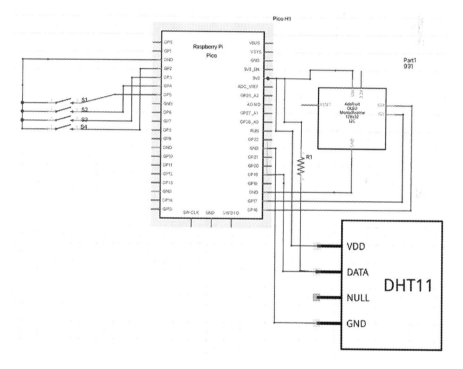

Figure 7-25. *Our badge circuit as a schematic diagram*

Now, here's the code.

Import the module with `import dht`.

Create a DHT11 object called `dsensor` on GPIO pin 18: `dsensor = dht.DHT11(Pin(18))`.

Read the sensor values (only once every second) with dsensor.measure().

Get the individual temperature and humidity values using dsensor.temperature() and dsensor.humidity().

Here's the code listing with the new code added to our original program to display temperature and humidity when we press buttons 1 and 2, respectively. It also displays a menu. Remember that pesky one second wait time? It turns out that it's a little unreliable and kept on crashing the program when it failed – so we have a try..except command around it to let our program continue even if the sensor read fails.

```python
from machine import Pin, I2C
from ssd1306 import SSD1306_I2C
from oled import Write, GFX, SSD1306_I2C
import time, dht

# create dictionary to set up pins
buttons = {
    "button1": Pin(5, Pin.IN, Pin.PULL_UP),
    "button2": Pin(4, Pin.IN, Pin.PULL_UP),
    "button3": Pin(3, Pin.IN, Pin.PULL_UP),
    "button4": Pin(2, Pin.IN, Pin.PULL_UP)
    }

# set up DHT11 data pin
dsensor = dht.DHT11(Pin(18))

# set up I2C pins connected to OLED
i2c = I2C(0, sda=Pin(16), scl=Pin(17), freq=200000)

# create OLED object
oled = SSD1306_I2C(128, 32, i2c)

# write something on the OLED and wait 2 secs.
oled.text("It works!", 0, 0)
oled.show()
```

```
time.sleep(1)

while True:
    oled.fill(0)
    try:
        dsensor.measure()
    except:
        print('error reading') # in case reading fails
        keep running

    if buttons['button1'].value() == 0:
        oled.text("Button 1 pressed", 0, 0)
        oled.text("Temperature: "+str(dsensor.
        temperature())+"C", 0, 20)
    elif buttons['button2'].value() == 0:
        oled.text("Button 2 pressed", 0, 0)
        oled.text("Humidity: "+str(dsensor.
        humidity())+"%", 0, 20)
    elif buttons["button3"].value() == 0:
        oled.text("Button 3 pressed", 0,0)
    elif buttons['button4'].value() == 0:
        oled.text('Button 4 pressed', 0, 0)
    else:
        oled.text("-Menu-", 0, 0)
        oled.text("1. Temperature", 0, 7)
        oled.text("2. Humidity", 0, 16)
    # update the display
    oled.show()
    time.sleep(1)
```

Again, test and save a backup of your working code on your computer. If something doesn't quite work, check your connections on the breadboard and try again. Pressing a button corresponding to a menu item should display the appropriate text (Figure 7-26).

Figure 7-26. *Displaying humidity*

Step 5: Our badge project now has a menu with buttons and a display. The obvious way to add more "bling" is to add LEDs – since we still have buttons 3 and 4 free, we can use them to set a pin connected to an LED to high or low. At this point, I added the breadboards to a piece of plywood to keep everything together. Since the LED is just connected to a pin and ground, with a resistor to prevent it burning out, we don't need to load any modules or do anything fancy this time. If you can get hold of a datasheet for the LED or know the resistance of it, you can use Ohm's law to calculate the value of the resistor you require. Alternatively, there are plenty of calculators online, for example, the Kitronik online store has such a calculator for the LEDs that they carry.[23] As I used a random LED that I happened to have, a 220 ohm resistor was enough to bring the voltage down to under 2V.

The code is quite simple with the LED positive anode (longer wire) connected to GPIO pin 0: `led1 = Pin(0, Pin.OUT)`

To turn the LED on: `led.high()` or `led.value(1)`

To turn the LED off: `led.low()` or `led.value(0)`

---

[23] https://kitronik.co.uk/blogs/resources/led-resistor-value-calculator

The complete code uses buttons 3 and 4 to turn the LED on and off, respectively, and this option has been added to the menu. As before, our debouncing is taken care of with the `time.sleep(1)` at the end of our code.

```python
from machine import Pin, I2C
from ssd1306 import SSD1306_I2C
from oled import Write, GFX, SSD1306_I2C
import time, dht

# create dictionary to set up pins
buttons = {
    "button1": Pin(5, Pin.IN, Pin.PULL_UP),
    "button2": Pin(4, Pin.IN, Pin.PULL_UP),
    "button3": Pin(3, Pin.IN, Pin.PULL_UP),
    "button4": Pin(2, Pin.IN, Pin.PULL_UP)
    }

# set up DHT11 data pin
dsensor = dht.DHT11(Pin(18))

# set up LED output pin and switch off
led1 = Pin(0, Pin.OUT)
led1.low()

# set up I2C pins connected to OLED
i2c = I2C(0, sda=Pin(16), scl=Pin(17), freq=200000)

# create OLED object
oled = SSD1306_I2C(128, 32, i2c)

# write something on the OLED and wait 2 secs.
oled.text("It works!", 0, 0)
oled.show()
time.sleep(1)
```

273

```python
while True:
    oled.fill(0)
    try:
        dsensor.measure()
    except:
        print('error reading') # in case reading fails
        keep running

    if buttons['button1'].value() == 0:
        oled.text("Button 1 pressed", 0, 0)
        oled.text("Temperature: "+str(dsensor.
        temperature())+"C", 0, 20)
    elif buttons['button2'].value() == 0:
        oled.text("Button 2 pressed", 0, 0)
        oled.text("Humidity: "+str(dsensor.
        humidity())+"%", 0, 20)
    elif buttons["button3"].value() == 0:
        oled.text("Button 3 pressed", 0,0)
        oled.text('LED switched ON!', 0, 20)
        led1.high()
    elif buttons['button4'].value() == 0:
        oled.text('Button 4 pressed', 0, 0)
        oled.text('LED switched OFF!', 0, 20)
        led1.low()
    else:
        oled.text("-Menu-", 0, 0)
        oled.text("1. Temperature", 0, 7)
        oled.text("2. Humidity", 0, 16)
        oled.text("3/4. LED switch", 0, 25)
    # update the display
    oled.show()
    time.sleep(1)
```

Here is the breadboard prototype with display, DHT11 sensor, buttons, and LED (Figure 7-27).

Figure 7-27. *Completed breadboard badge prototype*

Something I should add here is that one advantage of I2C devices is that each has its own address in hexadecimal (base16).

Note   Our decimal system uses base-10 where each column is a power of 10, that is, 234 in base-10 is $2\times10^2 + 3\times10^1 + 4\times10^0$. Where base-10 uses numbers from 0 to 9, base-16 (hexadecimal) uses 0-F, that is, 0-9, then A-F. So, 234 in decimal is equivalent to EA in hexadecimal, that is, $15\times16^1 + 10\times16^0$. Hexadecimal is used for representing numbers such as memory addresses in microcontrollers.

Next Steps

To take this project further, we could add more I2C devices easily because modules will usually know the correct hexadecimal address to automatically send commands to the correct device. To replace our breadboard with something more permanent, we can use a protoboard (Figure 7-28), which is just a solderable breadboard in the form of a PCB. But what if we didn't want to leave our Raspberry Pi Pico connected permanently? We would just solder in socket headers (Figure 7-29) to our protoboard. These would allow us to remove the Pico when the project is not in use and use it for other projects.

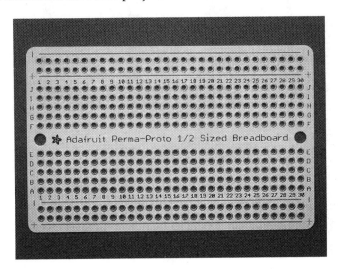

Figure 7-28. *An example of a protoboard; the Adafruit-branded Perma-Proto boards come in a variety of sizes (from Adafruit)*

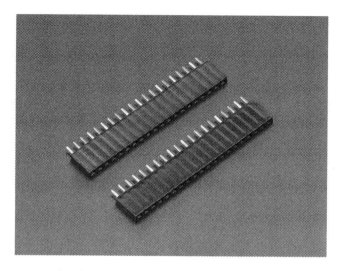

Figure 7-29. *Socket headers to fit GPIO header pins from a Raspberry Pi Pico H (photo from Adafruit)*

If we really wanted to make a truly fancy badge, we could transfer our schematic into a custom PCB that we could send away for fabrication. Although Fritzing does technically possess the functionality to produce the files required by PCB fabrication shops, I would recommend using KiCad.[24] KiCad is an open source software. If you would like a precompiled version, you can download it directly for a small fee that supports the project. Although technically out of scope for this book, transferring our circuit's schematic to KiCad (Figure 7-30) would allow us to map the electronic symbols to real components (represented by "footprints"). From this point, you can make your own custom PCB design to produce the files required for a fabrication service to produce your PCB. These files include Gerber files that describe the PCB, bill of materials (BOM) to describe the required components, and a drill file which specifies any holes that need to

---

[24] www.kicad.org/download/

be drilled. These days, obtaining a quotation is simple once you have these files, and if you're prepared to wait for cheaper postage, small runs can be quite affordable for your code club or maker group.

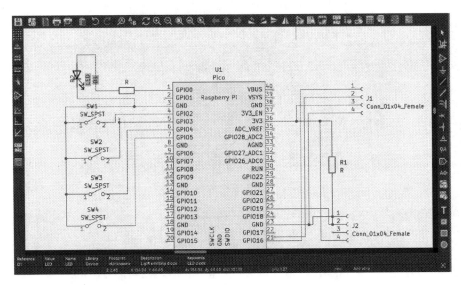

Figure 7-30. *Badge circuit schematic shown loaded into the Kicad PCB design software*

A passionate electronic badge community has grown up around the hacker conference scene – these are as much about making as breaking with conferences such as Hackers on Planet Earth (HOPE) and Defcon being prime examples of places where many unofficial badges can be seen.[25] The difference between a commercial vendor conference and these more grassroots conferences is that people attending are more about being passionate about their hobbies rather than only wanting to make money.

---

[25] https://hackaday.com/2019/09/19/pictorial-guide-to-the-unofficial-electronic-badges-of-def-con-27/

Summary

In this chapter, we have gained a basic understanding of some common component types and learned which features to consider when designing a digital electronic circuit. We have written embedded code in MicroPython and ran this on our own electronic badge prototype. This should be within the reach of your code club and maker group once they can program basic Python scripts with loops and dictionaries and leverage modules for more functionality.

Chapter 7: Cheat Sheet

Electronic Components

Concepts

- Schematics and datasheets
- Breadboards and circuit boards
- Through-hole vs. surface-mount components

Components

- Resistors
- Transistors
- Capacitors
- Diodes
- Light-emitting diodes (LEDs)
- Integrated circuit (IC) chips

Soldering Tools

- Soldering iron/station

    - Adjustable temperature, digital if possible

- Solder

    - Leaded and nonleaded

    - Flux core helps solder go where you want it

- Helping hands/mini vise

- Cutters

- Wire strippers

- Heat-proof mat or board

- Solder sucker/desoldering braid

Soldering

- Heat both the copper pad and component leg, then apply solder to both.

- Primary-aged kids should be standing and supervised.

- Practice with Veroboard.

- A good solder joint is shiny and concave.

Software Tools

- TinkerCAD

- Thonny IDE

- Fritzing

Other Useful Concepts

- Microcontroller breakout boards

- Communication protocols

Approaching a New Electronic Project (Digital)

- Compatible with our skills

- Good support

- Features match

- Within budget

Badge Project

- Raspberry Pi Pico W supports MicroPython and CircuitPython.

- Modules loading with Thonny to support components.

- Remember the common ground.

- Display: I2C (easy to daisy chain more).

- Buttons: GPIO.

- DHT11: GPIO.

- LED: GPIO.

Next Steps

- Read the Python module to learn more.

- Replace the breadboard with a protoboard.

- Look into KiCad and fabrication.

CHAPTER 8

Putting It All Together

Planning a Year of a School Maker Space/Code Club with Python

> *I guess you could call it a "failure", but I prefer the term "learning experience."*
>
> —Andy Weir, *The Martian*

In this final chapter, we'll walk through planning a year of activities, referencing what we've learned in previous chapters and putting these into the context of a kid's code club or maker group. Since we've already dived into these topics, I won't go too deep here, but the objective is to show where these fit into a real working schedule over a year. Although you may end up with kids staying at the code club for multiple years or even just a couple, I've chosen a year as a good sample for starting off. Rather than trying to add everything the first time, feel free to take your time and build things up – for this reason, I've included a range of ideas, including how to create your own workshops and other projects. This should give you a living plan that grows as you and your club progress over the years, limited only by your, and your maker kids', imaginations and skills.

© Martin Tan 2023
M. Tan, *micro:bit Projects with Python and Single Board Computers*,
https://doi.org/10.1007/978-1-4842-9197-9_8

The information here does not include any business advice, as this will vary depending on your circumstances. To prevent any conflicts, I have only covered the requirements of a nonprofit code club or maker space, as these have a clear objective to educate and facilitate creative pursuits.

Deciding on Communication Channels

To effectively coordinate both participants and volunteers for your code club or school maker space, you'll need to first establish communication channels for each type of communication. You can have an immediate communication channel and another for event notifications to parents/guardians; you may even find that it is helpful to have a way to distribute read-only information for kids.

Communicating with Parents/Guardians

These communications will often be at regular intervals, for updates, when information and permission slips are required for certain events and when tasks like account creation for online services need to be performed. There are paid subscription and free services, but when transmitting any personally identifiable information (PII), you will need to follow specific rules in your area, regarding transmitting and handling such information. In Australia and New Zealand, there are privacy acts.[1,2] You should avoid dealing with any of this information unless it is required – realistically, you will only need a contact email and phone number. If your code club or maker group is working in conjunction with a library or school, you may already have access to a suitable existing communication mechanism, for

---

[1] www.ag.gov.au/rights-and-protections/privacy
[2] www.legislation.govt.nz/act/public/2020/0031/latest/LMS23223.html

example, schools may already be using Compass[3] and others may already be sending out some information via email.

Although specific recommendations for your area will vary, it is important to understand the limitations and required setup of whichever communication mechanism you use for collection and storage of various forms of data, for example, Google Forms provides encrypted communications to connect to resources, but requires that you have the right settings to ensure that documents or form responses are not made public or inadvertently shared to those without a requirement. If you are in Europe, GDPR requirements will mean that you cannot keep data longer than it is needed and only request what is needed. Consent will also be required for some activities and events you may run in conjunction with your code club or maker group, for example, in Australia there are government requirements for information related to minors.[4]

Communicating with Volunteers/Teachers

For keeping in touch with volunteers/teachers, you can use the same mechanism that you are using with parents/guardians – this will be fine for the occasional email or note about whether your session has been canceled or moved for a week, but for organizing details relating to workshops, changes in processes, or just to discuss a new project or common error that kids are seeing, you will generate a high volume of chatter, quickly. The best way of keeping these high volumes of information in some sort of order is to have a chat system that allows separate channels and file storage. Again, find out about any privacy requirements before making a choice on what you will use.

---

[3] www.compass.education/

[4] www.oaic.gov.au/privacy/your-privacy-rights/children-and-young-people

For our code club, Discord[5] offered the features we needed; this included the ability to paste screenshots, photos, and link or transfer documents. It works on mobile devices and was friendly for the younger alumni volunteers who were mostly already using it at the time. For this, we set up our own free server and were able to limit access. If you have a large group of volunteers, you may consider implementing a code of conduct to maintain a welcoming environment and prevent any ugly conflicts. Online communities will often require reading and acceptance of a code of conduct before access to chat channels is granted. When we had a smaller number of volunteers for a given year and already had most of our content retained from previous years, we would often revert to email for these communications due to the lower volume of information needing to be transferred.

Communicating with IT Staff

In Chapter 1, we learned about the importance of setting up good relations with your IT staff. You should also understand the best way to engage them, for example, opening a ticket on one of their systems or however they prefer you to request something. Once you have established what the required processes are, a minimal list of requirements should be communicated:

- List any software that needs to be installed for your sessions.

- Understand any limitations of Internet access, that is, is anything blocked? This may be a limitation in school in some Australian states, where only an allowed list of websites can be used.

---

[5] https://discord.com/blog/starting-your-first-discord-server

- What the process is for logging in to laptops and where kids' projects are best stored.

- Whether they can stay for the start of your sessions, to help with any teething problems that may arise.

Setting Expectations

Setting expectations is important for participating kids, their guardians, and your volunteers. This also includes any new volunteers that may have been starting that year; in addition to parents/guardians and alumni volunteers, we also have had volunteers referred from Code Club Australia.

Expectations for Participating Kids

At the start of each year, our code club sends out a notice on Compass to inform parents/guardians about Code Club. Once submissions come in, a response is sent to advise when kids have secured a place in that year's code club and announce the dates and times of commencement.

Accounts Required

The response provides a list of accounts that parents need to set up, for example:

- Trinket.io for Python

- TinkerCAD for 3D design

Since our code club was an extracurricular activity for the school, some iPad apps would also be listed, but they were rarely used and ultimately were more as a distraction than any real maker-related activities. Dropbox was useful for delivering files, and grade 6 kids also had their own email, which helped for setting up accounts. Earlier on in the book, we went through the requirements to have your IT people set up Thonny and Mu editors on the computers. If you have kids bringing their own laptops, you can include this information as well.

Asking parents/guardians to set these up greatly reduced the instances of kids "forgetting" or otherwise not having accounts set up. This put the responsibility on the guardians and set an expectation that these were required for participation. It also increased value and continuity for kids as they would learn to save their work and were responsible for logging in. Previously, we were trying to help kids set up their accounts, and this would waste multiple weeks, with some years where kids could still not log in at the end of the semester.

If kids are bringing a mobile device, you may want to encourage the use of a local password bank for storing any account passwords required for your sessions. KeePass and Bitwarden are good examples of open source and free password managers that are widely used, with other solutions like 1Password also having good reputations at the time of writing.

Display of Projects, Photos, Blog Posts

In addition to the required accounts and other information, you will want to let guardians know that projects may be shared and displayed on various online media and allow opt-outs for these. This should include a statement that no PII would be shared online. Since our code club was associated with a school, it made it much easier to do these. Libraries and other institutions will have similar existing policies already in place, too.

Expectations of Behavior and Conditions of Attendance

As our code club evolved, we came across various challenges related to disruptive behavior, exploiting the club for free childcare, and refusal to participate (this was mostly related to instances that would preclude kids from being able to move forward to more advanced activities and often resulted in disruptive behavior). So, a clause that outlines expectations of behavior and consequences after "three strikes" was brought in to ensure a healthy and productive environment for those who valued our free code club activities. We never ended up having anyone with three strikes, but setting the expectation that attendance was a privilege and that we had eager kids on a waiting list was enough to put things in perspective (most years we did have a waiting list which meant that when kids decided not to attend, we could give someone else an opportunity to participate).

The other expectation we included was that code club wasn't the time to be playing video games. This was based on previous issues where one kid would start playing a game and others would become distracted, and soon the whole group was mostly unfocused. And so, we added to our expectations that disruptive behavior included playing games on iPads. A clear distinction was made that these were different to games that may be part of code club activities.

Setting Expectations for Volunteers

New volunteers will benefit from some history of your club, a list of objectives, and an understanding of the requirements of their role. Firstly, you will need any documentation required by law in your location – for Australia, you will need records of any required vetting for volunteers to work with children, which varies from state to state. Although the information we include has changed over the years, we also typically talk about the approach we use and give a summary of the expectations we make of the participating kids. As the year proceeds, we learn more about the strengths, weaknesses, and interests of our volunteers – this lets us customize how we leverage their help, as we progress through the year. Any information about the venue such as first aid, evacuation processes, and anything else relevant will need to be included. For any other requirements, you should reference the relevant government department.

We were lucky that we were able to tell Code Club Australia that we were after volunteers with Python skills. It was really nice to have a volunteer who ran her own team of developers at work, come into our code club, and be able to help our kids find their way.

A Note About Qualifying/Filtering Volunteers

Volunteers can be parents/guardians, your code club's alumni, or external sources. We also reached out to Code Club Australia at one stage which resulted in a couple of excellent volunteers who had already received training. It was interesting to hear comparisons between ours and other clubs that other volunteers they knew were attending. The initial expectation seemed to be that of leadership, but due to our club being more established than most, it changed into support, which worked well and even extended their stay for a bit longer.

Based on some of our experiences, here's some things to be wary of when assessing volunteers:

- Affiliations with groups that might be looking to recruit kids/parents

- An agenda that might not be in line with your code club or school maker space's interests/objectives

- Putting self-promotion before the best interests of the club

- Any misunderstanding of what your code club or school maker group is

- Disregard for what you've already established and built

Examples that come to mind include a prospective volunteer that appeared to be affiliated with a church that seemed to have an overly strong recruitment drive, one who said that all our activities were bad and boring and that kids just wanted to make games and a range of others relating to "we should sponsor the club" or "look at using X language instead." Although it is great to have input and enthusiasm, there's a point at which this can become overly aggressive or misguided. For instance, it would make more sense to first understand club objectives and the reasoning behind choosing specific programming languages and other choices.

On the positive side, we also had some great input to workshops and support for the things we were already doing. We had a university lecturer who worked with artificial intelligence (AI) and machine learning (ML) who was able to simply these into a short workshop for the kids. We had some great support from the school parent committee that allowed us to get our first set of BBC micro:bit boards.

Get a Benchmark of Skills Across the Group for Kids and Volunteers

Each year with a new group tends to give you a different spread of kids, all with their own individual experiences of technology and programming. Finding out where those levels of experience sit at the start of the year is important as it helps you to ensure that everyone is dealing with content that they understand and challenges them enough to keep them engaged. It doesn't take long to identify the kids who have been playing with micro:bits before, or have some Scratch programming experience, or have even just been teaching themselves programming using *Minecraft* mods or plugins.[6]

An easy way to start finding out what the skill levels are in a group is just to ask. You'll often get slightly subjective responses and mostly from the louder kids. However, something we learned as we progressed is that prior experience does not necessarily mean someone will excel in your

---

[6] www.idtech.com/blog/what-are-minecraft-mods

code club or maker group. It seems to come down to a combination of how kids approach the club and how they relate to you, and sometimes it takes a while for them to actually realize that they can do it. As I mentioned previously, the "posse" that may develop around a skilled kid may sometimes prevent other kids from struggling enough to push themselves to learn.

Another way to determine your benchmark is to just interact with each of the kids. Ask them what they are doing and what they are finding interesting, easy, or difficult. Talk to them about coding concepts and their ideas and look at how they work. This is another area where tracking progress as we initially skill up our group can tell us lots about how your club deals with challenges and solves problems.

I usually prepare some sort of refresher presentation at the start of each semester, both to see how much everyone has learned and to show the kids how much they have really learned. This helps to empower them when they realize that their time has been well spent and that they understand concepts that they didn't before. Pairing what they know with the correct terminology will mean that they can talk about their coding in a way that other coders would understand; often, kids will go home and talk to their parents/guardians about what they have learned, and we hear some great feedback from this.

Build Some Basic Skills to Equip Kids to Go the Distance

As we talked about in Chapter 1, getting kids to work in a structured way can help them quickly acquire some good skills that will enable them to move on to more advanced activities before they stagnate; this is preferable to letting kids plateau later, when it is difficult to get them learning anything more because they have invested too much time to see value. Make sure you check yourself when kids progress, by making sure that they understand the projects and can articulate these to you. It is all too easy for kids to say "oh, I finished this, it was really easy" but then not be able to tell you what was challenging or how they worked through errors or even how their program works.

It can become easier to persevere when you know what you're working toward. For this reason, it helps to outline some of the concepts and subject matter that kids will work through; they can then understand where they are going and what to expect. This can also prevent that feeling that they are coming in week after week to simply work on the Python lessons. It will feel like they are working toward something and give more of a useful context to the activity. I will often reiterate this by talking about something our code club kids might be working on and adding relevance such as "this racing game uses lists, which we can use later on for...." It also helps to show kids some of the real-world uses for Python at the start, for example, websites that are built on Python, scripts that do useful things such as automate downloading lots of images from a website or updating products on an ecommerce store. A Space Station (Figure 8-1) lesson from Code Club shows how to interact with application programming interfaces (APIs) online, and we were able to apply this to have one of our kids write their own interface to a different API. A quick online search for Python projects should uncover some good examples!

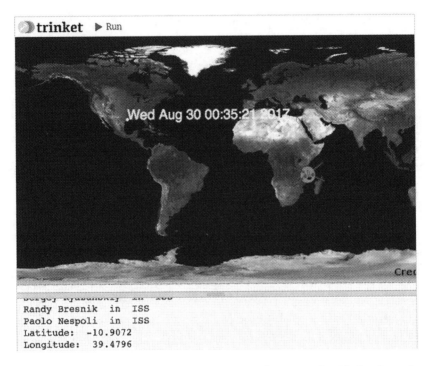

Figure 8-1. *This ISS Space Station lesson from Code Club plots the location of the International Space Station on a Google map*

Once kids are working well, I try to find some sort of small reward that is relevant to coding and technology. Getting a bunch of Python stickers that gave part of the proceeds to Python and helped a Python podcast was a good example of this. Other times, getting a roll of stickers from Code Club Australia really helped reinforce that they had achieved something. Other rewards have included drink bottles and t-shirts that came from Code Club Australia when we supported some of their events or contributed projects.

The period when you're just coming in each week and working on continuing lessons/projects can sometimes feel a little long at the start. But the focus you put into this time and those little debugging tips that kids will learn as they find solutions to errors that inevitably crop up as they program will pay you back once you get into group activities and workshops later in the year. The trick is to be efficient at this time, so that kids are getting things done, but without rushing past the important bits, which include completing each lesson/project; if you find that everyone gets a bit behind, it doesn't hurt to just put aside another couple of weeks where you encourage kids to finish any unfinished lessons and can seek volunteer help if they may have missed out earlier on. One of our volunteers, Glenn, suggested this one year – it made a huge difference as kids felt less pressure and could ask any questions or for help needed to complete their projects.

Group Activities

Even before everyone completes many Python lessons/projects, group activities can come in handy. Oftentimes, we find ourselves with a group tapping away with Python and several kids who have gone home, completed all the projects a couple of weeks earlier, and are chomping at the bit for something to do. Although we can have them talk to the group about some of the challenges they came across and how they solved them, it helps to have some smaller group workshops up your sleeve for these kids.

This is a good time to bring out the Devs and Testers project that I described earlier in the book – it runs for two weeks and can be an interesting way to change the pace of things and allow kids a bit of leeway to start coding creatively. It also helps develop skills in collaborating with others on code. In the book *Coders* by Clive Thompson,[7] he talks about codebases that were initially written by single programmers (developers) that end up being improved and much easier to maintain after being rewritten by a team of developers.

---

[7] www.goodreads.com/en/book/show/40406806-coders

A small group project can also cater to some niche interests within subgroups of your code club and maker group. This may be a good opportunity to explore an area that may not be of interest to everyone, but might attract several kids, for example, 2D game programming principles can be taught in Pygame Zero within the Mu editor, or interested kids can purchase a programmable console such as the many MakeCode Arcade-compatible ones.[8] MakeCode Arcade has a Python tab that allows the code to be represented as Python, allowing Python kids to implement game design concepts using a language they understand without getting too low level at the start.

Group activities can also be a more engaging way to bring some skill parity to your code club by identifying those feeling challenged by a specific concept; you can revisit this in a way that might be easier to understand for a small group. I built a "capture the flag" game in Python (Figure 8-2) which has been great fun for groups who have completed a majority of the Code Club Python modules. I haven't published the code for this online to discourage some kids who may have been tempted to look up the solutions rather than collaborate with their peers to solve the levels - at the time of writing I have been talking to Code Club Australia to hopefully find a home for this project so others can contribute.

---

[8] https://arcade.makecode.com/hardware

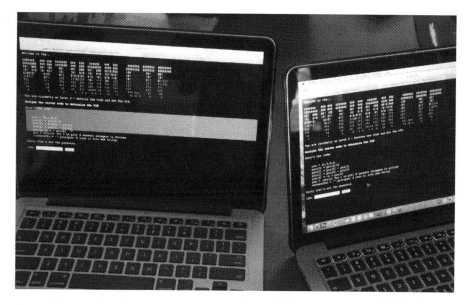

Figure 8-2. *A Python "capture the flag" group challenge I wrote, based on the Code Club Python curriculum*

Develop and Deliver Workshops with Scalable Projects

Once everyone has at least a basic understanding of programming, the best thing to do is capitalize on that knowledge by applying it. When the timing has been such that there is a school holiday gap, I'll normally just do the quick presentation recap thing. This reminds people of what they've done, and sometimes we will even do a single short lesson from Trinket.io just to get everyone back into things. It can help to reiterate some of the advantages of Python by picking a set project that leverages a module to apply Python to something; whether this be a built-in module or an external module depends on whether you are using a Mu or Thonny editor or are in Trinket.io on a free account.

At this point, it helps to plan multiple workshops and present them in a short slide deck – these can be run in series or parallel, depending on the number of kids and volunteers attending. Letting the kids know up front what they will be doing helps them understand that they are into the next phase of their code club/maker group journey. It is also a great way to show that the time they invested was well worth it because now they can create fun and interesting projects using what they've learned. As you cycle through a few iterations of workshops, be sure to take photos and videos as these can be incorporated into future slide decks when introducing workshops. Running through the guided workshops is also a nice way to ease yourself into a more hands-on phase of the maker journey. At this stage, it will be easier doing this as groups and getting that computational thinking happening but without so much freedom that the kids feel overwhelmed. A good number of workshops to have here is four to five before taking the next step into a more design-orientated freeform phase.

A cost-effective solution for hardware is the micro:bit. Although these have had some supply chain issues, the Microbit Foundation appears to have swapped out a component that was proving difficult to source, and these are available at the time of writing. A class set of micro:bits can be a cost-effective way of applying Python skills and integrating a more tactile approach that can prove refreshing after initial curriculum–style lessons/projects. The micro:bit emoticon switcher project from Chapter 2 is a good way to get started with your workshops – this project can be completed in around an hour. This project scales nicely since kids who put their micro:bits on the same wireless channel can enjoy seeing their emoticons displayed on their friends' micro:bits. The next workshop (or one run in parallel with rotating groups) could be the self-watering plant. Depending on how many micro:bits you have, you can choose to display this one somewhere as it is quite visual. Even displaying it to others between code club sessions can prove interesting for outsiders to see some output from the club. Other workshops could include e-textiles and TinkerCAD with a conductive tape (use the introductory lessons, shown when you sign up, to get started) – these can also be adapted to any microcontroller board that supports MicroPython or CircuitPython.

We had some great successes when we combined these workshops to build a smart city. By presenting the smart city idea and breaking it down into multiple workshops, kids felt that they were working together to contribute to a larger project (Figure 8-5). This created a great feeling of building something big and incorporated 3D-printed houses (Figure 8-4) and trees, self-watering plants (Figure 8-3), and traffic light pairs on a paper city map. We also had a banner made of three squares of multicolored (RGB) LED tiles[9] controlled by a micro:bit.

Figure 8-3. *Python self-watering plants ready for adding to the city project*

---

[9] https://kitronik.co.uk/products/5645-zip-tile

Figure 8-4. *3D-printed houses and trees ready for the city project*

Figure 8-5. *A view of the city being populated*

Once you have run a few of these prepared workshops, you should
have a reasonable idea of how to write your own. Just like the exercises I've
included for you in this book, the rough structure goes something like this:

- State what your audience will learn.

- State what is required in terms of skills, electronic hardware, installed software, and other parts.

- Include a photo or working example of the finished project, so your audience understand what they are working to.

- Break your project down into numbered steps, explain any concepts involved with examples if required, and within each step list the required tasks.

- If what you are explaining can be better explained with a screenshot or image, use that and make sure what you are communicating or referring to is clear (crop your image if required). If you can better explain something with one line of text, use that instead, and save the screenshots for when they are best suited.

- After each step, remind your audience to test and save, giving hints for debugging and troubleshooting if something goes wrong.

- Remember to show examples of the results of each step, so that your audience can check their work.

- And finally, include a challenge with a few clues for those who finish early.

If this goes smoothly, and there's time left in the year, you can look at more freeform development of ideas. At this point, you can help kids to brainstorm for problems for which they can provide solutions. Alternatively, look at improving on existing solutions. A whiteboard can come in very handy or something similar that allows whiteboard collaboration online.

Remember that depending on the scope of your code club or maker group, you may end up having kids staying for multiple years, in which case you can dive more deeply into topics and projects if you keep kids engaged. Don't forget to suggest the opportunity for older kids to return as volunteers – they are often the best candidates as they understand how things work and often can relate well to the code club participants, including their doubts and challenges.

Club Excursions/Events, Community/ School Events

As your club starts to gather momentum, and kids talk about what they are learning, more people will become interested in what you are doing. Our first exposure of this sort is when some of our first group of code club kids spoke in a school assembly. One of the comments that has stuck with me was, "At first I thought code club was just going to be about games – but we learned that coding can be used to solve real-life problems and create useful software." We felt quite proud that these kids were actually gaining some benefit from our then bumbling way of helping them to learn. We had a few of the kids demonstrate Scratch programs that they had made, and soon we had more people lining up for the next year's group.

There is often some overlap with school projects from code club/ maker group projects, where kids can use some of the skills that they learned for their school projects. My son collaborated with Tom, one of our earlier code club volunteers, to create a walkaround tour of the school; although this was at a point when we were only using Scratch, it is possible to do the same exercise with Python and Flask, a module that facilitates creating website applications (web applications). Other projects served as promotional material for the school – such as the smart city being displayed in the main school office, where prospective students and school tours would pass.

Open nights were also a time when kids would show off various projects they made, both for their parents and prospective students looking to attend. Sometimes, these projects had been used to communicate concepts or in augment artwork as part of school assignments. One year we were lucky enough to have an art teacher with a keen interest in paper circuits, who helped kids use these with their art projects to include lighting effects with switches. Another year we were asked to do a series of small 15-minute introductory projects which I wrote for the BBC micro:bit. Kids could sign up for a workshop and create working code quite quickly – since this was for the school committee, we ended up having the purchase of ten micro:bits funded, which helped to fuel our journey using these in code club. With working models to show how these could be leveraged by teachers for computing topics in their classes, we gained a few more, with some add-ons such as traffic lights and moisture sensors. Two electronic kits for the micro:bit also came in handy when we had a couple of kids pulling ahead in code club. These were some of Simon Monk's kits for the micro:bit – if you're interested in more projects for these, I highly suggest checking out some of Simon's books, too.

One of the major events each year has been Code Club Australia's Moonhack event. This initiative started in 2016 to get over 10,000 kids coding at one time to break a world record, where I was asked to put together Scratch and Python projects. Later, this led to our code club kids attending a few live events, including two being featured on *That Startup Show*, both of whom became volunteers, programming in Python – Emily and Ethan. For us, it was not so much networking at a business level, but rather showing enthusiasm to help out and volunteer to create educational content. Sometimes, it may not even be content aimed at kids – another time, I was flown to Code Club Australia's office, which was in Sydney at the time, to deliver a Python Flask project to help volunteers.

Above all, one of the best ways I've found to help kids understand the benefit of being able to code is by doing it myself. Being able to show kids that you are using Python to solve problems and automate tasks is one of the easiest examples to demonstrate how programming can be useful even if you're not a professional software developer. If you're a teacher, one of the best ways to encourage kids with programming is to use it for everyday automation, for example, grabbing data from websites and transferring it into a spreadsheet or automating a task to create a visual representation, such as with our self-watering plant project where you can add wireless communications to turn on the light, display a picture on some LED tiles, or even move a servo motor to make a clown wave back and forth when the plant is being watered.

Demos

If your code club is affiliated with Code Club Australia, or another group, they will often ask for clubs to test some material they have written or attend their own workshops or volunteer training sessions. These can be an easy way to get to know people in the same community and share ideas and get advice or support. You may even get asked to take some kids to demonstrate at an event – you can read about some of the events we attended in a blog post I wrote for Code Club World.[10]

As time went on, we were eventually asked to become a star club – which meant that Code Club Australia could send people to attend our weekly session and see how they were run, ask questions, and consider running their own. This also involved a few fun visits from Code Club Australia and some fun pizza days. Of course, we would also set these up some years and invite parents/guardians to help celebrate a successful year.

Some of the other events we were asked to attend included Parliament in Victoria for several demos, the Future School Conference where the kids demoed Makey Makeys and Python in the micro:bit emoticon switchers,

---

[10] https://blog.codeclub.org/2018/04/27/practicing-real-world-programming-in-a-code-club/

and Kid Inventor's Day at one of the local libraries where we created a robot arena and talked about the self-watering plant project that the kids had built and some capacitive touch drums with a Circuit Playground Express board. As you can probably see, progressing with workshops can easily morph into helping your code club and maker group kids to eventually create their own projects – and with a bit of luck, these projects can be leveraged to open doors to lots of events both locally and external to your group.

Contribute Back

Contributing to Code Club was initially made possible due to early efforts to make the content open source. Early on, I got the opportunity to brainstorm some ideas with Rik from Code Club UK. Back then, all their projects were written in text, using Markdown[11] formatting to represent code blocks and headings which would call some open source software called Pandoc[12] to create a `.pdf` file of the lesson. These days, things seem to have changed although I personally still do use a similar method to create projects. Back then, contributing to Code Club projects was similar to how you would contribute to any other open source project; you would open an issue, discuss what your enhancement or idea was, then do a "pull request" which is essentially submitting a request to have your change merged with the project. These days, I suspect most of the work is done using something as mundane as Microsoft Office, which makes it even easier if you were to contribute. However, even if you're not contributing to a group such as Code Club, you may just want to contribute to the community; there's many teachers out there who welcome projects that they can use to teach with and other code clubs or maker groups that

---

[11] `www.markdownguide.org/`

[12] `https://pandoc.org/`

welcome extra projects. A good way to get involved is to first look around for what is available. Find something for which there is a gap and see if you can make something to fit. Test it out with your maker group kids and make a few changes, and I also usually get other volunteers to have a read through if they have the time. If your project requires it, you may like to add some teacher/volunteer notes, which help those running the project to understand it in more depth. Once you have something written up and you are confident that it provides enough information for someone you've never met to successfully reproduce your project, socialize it around and maybe even get other groups to try it out. If you use a Raspberry Pi or Raspberry Pi Pico, you can even talk to someone at Raspberry Pi, CoderDojo, or Code Club to have it included in their resources.

These days, it is still possible to collaborate with many nonprofit groups, and all it takes is to ask. Behind the scenes, I was lucky enough to create projects for some businesses that were working with Code Club Australia, Moonhack, and some other Code Club Australia events and be the technical editor for a couple of awesome books for kids, one of which was a revision of the book that my son first used to learn to code! As one of the group projects, I developed a Python *Capture the Flag* game that kids can play online, based on the Code Club Python curriculum – hopefully, that will be something I can hand over to Code Club Australia to host, since I had one of their staff play it a few years back, giving some positive feedback on it. Time will tell whether this happens – otherwise, it's possible that I may just open source it or find somewhere cheaper to host it. The side effect of making the source public will be that the solutions will be searchable by kids, and they would also just be able to grab the URLs for the next level quite easily which would remove the challenge of the game.

Sometimes, I have been paid for contributions. This happened when we needed something that was quite time-intensive for a specifically tight timeline or if there was travel required. As Code Club Australia gained more resources, this was not required as much. When I've been asked to work as a technical editor on books, these were also paid, and these may vary depending on the publisher you are working for. Blog posts or interviews have not usually been paid although there are many online publications that do pay per word for these. Open source contributions are typically not something anyone pays for, although there are companies that employ people who contribute code to major projects and pay their employees a salary.

Encouraging Alumni to Volunteer

Our code club volunteers originally consisted of myself and an alumni student from the school where our code club is based. We worked with David, the teacher who originally registered the club, and muddled our way through. Even with the three of us, we did manage to somehow cultivate a small group of kids working with an adapted Lego Mindstorms robot programmed with Scratch, while the other kids forged forward with basic Scratch lessons. Fast-forward a couple of years and we had moved into a much larger space, with a handful of parent volunteers. Although having parents help is great, we only really retained a couple of parent volunteers for more than two years. Some had kids that didn't really manage to persist at that early stage – I'm a bit surprised that many of the kids persisted through those early days with our fumbling around trying to get passwords reset and working out where to save things. Often, kids would leave without saving their projects only to return the next week and need to redo all the work they did the previous week. When we tried to move kids on to Python at first, we had many false starts and frustrations, too.

Somewhere along the way, we somehow figured things out with volunteers and the way we planned, communicated, and documented things for them and the kids. Much of it seemed to come down to planning, and that helped us work out ways to strategically stack things in our favor, so that we could keep everyone engaged and having fun while learning.

There were times when our numbers were high enough that I really wondered how it did not all fall apart – at peak numbers, we had two code clubs each with different year levels, and we tried running these both in parallel and in series, that is, the latter being one group per semester and the former with two groups on the same day or separate days. I've done my best to outline many of the things we found worked for us in this chapter and the rest of the book. You will likely find that there are still challenges specific to your setup, but at least these should reduce the number of variables so that you can focus on the hard parts.

The good thing was that we always had kids coming back year after year. Although it varied with whatever configuration we were running at the time, we generally had a new group of kids come in at least every two if not each year when we were running dual clubs. Even with two clubs, and lots of kids learning, there was still something great about having a slightly smaller group with enough volunteers to make sure more kids got their heads around Python better. Having a waiting list seemed to increase the perception of value that our code club had. Eventually, our first kid volunteer moved on as he got a part-time job, and we even wrote him a decent reference reflecting on his positive time at code club. By then, we already had a few other alumni kid volunteers, and when I think back, I can roughly pinpoint the time that I noticed their enthusiasm rise while they were in code club as participants. After that, it was simply a matter of suggesting to them and their parents/guardians that they were welcome to come back each week as a volunteer. At this point, most of the volunteers had departed for different high schools, and so it was something of a mini reunion every time they came back for code club sessions. There was a certain persistence when working through debugging their programs that I've noticed in every kid who came back as a volunteer. They each had a time when we would almost have to kick them out at the end because they were trying to get something finished in one of their projects. It always brought a smile to my face when we got to that point where we had to forcefully tell kids to finish up at the end of the session because they were so focused and wanted to keep building things. That persistence seems to be something that helped those keen volunteers keep pushing younger kids to get through things. Of course, there were those days when some volunteers were visibly tired or unmotivated, but they kept turning up. Eventually, we knew when someone's time was up at code club, and we would thank them, and new volunteers would walk in to fill their places the next year.

Our parent volunteers varied in experience and attitude. Some would want to change everything without understanding why we were doing things a specific way that had evolved over a few years. Others would find things difficult which tends to pass this onto the kids. The longer-lasting volunteers would generally ask how we did things and roll their sleeves up and just help. Later, they would suggest improvements based on what they had observed and understood about our reasoning for things – this was the most valuable help for us. Other volunteers were just happy to turn up and do whatever we needed them to do, which was great too. When we got Python-trained volunteers from Code Club Australia, we felt very lucky, and it was also sad to see them go at the end of their allotted time. Throughout all this, I should mention that we also had most of the local high school teachers come along to visit our code club. It surprised me that they were keen to see what we were doing and later found that some had taken on some of what they saw us doing in their own formal classes that they were teaching at a high school level.

The other category of volunteer we had over the years was student teachers and other teachers keen on digital technology areas. This was also a wonderful addition to our body of expertise – I recall that one of our teachers, Noam, would put a huge QR code on the projector screen. Kids were then able to scan the code from their seats using their iPads and access the documentation. It always impressed me how well our teacher volunteers would dispatch any behavior problems or grab control of the group so quickly. It helps to learn whatever techniques the kids are familiar with for getting their attention, especially when their teachers are helping.

I would say that sometimes the kids who struggle a bit at the start and eventually learn some good skills can often make the best alumni volunteers – so make sure you leave that door open for them to come back. Even those who you might not expect to volunteer should still be encouraged as they will understand the kids and the content well. If you can get pre-trained or experienced volunteers as we did from Code Club Australia, they are worth their weight in gold, so leverage that to both give yourself a reference point to compare against and free your other volunteers up to do as much planning as you can.

Learning from Mistakes and Learning More

One of the recurring things in our journey with a code club was probably frustration. It was frustrating when we discovered someone who still didn't know their login after six months of attending. It was frustrating when I spent hours of time preparing something and then a small detail prevented it from working during code club. It was frustrating when the laptops had issues at the school and frustrating when robots were not able to connect to the Wi-Fi. It was also frustrating when problems prevented kids from staying engaged and they started playing games on their iPads.

Out of each one of these frustrations were born strategies that we used to improve how our code club ran and increase the value that participating kids would get from attendance. We could explain why and how things worked and the advantages of using Python. Once we just approached it from the perspective of a more scalable language, which allowed us to get out of just doing things on a screen, kids would just treat it as the thing we did. We gradually took our club from something kids would come to and expect the same thing each week to something that was working toward bigger things.

Keeping Yourself Motivated and Kids Engaged

Based on one session per week, it can be challenging to make sure that everyone has something to do each week. Kids need to stay engaged and challenged sufficiently to persevere over time. Much of this is driven by our own excitement and journeys as volunteers and teachers. Speaking to some of our volunteers, many told me that one of the reasons they started volunteering was to learn and challenge themselves, in addition to helping kids learn. With alumni code club kids, some said that they really enjoyed code club and the doors it opened for them, and they wanted to give back to help others do the same. For me, I wanted kids to feel empowered to make their ideas real – to prove to others that their ideas really worked and show them how they worked. To do this, we first needed to equip them with the required skills, including the most important skill – teaching yourself to learn, so that boundaries become limitless. In pursuing these goals, one of the biggest challenges was trying to show teachers why coding was useful to anyone, not just professional developers of software; it turns out that this last one was the biggest challenge of all.

In the long term, we learned that solving most of our issues hinged around a failure to plan. Of course, we also had many lessons to learn before we could plan things. The better we planned, the less we failed, both in the long and short terms. Planning allowed us to run workshops and know what we would be doing weeks and months ahead, opening more time for creating more interesting activities and making sure we the time available to us as effectively as possible. We were able to consider events such as the yearly Moonhack and attend the occasional field trip when we were invited to these.

Eventually, collaborating online allowed us to leverage our time and made us more efficient at planning. I could distribute workshop notes, we could keep our ideas in separate channels, and it made it a little bit easier to catch up with our different timetables when our team of volunteers grew. When people were going to be absent one week, they could let everyone know easily. Over several years, we leveraged various other tools for various tasks, for example, kids tracking their progress, explaining concepts, and exhibiting their finished projects. Many of the tools worked on mobile devices as well, making it even easier for everyone to collaborate.

Preparation

Many of our failed sessions can be attributed to time wasted trying to set things up once the session had already commenced. This left the kids waiting around, and often we would discover we were missing a cable, or the Wi-Fi network would not connect, which only added to the frustrations. The IT people were not available to help with laptop and network problems, and there was just not enough time to accommodate any problems. We found that we had to have everything ready to go prior to each session. All the volunteers needed to know what their role would be, whether that be hosting a workshop, supporting the code club lesson curriculum, or any other activity.

It wasn't enough to "wing it" anymore, we needed to make sure that everything we required was in the room and ready. This meant messaging teachers ahead to ensure someone knew where the required equipment was and brought it to the room before we started. Because of the tight timeframe, we needed to make sure that everything was prepared so we could start each session as soon as the kids were seated and ready. We also needed to consider the most effective way for kids to save their work and retrieve it to maintain continuity. Later, we also managed to have an IT person from the school stay a bit later to help with any problems. This offloaded any school-related technical issues and ensured that everything was up and running most of the time. For our workshops, I would have handouts ready, and we would leverage some freed-up time to ensure that the right quantities of required hardware were ready beforehand. For any activities that required parental/guardian support, we would communicate these over a previously agreed communication channel; this started off as email, but eventually the school got their own tools that we were able to use. We had to ensure that kids had their logins ready and developed processes to accommodate any contingencies that we had dealt with over the years.

Scaling Things Up

As our numbers grew, we employed the strategies described earlier in this chapter to address the following areas:

- Varying skill levels in both the kids and volunteers

- Consistency in our approach based on our previous collective experience

- How to effectively run workshops so that most volunteers could run them

- Communicating to a larger group of participants and volunteers

- Setting expectations for parents, kids, and volunteers

- Ways of building up club hardware and tools

When you start seeing these, they are very good problems to have because it means that your code club is growing and evolving. Be prepared to adapt as you go and try to anticipate as much as possible. Obviously, you will encounter surprises, but being prepared to adapt quickly and manage these changes across your team of volunteers will increase the likelihood of a good long-term outcome.

My Experience Highlights

For me, highlights that come to mind include all the breakthroughs whenever one of our kids "got it" – the point where they realized that they knew something before I needed to tell them or getting to the point where they figured out how to debug something by following the steps before I needed to say anything. Or the times when one of our kids, who later became a volunteer, almost gave up on Python because he missed a week of code club, and I reminded him that everyone misses a week here and there, and he persisted and completed his Python modules and helped create the self-watering plant project with us. Sometimes, we were able to identify kids that appeared to be unfocused, having more understanding of programming concepts than we expected. In some of these cases, we were able to call upon them to solve bugs and eventually have them reengaged with their coding.

For many highlights, I ended up not being present, for example, for Moonhack, I ended up being in New Zealand for work and only saw that 10,000 kids had built my projects after the event occurred; for the filming of *That Startup Show*, I was also not able to attend; and there were other Moonhack events that I helped arranged but was not able to attend. Even though I couldn't be present to see the results of these events live, these will remain as highlights of our code club!

As part of volunteering for code club, I also started a blog.[13] Our code club kids would ask some of the same questions, and it seemed like a good way to answer some of the questions. As it turned out, and as David our teacher volunteer had warned me, the kids didn't really read the blog. I found that other people running code clubs and maker groups did though and would sometimes reach out on social media to ask questions.

---

[13] http://jafine.github.io

It's Up to You, Now!

There you have it – a year of activities that you can run for a kid's code club or maker group – although not everything will come together immediately as every club will have their own unique challenges, requirements, and goals. However, this should at least give you an idea of how to get started and some ideas of what to aim for. You can use some of the linked resources to get kids skilled up and prepare your own workshops from the prepared ones that I've supplied in this book. You will have some guidance on setting expectations for the participating kids and your volunteers and setting up your communication channels from the start. Feel free to change things up as required and adapt what I've suggested to fill your group's requirements and interests. Once you have a solid way to skill kids up and keep them engaged, then you will be able to look at some of the more advanced workshops, such as the electronic badge prototype or a smart city. Soldering may or may not be something you want to tackle in your first year, but I've provided scope for this for when you are ready. If you have access to a 3D printer or laser cutter, you may also decide to get started with some copper tape circuits or even investigate building a digital circuit within a 3D-printed case. There are really no limits if you are careful to maximize the value that kids get from your sessions by planning ahead and preparing effectively. From this point, it's up to you, and I wish you all the best. If you've got this far, I'd like to thank you for reading my book and hope you got some good ideas from it. It has been interesting to brain dump what people have been asking me about, but hopefully I have covered most of it. Please do reach out if you have any questions or want to share some of your code club or maker group's achievements – I'd love to hear about them!

Chapter 8: Cheat Sheet

Communications

- Choose appropriate or available communication channels and set these up for volunteers, parents/ guardians, and IT staff. Look at different channels for immediate vs. nontime-sensitive communications.

Expectations

- Set expectations for volunteers, participants, and their guardians regarding goals, the year's road map, volunteer roles, and behavior.

- Create accountability by having guardians sign up for required services.

Setup

- Ensure that computers are set up and charged before each session.

- Arrange for an IT support person to be present for at least some of your earlier session to sort out any problems with the network or computers.

Skill Building

- Use a curriculum of lessons/projects that will equip participating kids with programming skills in Python.

- Check for completion and assist where required; do quick refresher presentations to reinforce and remind people of what they can do.

- Have a way of tracking capabilities during this time, so kids are ready for moving into workshops.

Interim Group Projects for Those Ahead

- Use small workshops for those who might finish the curriculum modules a bit earlier.

- Let others complete their curriculum before moving into larger workshops.

Workshops

- Use prepared projects for workshops to get started.

- You can either run these in series or parallel rotation of subgroups, depending on volunteer to participant ratios and available hardware.

- Leverage workshops for demos and displays to promote your code club or maker group.

Events

- Sign up to newsletters and mailing lists to stay in touch with relevant local events and keep your ears open for any school or events, or events related to where you run your code club or maker group.

- Schedule in events like Moonhack or similar and reach out to organizers in case there are opportunities to contribute/collaborate and attend live events.

- Look for competitions or conferences that may be relevant to your code club or maker group objectives.

Start Making Your Own Projects

- Once you have done some written workshops, look at making your own.

- Help kids work from basic ideas and keep adding and scaling these up.

- Write about them to communicate back to parents/ guardians and any community around your code club or maker group.

Contribute to Community Projects

- Provide feedback and other updates to community projects you might be leveraging.

- Encourage kids to contribute where feasible or at least understand the opportunities.

- If you or your participants make something cool in your code club or maker group, consider writing it up for others to use.

- Be open to contributing blog posts and sharing tutorials with communities that you have found useful.

Encourage Alumni to Come Back As Volunteers

- Look for those kids that have overcome challenges and are good at sharing.

- Don't forget the quiet kids as many do really well without saying much and can be relatable to similar kids in future code clubs.

EXAMPLE VOLUNTEER HANDOUT TEMPLATE

Code Club volunteers handout

Thanks for volunteering for our Code Club this year! Your efforts make a huge difference to our student coders, and we have a lot of fun along the way. To make things work a bit smoother, we have put together some information for this year's club.

General structure of each meet

Code Club starts at 3:45 PM and runs through until 4:45 PM, so this gives students time to go to the bathroom, have a snack, and relax a bit before starting. Sometimes, some students decide to voluntarily use this time to work on their projects, especially if there's areas they want to push through and get finished by a certain time. At the start of Code Club, students are required to gather on the floor, where we briefly explain what will be happening that session and mention any good achievements. Then each student must go get a computer and take a seat and continue with their activities.

As we have a variety of skill and experience levels at Code Club, students are often working on a variety of different projects at any given time. In order to keep track of progress, we are tracking this through an application called <insert communication app>, which will house the activity documents and where students can record their progress. To enable students to collaborate easier, and to make it easier to assist, most students working on the same project will be seated together. Occasionally, there are exceptions, for example, if a student needs a quiet space to focus, they can go into one of the classrooms set aside for this.

Before students move on to other activities, we need to confirm that they've updated <insert communication app> and have completed their current activity with a screenshot and description. Any challenges they had could also be added in here. With each activity completed, we'll be giving out a small achievement certificate to acknowledge progress.

319

Responsibilities

As volunteers, we collaborate with <insert volunteer communication app>. If you don't already have access, please provide your email address, and we can add you. <insert volunteer communication app> is a chat system that also allows storage of files and information. No personal student or school information is to be stored there, but we use it to share the upcoming week's learning material or tricks and tips for various activities. It is arranged by subject, in channels. This is also a good place to ask for help or share a problem or interesting solution that may have come up during Code Club. Often, it can be hard to get time to have in-depth discussions during Code Club, so this gives us a way to have these while being flexible since it works both in a browser and using software on your computer and phone.

Helping to troubleshoot

A good way to show students how to troubleshoot their code is to first ask what it is supposed to do and have them explain any problems they are having. As you walk through the code, it helps to verbalize your thoughts, for example, "OK, so we're increasing X when this key is pressed…," so students can understand the process. At some point, they may even stop you if they work out what the issue is. Also, look out for a potential root cause of the issue, or if there's a skill gap, sometimes it can help to suggest an easier activity be completed first.

If we see a common issue that is recurring, we can discuss on <insert volunteer communication app>, and sometimes I can do a blog post, or as with bugs we've found in the Code Club activities themselves, we can contribute the fix back to Code Club themselves. Please talk to me about how to do that if that is something that sounds interesting to you, and I'm happy to assist or walk you through the process.

Participants working on their own game/program

<add any cases where some kids may be working on more advanced projects or other activities>

Acceptable and unacceptable behavior

If students engage in unacceptable behavior, we now have a three-strike rule to reduce the impact to others' experience at Code Club. It is important to report any unacceptable behavior to attending teachers/staff.

Unacceptable behavior includes

- Interfering with other students' computers in a way that prevents them from participating

- Ball games or other games indoors that are disruptive or could damage equipment or result in injuries

- Anything deemed unacceptable under school rules

- Continuous playing of games or other activities unrelated to Code Club

- Anything disruptive to others

- Not participating and progressing in Code Club activities: In this case, it is important to ask some questions to determine whether the student is new to Code Club or whether there is something they need explained, and if you need help, please feel free to ask another volunteer to assist.

Volunteers' kids

<details for volunteers' kids to come along to sessions>

APPENDIX A

Traffic Light Workshops

I developed a variation on these micro:bit traffic light projects for our Code Club workshops and also incorporated this into our city project. Given there are sufficient numbers of participants, we usually run these in parallel with other workshops, using one hour per week for two to three weeks, which adds up to two to three hours overall.

Since our workshops were always quite popular and really got kids engaged, I wanted to include this project. We use the Kitronik STOP:bit board with the micro:bit, but I've also included an alternative (Figure A-1) if you'd like to make your own traffic lights – it uses 220 ohm resistors to reduce how much power goes to each LED, but you can use the resistor calculator on Kitronik's site[1] to calculate what you need for your LEDs.

---

[1] https://kitronik.co.uk/blogs/resources/led-resistor-value-calculator

© Martin Tan 2023
M. Tan, *micro:bit Projects with Python and Single Board Computers*,
https://doi.org/10.1007/978-1-4842-9197-9

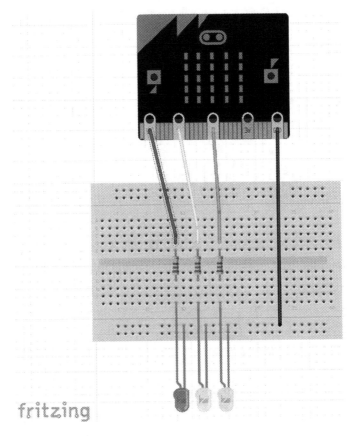

Figure A-1. *LED and resistor connections as an alternative to the STOP:bit*

With regard to running the workshop yourself, we typically have kids working in pairs, and then they would coordinate with the group to ensure that they all had their traffic lights on different radio channels. Part of this project is the introduction of truth tables to help kids manage the increased complexity as they add a second traffic light to run in conjunction with the first traffic light.

PROGRAM A MICRO:BIT TRAFFIC LIGHT WITH PYTHON

We see traffic lights all the time, but we don't think all that much about the logic behind their changing lights – this project lets you create a traffic light model using a BBC micro:bit and some Python code (Figure A-2). Later, we will make things a little more interesting and add a second traffic light!

Figure A-2. *micro:bit with a battery holder and Kitronik STOP:bit fitted*

In this project, you will learn

- How to create structured data state tables to help model events and logic

- Write a function to turn on individual traffic light LEDs

- Call the function in your main loop

<u>You will need</u>

- One Kitronik STOP:bit, assembled with a micro:bit, or your own LEDs and resistors connected to micro:bit pins 0, 1, and 2

- Micro USB cable for programming the micro:bit

- Battery pack (2x AAA batteries) for the micro:bit

- Mu editor[2] installed on your laptop

Step 1: Launch the Mu editor and enable micro:bit mode.

- Go to **Applications** in Mac, or the **Programs** menu in Windows, and launch the **Mu editor** by clicking the icon that looks like this: .

- Once the editor is running, click the **Mode** button .

- Click **BBC micro:bit** so it is highlighted, then click **OK** (Figure A-3)

---

[2] https://codewith.mu/

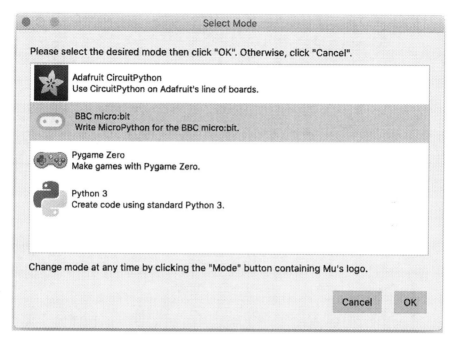

Figure A-3. *Select "BBC micro:bit" mode in the Mu editor*

Step 2: Write your code.

Each traffic light is made up of three colored light-emitting diodes (LEDs). Each LED has two wires; one connects to the ground (GND) and the other to pin 0, 1, or 2 on the micro:bit.

- Type in the code from Listing A-1 into the **Mu editor**, then connect your micro:bit USB cable, and click the **Flash** 🔘 button to download the code onto the micro:bit.

Listing A-1. Set pin 2 on the micro:bit to 1

```
from microbit import *

pin2.write_digital(1)
```

327

- If all went well, the green LED connected to pin 2 should be lit! Try changing `pin2` to `pin1` and the amber LED connected to pin 1 should now be lit.

- Change the `1` in `.write_digital(`**1**`)` to **0** and it should turn the LED off.

- Now click the **save** ⬇ button on the Mu editor to save a copy of your code as "`stopbit.py`" on your computer.

What our code does

- The LEDs have one wire connected to the ground, and one connects to a pin 0, 1, or 2. We switch the power from low (0) to high (1) with our `digital_write(1)`.

- By sending to a different pin, we can turn on a different LED.

- Writing zero to the pin will set it to low and turn off the LED.

Step 3: Write a function to turn one LED on and the others off.
We can reduce the amount of code we need to write by creating a *function* in Python. Then, instead of rewriting all our code again, we just call the function by typing its name and customizing what it does by giving it extra information in a *parameter* inside the brackets.

- First, delete the line `pin2.write_digital(1)` from your code in the Mu editor (leave the `import` line there). Now that we know how to turn LEDs on and off, we'll make a function to turn on an individual LED and turn the others off.

- To start defining our `stopBit()` function, we add the following line and add a parameter called color. The parameter will let us tell our function which color LED to turn on when we later call our function.

```
def stopBit(color):
```

328

- To put code in our function, we'll **indent**[3] it by four spaces (the **Mu editor** will do this for us automatically). We indent it again to put it inside an **if** statement. So now our code should look like Listing A-2. (Note: The new lines you need to add are always in **bold**.)

Listing A-2. Turn off all LEDs except for the green one connected to pin 2

```
from microbit import *

def stopBit(color):
    if color == "green":
        pin0.write_digital(0)
        pin1.write_digital(0)
        pin2.write_digital(1)
```

- Now that we have our function defined, we can call it and tell it what color we want lit. Add the next line under your function and make sure it isn't indented, so it's outside of the function definition:

    ```
    stopBit("green")
    ```

    Now save your updated code in your mu_code directory again, then click the **flash** button to send it to your connected micro:bit. Only the green LED should turn on.

- We still need to add two more if statements to let us turn on the amber and green LEDs – you can extend your code to use **elif** to add **amber** and **red** colors to your function.

---

[3] "Indent" means to move text four spaces to the right – the tab key will work as well in Mu (although there's huge arguments between using tabs and spaces)

- Once your function can handle "green," "amber," and "red" colors, make them loop forever in a while loop. In your loop, make sure to tell the traffic lights to wait for some time between changes!

- Test your code by flashing it to the micro:bit. It should cycle through green, amber, then red, waiting about 5000 milliseconds between each. **Hint:** Use sleep(5000) for that.

What our code does

- Defines a function that accepts a color parameter, which can accept three different *arguments:* "green," "amber," and "red."

- An endless loop calls our function to change the traffic light between three different **states**, shown in the **truth table** (Table A-1).

Table A-1. *Truth table for one traffic light, showing LED*

State	Red LED	Amber LED	Green LED
green	off	off	on
amber	off	on	off
red	on	off	off

Congratulations! You've successfully programmed a single Australian traffic

light!

MAKING TWO TRAFFIC LIGHTS WORK TOGETHER

One traffic light is simple – we just have three colored lights that light up for a given time in sequence. But what happens when we want another traffic light to coordinate with our traffic light, that is, if we had two traffic lights controlling traffic at the intersection of two roads? Now things become a bit more interesting! In this project, we'll add another traffic light and make them work together - you can see a photo of these in Figure A-4.

Figure A-4. *Two traffic lights controlling traffic at an intersection*

In this project, you will learn

- How to extend our truth table to represent the different changes between two traffic lights

- How to reuse our function to save time

- How to coordinate our light changes with another traffic light or radio, representing all the states in our truth table

You will need

- To have completed Project 1: Single Traffic Light first

- 2 x STOP:bits and micro:bits with USB cables

- 2 x battery packs for our micro:bits

- Mu editor installed on your laptop

Step 1: Extend our truth table to use two traffic lights.

Here is our previous truth table that shows three states with one traffic light (Table A-2).

Table A-2. *Our original truth table for one traffic light*

State	Red LED	Amber LED	Green LED
1	off	off	on
2	off	on	off
3	on	off	off

We can add another traffic light to our truth table – T1 is the first traffic light, and T2 is the second traffic light (Table A-3). These traffic lights are arranged on different streets at an intersection (they need to work together to make sure traffic runs smoothly).

Table A-3. *Truth table for two traffic lights working together*

	T1	T1	T1	T2	T2	T2
State	**Red LED**	**Amber LED**	**Green LED**	**Red LED**	**Amber LED**	**Green LED**
1	off	off	on	on	off	off
2	off	on	off	on	off	off
3	on	off	off	off	off	on
4	on	off	off	off	on	off

Note   When one traffic light changes to amber, the other traffic light stays red – this gives the traffic enough time and warning to stop before the traffic from the other street gets the green light to go.

Step 2: Reuse our code.

We need to remove the main while loop from our previous code, so that we can make it into a **module** that we can import.

Launch the **Mu editor** as we did in Step 1 of the **Single Traffic Light** project. Click the **load** button in Mu to load our stopbit.py script. Delete the while loop from the bottom of the script so it looks like Listing A-3.

Listing A-3. Reusing previous code

```
from microbit import *

def stopBit(color):
    if color == "green":
        pin0.write_digital(0)
        pin1.write_digital(0)
        pin2.write_digital(1)
    elif color == "amber":
        pin0.write_digital(0)
        pin1.write_digital(1)
        pin2.write_digital(0)
    elif color == "red":
        pin0.write_digital(1)
        pin1.write_digital(0)
        pin2.write_digital(0)
```

333

- Save your script to your computer.

  Congratulations, you just made a module that can be imported into other scripts!

Step 3: Copy our module onto the micro:bit.

- Connect the first micro:bit and click the Files 🔗 button in Mu. You'll see two boxes open up at the bottom of Mu. Find your `stopbit.py` module file in the right box, and drag it to the box labeled `Files on your micro:bit` (Figure A-5). If you've already got some code **Flash**ed on your micro:bit, you'll see a `main.py` file there, too.

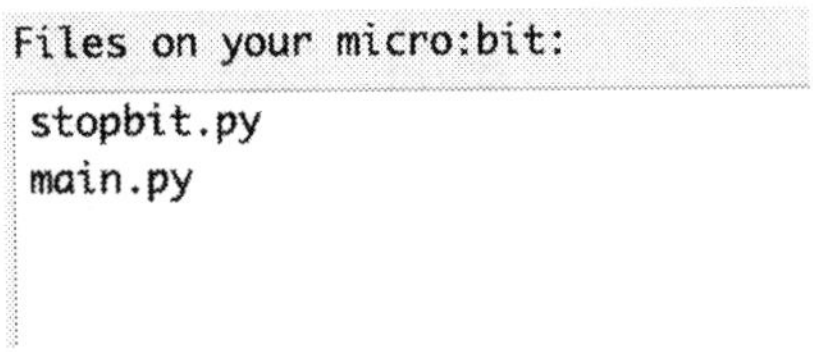

```
Files on your micro:bit:
stopbit.py
main.py
```

Figure A-5. *Copy stopbit.py file to the micro:bit filesystem*

- Repeat the process by plugging in the second micro:bit and clicking **Files** again to drag the `stopbit.py` module to that micro:bit too.

Step 4: Write code for the first micro:bit.

Now we can convert the new truth table into our main loop on the first micro:bit (Table A-4).

Table A-4. *Truth table for two traffic lights working together*

	T1	T1	T1	T2	T2	T2
State	Red LED	Amber LED	Green LED	Red LED	Amber LED	Green LED
1	off	off	on	on	off	off
2	off	on	off	on	off	off
3	on	off	off	off	off	on
4	on	off	off	off	on	off

It looks like a lot of work, but don't worry because the stopBit() function in our module does most of the work for us!

- Click New in the Mu editor to open a new tab and add these two lines of code at the top:

```
from microbit import *
from stopbit import stopBit
```

- Add the main while loop below that – this time, we have the red and amber function calls too in Listing A-4 (**Remember:** The new lines you need to add are the bolded ones.)

Listing A-4. Add additional states to your code

```
from microbit import *
from stopbit import stopBit

while True:
    stopBit("green") # state 1
    sleep(5000)
    stopBit("amber") # state 2
    sleep(2500)
    stopBit("red") # state 3
```

```
sleep(2500)
stopBit("red") # state 4
sleep(2500)
```

Flash the updated code to the first micro:bit and check that it cycles through the different colors. The comments help us remember that each stopBit() call corresponds to each of our states.

Step 5: Use radio to send signals (first micro:bit).

- We need the radio module to be able to send our signals from the first traffic light. Add import radio and code to set up the radio under that. If you're near other micro:bits using radio, make sure to set a different channel (Listing A-5).

Listing A-5. Add radio commands

```
from microbit import *
from stopbit import stopBit
import radio

radio.on()
radio.config(channel=7)
```

To send a message to the second micro:bit, use the radio.send() function. For example, to send the message "green," use radio.send("green").

In our truth table, when Traffic Light 1 has "red" lit, Traffic Light 2 has "green" lit.

Looking at the truth table, send the corresponding message for Traffic Light 2 under each stopBit() function call. The code for the first micro:bit should now look like Listing A-6.

Listing A-6. Listing with additional states and radio

```
from microbit import *
from stopbit import stopBit

import radio
radio.on()
radio.config(channel=7)

while True:
    stopBit("green") # state 1
    radio.send("red")
    sleep(5000)
    stopBit("amber") # state 2
    radio.send("red")
    sleep(2500)
    stopBit("red") # state 3
    radio.send("green")
    sleep(2500)
    stopBit("red") # state 4
    radio.send("amber")
    sleep(2500)
```

Save this code in your mu_code directory as t1.py and then flash it to the first micro:bit.

Step 6: Write code to receive radio (second micro:bit).

The only difference in the *second micro:bit* is in the main while loop. This time, we just need to call stopBit() whenever we receive a radio message.

- Connect the second micro:bit to your computer, and click the **New** button in the Mu editor to open a new tab and copy over the code from t1.py. Now, remove everything after the while True: line in this new tab. The code in the new tab should look like Listing A-7.

Listing A-7. Code for the second micro:bit

```
from microbit import *
from stopbit import stopBit

import radio
radio.on()
radio.config(channel=7)

while True:
```

- Now just add three lines to receive and set the LEDs on the second micro:bit, as shown in Listing A-8.

Listing A-8. Add code to receive incoming radio messages

```
from microbit import *
from stopbit import stopBit

import radio
radio.on()
radio.config(channel=7)

while True:
    incoming = radio.receive()
    if incoming:
        stopBit(incoming)
```

Save the tab with the preceding code in the mu_code directory as t2.py. Flash the code onto the second micro:bit and use the **Files** button to drag the stopbit.py module on.

With the STOP:bits connected to each micro:bit, you can now attach a battery pack to each and draw a mini intersection on a piece of paper and watch the lights work!

Congratulations, you've just made a working set of Australian traffic lights!

Index

A

Application programming
　　interfaces (APIs), 293
　accounts, 180
　concepts, 179
　data requests module, 183
　description, 181
　dictionary structures, 179
　features, 181
　JSON data, 184
　modules, 179
　objectives, 180, 181
　random.shuffle(), 184
　search online, 181
　shuffling code, 184
　Trinket.io, 179
　URL generator, 182

B

BBC micro\:bit
　amplified speaker, 69
　challenges, 62
　edge connector, 67
　editor option, 41
　emoticon switcher
　　dictionary, 48

events, 50
features, 47
.hex file, 54
indentation, 48
index creation, 49
learning process, 46
library modules, 47
light-emitting diode
　(LED), 53
loop/receive data, 49
Mu editor, 52
Python code, 47
Python source code, 50, 51
testing code, 54
Thonny editor, 52
web browser, 53
working process, 54, 55
external components, 65–70
features, 64
firmware, 41
ground (GND), 68
.hex file, 41
input/output pins, 66, 67
library module, 68
MicroPython
　Mu editor, 56
　radio module, 57–59

© Martin Tan 2023
M. Tan, *micro:bit Projects with Python and Single Board Computers*,
https://doi.org/10.1007/978-1-4842-9197-9